BUSINESS ONE IRWIN GUIDE TO KEOGHS

Revised Edition

James E. Cheeks

BUSINESS ONE IRWIN
Homewood, IL 60430

© JAMES E. CHEEKS, 1991

This publication is designed to provide accurate and
authoritative information in regard to the subject matter
covered. It is sold with the understanding that neither the
author nor the publisher is engaged in rendering legal, accounting,
or other professional service. If legal advice or other expert
assistance is required, the services of a competent
professional person should be sought.

*From a Declaration of Principles jointly adopted by a Committee
of the American Bar Association and a Committee of Publishers.*

Project editor: Gladys True
Production manager: Mary Jo Parke
Compositor: TCSystems, Inc.
Typeface: 11/13 Times Roman
Printer: Arcata Graphics/Kingsport

Library of Congress Cataloging-in-Publication Data

Cheeks, James.
    The Business One Irwin guide to Keoghs / James E. Cheeks.—Rev.
ed.
      p.   cm.
    Rev. ed. of: The Dow Jones-Irwin guide to Keoghs. c1989.
    ISBN 1-55623-684-0
    1. Keogh plans—United States. 2. Investments—United States.
3. Finance, Personal—United States. I. Cheeks, James. The Dow
Jones-Irwin guide to Keoghs. II. Title.
HD7105.45.U6C44   1991
332.024'01—dc20   91–38022

Printed in the United States of America

1 2 3 4 5 6 7 8 9 0 AGK 8 7 6 5 4 3 2 1

CONTENTS

INTRODUCTION—
THE KEOGH PROGRAM

This book is about wealth building, estate building, and retirement security. It's about how people who earn income in some kind of self-employment activity reach those goals through investing in government-sponsored Keogh plans.

It's mostly about how *moonlighters*—employees or home-makers with a self-employment sideline—can achieve these goals. But the Keogh advice in these pages works as well for those who are self-employed full-time.

I use the program and benefit from it myself; others can benefit from it more than I do. As you read, you'll meet Harold, Peter, and Elaine, three moonlighters among the millions who I think are going to profit greatly by adopting Keogh plans.

Are there Keogh millionaires? Of course. Keoghs have been around since 1962. Some Keogh investors have already reached the Millionaires' Club.

But soon many more will, because of what I would call the Keogh Revolution of 1984, the year the shackles came off Keogh investments. Thanks to the Keogh Revolution, you can

- Invest much more than before—several times more, in some cases.
- Take larger tax deductions than before—again, sometimes several times more.
- Take personal control of your investments if you wish; you no longer have to invest through a bank, insurance company, or other faceless institution.

"All right," you may answer, "but what about me? Can *I* become a Keogh millionaire?"

My answer, hedging as all lawyers must, is this: No sensible person, however expert, can guarantee you'll make a fortune from your Keogh investment. But it's easy to tell you how *not* to become a Keogh millionaire. If you make any of the following wrong moves, you can be sure that Keogh riches will never be yours.

WRONG MOVE #1:
DON'T LEARN ABOUT KEOGHS

Keoghs are plans for building personal wealth, accumulating an estate to leave your family, and ensuring a secure retirement. If you already have all you need in these departments, read no further. If you're still working toward these goals, a Keogh may be what you need to reach them. But it will take effort.

All or most of the wealth you have now you had to work for. If you want the added wealth a Keogh can give, you first have to learn about Keoghs. You must learn some terms and concepts that are new to you. And above all, you must be willing to *think* about your financial situation, think in a systematic way with specific objectives. We'll say more about that later.

WRONG MOVE #2:
DON'T ACT ON WHAT YOU KNOW

We all know how easy it is to put things off. I must have heard all the excuses. Here are some perennials:

"The tax law may change." Sure it will. The tax law is always changing. No one can be sure they won't cut back on Keogh benefits sometime. All the more reason to get in now. You can get every benefit going, up to the moment of cutback. And thereafter, some benefits will be grandfathered in for you even if they're denied to newcomers.

"I don't understand investments. All I know is bank deposits and CDs." I think you should learn about more than these, and we'll examine other investment approaches later. But that is no excuse for inaction. If bank accounts and CDs are all you know, then do them through your Keogh. Millionairehood is a distance away if that is all you do, but you're better off doing them through your Keogh than without one.

But enough of excuses. Delay is costly. Any investment program is time-sensitive. Keoghs are especially so. Every dollar your Keogh makes is tax-free, so the sooner you act, the greater your wealth in almost every case.

WRONG MOVE #3:
ACT ON YOUR KEOGH, BUT ACT TIMIDLY

A modest Keogh is better than none at all. But make the most of your Keogh opportunities. Find or create a plan that lets you invest the maximum the law will allow in your case. And then fund it to the limit.

Am I advising reckless investment? I am not. With today's Keogh, you can pick whatever investment suits your temperament. I'll have something to say later about whether your Keogh investments should be conservative or high risk and where you might consider putting your money.

Keogh enthusiasts make mistakes, too. I'm a Keogh enthusiast, and I now see my mistake was to talk about Keogh "millions." Keogh millions are unlikely for people whose self-employment is a sideline. I don't expect to become a Keogh millionaire. But it's not hard to build a Keogh fund of more than $100,000 out of a self-employment sideline. And Keogh funds of $200,000 to $500,000 are within reach of many with self-employment sidelines. If you're skeptical about Keoghs, that's fine. Healthy. I expect it. In Chapter 1 you'll meet three moonlighters, skeptics all, with searching questions about Keoghs and Keogh claims.

CHAPTER 1

WHAT'S A KEOGH?

Maybe you've seen Keoghs advertised in the financial pages of your newspaper, touted by your bank, pushed by stock brokerage firms. Keoghs are a government tax and investment program, *for those who qualify*. Many millions of people qualify. If you're in a Keogh plan, you can do *all* these things:

- Put money in the plan each year toward retirement or investment goals.
- Take a tax deduction for that amount.
- Postpone tax on your investment earnings.
- Have complete personal control of your investment assets.
- Enjoy tax benefits when you cash in your Keogh investments.

WHERE KEOGH BENEFITS COME FROM

A Keogh is a government program, but don't ask Uncle Sam for any cash. You get tax relief. Without it there's no Keogh plan, but that's *all* the government provides.

The seed money—the Keogh contribution—comes from you. You put in money every year, sometimes more than once a year. You invest those contributions in something that pays interest, dividends, or rents, or in some other productive way. Year after year you will contribute, invest, and reinvest.

Your Keogh wealth consists of the investment assets you acquire from the Keogh contributions and the reinvested investment earnings. Much of your Keogh wealth will come about through what bankers like to call "the magic of compound interest." But your Keogh fund is likely to be larger than what you'll have on deposit with any banker.

The longer you're in Keogh, the more your Keogh fund grows each year. Say you put in $4,000 at the end of each year, which you manage to invest at 8 percent. During the second year your Keogh fund grows $320. In the 10th year it grows $7,996, or 99 percent more than you put in that year. In the 20th year it grows $17,263, or 332 percent more than you put in that year.

Your Keogh benefits are what you buy—retirement annuities, for example—with your Keogh wealth.

WHO NEEDS KEOGHS?

Harold is 54 years old. He's an accountant with a manufacturing firm, making $50,000 a year. His wife, Judy, has a part-time clerical job. They have an adult son, a college graduate now on his own.

Harold's moonlighting earnings come from tax return preparation at tax time and fees from occasional accounting or bookkeeping work or consultation the rest of the year. In a good year, moonlighting earnings total about $7,000.

Harold is in his company's pension plan. Accountant that he is, he has been calculating what his income will be when he retires at age 65, 11 years from now. And he's not happy with what he finds.

His company's pension plan states a retirement benefit of 35 percent of his salary. Technically, his average salary during his last five years of employment will be used. Harold is aware of that but uses his present salary, $50,000, in his calculations; 35 percent of $50,000 is $17,500. The plan is integrated with social security, which in Harold's case means the $17,500 annual pension consists of two parts: the social security portion, $10,000 a year, and the $7,500 balance from his company's pension plan.

Is $17,500 a year enough to live on? Well, maybe, but just scraping by.

Another thing: The company's pension benefit is based on Harold's life expectancy—Harold will get 35 percent of salary as an annuity during *his* lifetime alone. If there's to be any company pension left for Judy after he dies (the technical term is *joint-and-*

survivor annuity), the two of them will have to take less while he lives. A joint-and-survivor annuity in Harold's case means their retirement income will be $16,830 rather than $17,500 ($10,000 plus $6,830).[1] Not the most comfortable retirement income, even when supplemented by the investments Harold has built up.

Harold is cautious, as most accountants are, but not a pessimist by nature. All the same, he has gloomy moods about his retirement years.

"I've seen 14 percent inflation," he says, "and not all that long ago. What is my $16,830 a year worth if that kind of inflation should return? My company, I think they're sound, but what if they should go under in a few years. I know my *vested* benefits are guaranteed by Uncle Sam, but I still won't get all of the annual $6,830 of company payments I'm figuring on now. And sometimes I even worry about social security. Many say it's OK, but some experts sound dubious. I *want* to believe my pension and my social security will be there, and I *expect* them to be there. But I still don't like trusting my future to other people's promises.

"I want to take control of my retirement security."

As you expected, I intend to prescribe a Keogh plan for Harold. But people in Harold's situation—in need of retirement security—aren't the only ones who can use Keoghs.

Elaine is 33 years old. She would describe herself as a housewife, and with two school-age children she's usually at home during the day. Elaine works at home, too, and not just doing housework. She's a free-lance book indexer for several New York publishing firms. She earns about $15,000 a year from this work. Elaine's husband Frank is an engineer with a local utility. He makes $40,000 a year and is in his company's pension plan. Elaine includes her free-lance income on their joint tax return. She'd do so even if she didn't know the publishers had to report what they pay her to the federal government.

"I can see why Harold is interested in Keoghs," Elaine says. "He's a man—a breadwinner, as they used to say—in his 50s. Of

---

[1] This assumes a joint-and-100-percent-survivor annuity. See Chapter 12 for an explanation of this concept.

course he's thinking about retirement and what he and Judy will live on after that.

"My situation is different. Frank and I are under 40. Oh, I know you're supposed to think about your retirement years however young you are. But it's really too far off for us to do that.

"I'm worried about something else. Well, maybe it's more annoyed than worried. I work at home, indexing, and earn $15,000 or so a year at it. I'd like to invest that money to build a family nest egg. But I lose so much of it in taxes every year. It's frustrating. Do you have any suggestions for *my* situation?"

Do I? Sure, a Keogh. A Keogh doesn't have to be *just* a retirement plan. But even those that are pure retirement programs are still *investment* programs for as long as you keep the funds invested. Keoghs cease to be investment programs only when you take the funds out of investment and put them to personal use.

Do you, as Elaine does, lose too much of your moonlighting income in taxes? Does that limit what you are able to invest?

This may sound like the old TV commercial: "How do you spell relief?" K-E-O-G-H. Keoghs relieve both problems. You pay no tax on the moonlighting income you put into your Keogh. Then you invest that income, tax-free.

And now for Peter, our third Keogh candidate. Peter is 41. He holds a Ph.D. in biochemistry. He's a professor of toxicology at a state university, with a salary of $50,000 a year. Peter is often engaged as consultant and expert witness by defense attorneys in product-liability cases. His fees, this year and for the past two years, have averaged $30,000 a year. Peter is enrolled in the university's pension plan. He's unmarried but has a live-in woman friend who also works at the university.

You couldn't get Peter to talk about retirement. He tunes out. But he's plenty interested in money and takes an understandable pride in what he's able to earn in addition to his salary. Peter doesn't need his outside earnings to live on. He's an active investor, investing all of the outside earnings he has left each year after taxes. Keoghs, I need hardly say, are for Peter, too.

A Keogh is a wealth-building machine because it harnesses three driving forces: (1) your ability to earn income in your self-employment activity, (2) your personal savings and investment program activity, and (3) tax relief.

There are no "typical" Keogh investors. Harold, Peter, and Elaine are three among millions of Keogh candidates. But their situations are illustrative. Harold's case will help show how Keoghs are used for retirement security. Elaine's situation will illustrate how Keoghs contribute to a modest family nest egg. We'll work with Peter to see how Keoghs help wealth accumulation.

WHAT CAN KEOGHS BE USED FOR?

You should plan to accumulate tens of thousands of dollars or hundreds of thousands of dollars in your Keogh. You should use your Keogh only for projects that call for that much money: retirement, an investment fund, a nest egg for a secure future, an estate for your children or grandchildren.

Those uses are OK. Other uses are discouraged or prohibited unless you terminate your plan at the same time. For example, you can use Keogh assets to buy a house if the plan you've chosen is the profit-sharing type. But in most cases you'll have to pay an extra tax on the Keogh funds you withdraw to spend on the house. If you've chosen a pension plan, you won't be allowed to use funds for a purpose such as buying a house until you reach your plan's retirement age or you terminate your plan.

WHO QUALIFIES FOR A KEOGH?

To be allowed a Keogh, you will have to make money in some kind of *self-employment* activity. That activity can be full-time self-employment, or you can be a full-time employee with a moonlighting self-employment sideline, or you can be a homemaker with a sideline. In each case you can have a Keogh for your self-employment activity. If you have two self-employment activities, you can have two Keoghs.

You must have *income* from this self-employment activity, but the source of that income doesn't matter. It can be fees, hourly, weekly, or monthly charges, retainers, royalties from writing or inventions, or other income for any kind of service, as long as it isn't investment income, or wages or salary as an employee.

To have income, your self-employment must be *profitable*. In technical terms, you must have "net earnings from self-employment." If you're a sculptor but no one buys your work, you're self-employed, all right, but you can't have a Keogh because you have no net earnings. If you have some income but spend more on the activity than you take in, again, no Keogh because no net earnings.

ARE *YOU* SELF-EMPLOYED?

See if you're on this list of the most common self-employment activities of moonlighters:

Accountant

Actuary

Arbitrator

Architect

Author

Barber, beautician, manicurist

Bookkeeper

Composer

Consultant, any subject

Court reporter

Craftsman

Creative artist

Direct seller

Engineer

Fisherman, even if employed (a quirk in the law)

Foster parent

Free-lance activity of any sort

Independent insurance agent

Insurance adjuster

Inventor

Lawyer

Lecturer

Model

Musician

Nurse: private duty, registered or practical

Psychologist

Process server

Real estate agent

Stenographer, public

Tax return preparer

Telephone solicitor

Therapist

Tutor

Typist

Word processor

It's not always easy to know exactly who is an employee and who is self-employed. But that is a problem for the lawyers and tax accountants, not for you.

For you, the answer is easy. If the person or business you work for withholds tax on your earnings, you are an employee. You can't consider those earnings self-employment income. You can't use them in your Keogh. If no tax is withheld, you're self-employed. You can use those earnings in your Keogh.

Well, it's not quite *that* simple. The person who pays you has the duty to determine whether you are an employee or self-employed. But the Internal Revenue Service (IRS) can review that decision. It could turn out that the person you worked for is wrong. If he or she considered you self-employed when the tax regulations say you're an employee, you are bound by the regulations.

A Keogh based on income as an employee won't be valid. That rarely happens. When it occurs, it's generally because you work on the premises of the person who pays you.

KEOGHS AND THE UNDERGROUND ECONOMY

Now for a sensitive issue. The term *underground economy* is sometimes used for moonlighting income that is not reported for tax purposes. Those who try to hide their moonlighting income will get nothing from this book. Income a person seeks to hide from the

tax authorities can hardly be invested in a Keogh. Keogh investments can be made only when self-employment earnings are
reported for tax purposes.

No reader of these pages needs reminding that tax cheating is a
crime. Tax experts will tell you it's a crime becoming easier to
detect. Federal law now requires a business to tell the IRS when it
pays a self-employed person $600 or more during the year. The IRS
can now track down more of those who try to hide moonlighting
earnings.

I think it's right that moonlighters' tax cheating should be
punished. But for moonlighters, tax honesty offers more than an
easy conscience. It offers a financial reward: the opportunity for
Keogh benefits.

Self-employment earnings invested in Keogh plans are tax-
deductible. Any allowable Keogh deduction eliminates tax on an
equivalent amount of earnings. But that's not all. Keogh money
can be invested almost anywhere, and all income is tax-free as long
as if remains invested. The person who hides his moonlighting
income has few opportunities to invest it in a way that won't
eventually disclose his crime.

I'm not trying to argue that Keogh benefits make tax honesty
profitable for moonlighters who might otherwise try to hide their
income. Tax honesty is a matter of conscience and respect for or
fear of the law. But Keogh investment reduces in a legal way the
tax some moonlighters try to avoid by illegal means, and profitable
investment becomes possible for moonlighters who come out of the
closet.

SELF-EMPLOYMENT AND SOCIAL SECURITY

The following are remarks for those who are just starting their
self-employment activity and maybe for readers who failed in
previous years to report their self-employment income on their tax
returns. Other readers probably know it already.

Income from self-employment is sometimes subject to the
federal *self-employment tax,* a tax used to provide social security
benefits for self-employed persons.

A self-employed person owes no self-employment tax if he or

she has paid the maximum social security tax as an employee. A person pays the maximum if his or her wages, salary, or other income as an employee exceeds the social security base. For 1991, that base is $53,400 for the old age portion and $125,000 for the Medicare portion.

Your social security benefits depend largely on the amount of social security and self-employment tax you pay. The larger your tax, the larger your benefit. Most retirees get back from the social security system much more than they put in. (As you can see, I don't share Harold's worry that social security may not be there at retirement.)

WHO'S INVOLVED IN YOUR KEOGH?

A Keogh always involves two people: an employer and an employee.

"Then how can *I* use a Keogh?" Elaine, the free-lancer, asks with a note of exasperation in her voice. "You know *I* don't have any employees. And I don't consider the publishers I index for my employers. I work at home, at my own pace, and in my own way, without any direction from anyone. I'm neither an employer nor an employee."

No problem. "Employer" and "employee" are legal technicalities here. A Keogh plan is a plan *for employees*. But self-employed persons are considered employees under the Keogh law. And if by this legal fiction the self-employed person is an employee, he or she must be employed by *someone*. A moonlighter or other business owner is also the *employer*. (If the self-employed person is a partner, the partnership is the employer.) So Elaine, like every other moonlighter, is both employer and employee.

There is also always a third party to a Keogh plan. That party is either a trustee or an insurance company. As a moonlighter you can make yourself your own trustee. In fact, I recommend it unless you decide you want an insurance company plan (see Chapter 9).

But the legal fictions and technicalities that make you both employer and employee have an important practical effect. A Keogh plan is a legal document, a kind of contract between employer and employee. Even though it's a contract between yourself and yourself, to be administered by yourself, that doesn't mean you don't have to do it correctly. It must be as carefully done as if there really were three different parties.

In a sense the U.S. government also is involved. Keoghs are government programs. The government will always claim the right to review your contract—your Keogh plan—to see that it satisfies the rules. And the government also can check to see whether you're actually doing what your contract says you should.

You might want to involve others, such as an investment advisor, a legal advisor, or in some cases an actuary. And of course your family is involved, as persons who may take or share in your Keogh wealth after your death. But at all times the key player in your Keogh, the person most in control, is you.

"HOW MUCH CAN I MAKE ON MY KEOGH?"

There's no ceiling. There are Keogh millionaires. The more you put in, the longer you keep it in, and the better your investments perform, the more you'll have. Start early, stay long, invest as smart as you can.

Consider Peter. He could reasonably expect to build a Keogh fund of over half a million dollars. Say he sets up a Keogh money-purchase pension plan. He puts $6,000 a year into the plan out of his consulting income. Say he does this each year until he reaches 65 (in other words, every year for 24 years). And assume he earns 10 percent each year on his Keogh investments.

At age 65, Peter would have a fund totaling $530,983. He could keep it invested, where it would continue to grow at a tax-free 10 percent a year. Or he could take out some or all of it. Let's say he took it all out at once. Tax on this could be $104,496,[2] so Peter could have $426,487 after taxes.

---

[2] No one can be certain what the tax rates will be in future years. The tax liabilities here reflect realistic assumptions of combined federal and state tax rates.

Peter actually put in $6,000 a year, or a total of $144,000. The rest, well over a quarter of a million dollars ($282,487), is investment earnings.

This is a strong case for Keoghs, at least in Peter's case, but it's not yet wholly convincing. We need more. We need to compare what would happen if Peter had invested without a Keogh.

So this time we assume the $6,000 a year is invested outside a Keogh, right? Well, not really. That is, not $6,000. Peter can't come up with the $6,000 because outside a Keogh this $6,000 is taxable. In the 30 percent tax bracket, $6,000 becomes $4,200. So he has $4,200 to invest each year, not $6,000.

No, it doesn't weaken my point that Peter could invest $6,000 by raising $1,800 elsewhere, which he could add to the $4,200. He would have $1,800 anyway and could invest it outside the Keogh plan in any case.

So Peter invests $4,200 each year, on which he gets a 10 percent return? No, not *10 percent*. Outside the Keogh, he must pay tax on his investment income. So his after-tax rate of return, in the 30 percent bracket, is 7 percent, not 10 percent.

After 24 years Peter's nest egg outside a Keogh would total $244,341. In this case the $244,341 is fully tax-paid. So the proper comparison is with the $426,487 *after-tax* assets he would have under the Keogh plan, which still leaves Keogh investing $182,146 ahead.

In fact, Keogh investing is favored from almost every angle. The Keogh investor puts in and invests more because he or she has more left after taxes. In the case illustrated above, Peter could invest $43,200 more through the Keogh plan than outside it ($144,000 in the Keogh compared to $100,800 outside).

And more is earned on a Keogh investment, $138,946 more, even *after taxes are paid* on a lump-sum withdrawal, than outside the Keogh ($282,487 in the Keogh compared to $143,541 outside).

Look at it this way: Starting with the same dollars ($6,000 before taxes) and investing them the same way (in an investment yielding 10 percent before taxes), Peter makes 97 percent more by investing through a Keogh than outside a Keogh.

"WHAT WILL A KEOGH COST ME?"

There are two kind of costs;

1. There are the amounts you put into the plan—your Keogh "contributions." How much you want to put in is entirely up to you. The more you put in, the more you'll have. These are *investments*, after all, not *expenses*. (In the pages to come, you'll find plenty of advice on planning your tax-deductible Keogh contributions, using Harold, Peter, Elaine, and others as examples.)

2. There's the cost of setting up or getting into a Keogh plan, which can be little or nothing. Or if you want the most aggressive plan, with complex options and opportunities tailored to your individual situation, first year start-up costs can be substantial. (We'll say more about that in Chapter 15.)

"HOW CAN I BE SURE IT'S THE RIGHT MOVE?"

I think Keoghs are the best deal going for moonlighters now. If you obey the rules, your only risk is making the wrong investment decisions. And you risk that anyway. The rules may change, of course. But even if they do, they aren't likely to hurt what you've done already. They probably would affect only future benefits. You can be as sure with Keoghs as you could be with any investment or retirement program.

But be careful about financial projections of future Keogh benefits. Be careful even of *my* financial projections, although I've nothing to gain or lose by whatever you choose to do. Financial projections tend to assume certainty in an uncertain world. Mine do that. Projections in these pages may assume that Peter or Elaine or Harold or someone else earns a specified sum each year from self-employment activity. Yet everyone knows that moonlighting income fluctuates from year to year. You gain a client or lose one, they give you more work or less, they pay late, you increase your fees. In the real world you can't *assume* the same amount each year. Nor can you assume a specific rate of increase.

The same goes for your Keogh contributions. The amount you earn controls the amount you are able to contribute. If self-employment income fluctuates, so will your Keogh contributions (more for some plans than for others).

Something similar happens to projections of investment income. Investment earnings tend to fluctuate, too. Interest rates rise in one year and fall in another; a corporation pays a dividend in one year and not another; you sell one investment at a profit in one year and another at a loss the next year. There are ways to minimize fluctuation, for those who want to (see Chapters 8 and 9), but to assume a constant rate of return, as most projections do (mine included), is to assume something that rarely happens.

What about taxes and tax rates? Aren't these fixed by law? Yes. We can be certain what those will be until Congress and the president agree to change the law. But they *do* change the law. They sometimes raise tax rates and sometimes lower them. They sometimes grant tax benefits—they granted a host of Keogh benefits effective in 1984—and sometimes reduce them or take them away.

And to some extent individuals make their own changes in tax rates. As income rises, so do the rates that apply to that income. It's called tax progressivity, and we've had it since the income tax came in. And the rates fall as income falls

Every element of a Keogh financial projection is subject to change. No, not just *subject to* change; it *will* change. The amount you actually will earn from self-employment *will* differ from what you predict. So will what you actually contribute to your Keogh and what you earn on your Keogh investments. And tax benefits are pretty certain to differ in some way from what they are today.

But there's really no alternative. Financial projections give you *some* idea of what you can expect, which is better than no idea at all. Tax rules 15 or 25 years from now won't be what they are today. But who believes we'll have *no* tax system then? The system we have today is probably the best guide to what it will be in the future.

"CAN CREDITORS GET AT MY KEOGH ASSETS?"

In general, your Keogh is "judgment-proof," immune from claims of your creditors. No attachment, no garnishment, no levy.

There are a few exceptions:

1. The U.S. government can attach your Keogh assets for your personal back taxes. (Well, you expected that.)

2. Your spouse (if you are legally separated), your ex-spouse (if you are divorced), or your child may be able to attach a portion of your Keogh assets by means of a court order called a qualified domestic relations order. This could entitle him or her to a payment out of your Keogh assets when you become able to withdraw retirement funds. That can happen even though you have not retired.

3. Once you have started to collect an annuity under your Keogh, you can assign up to 10 percent of your future benefits to creditors.

Any funds you withdraw from your Keogh can be reached by your creditors, except that the law in your state may limit what retirement funds a creditor can reach.

KEOGH PLAN TAX BENEFITS

A Keogh plan is the ultimate tax shelter. A Keogh gives you four distinct tax benefits.

1. You take a tax deduction for the amount you put into your Keogh (your Keogh contribution). You deduct it in the year you make the contribution (or in some cases, the year *before* you make it; see page 49). That is better than the usual tax rules, in which an employer must put off tax deduction until the employee collects his or her benefit. Deduction today is worth more than deduction tomorrow.

2. You pay no tax on the contribution you made for your *own* benefit, even though you have an absolute right to collect it eventually. That is better than the usual rules, which tax employees *immediately* on amounts they will collect only in the future. You will be taxed only when you collect on your Keogh at some future date. Tax tomorrow is preferable to tax today.

3. Investment earnings on amounts you contribute to your Keogh trust[3] are not taxable to anyone until you or your heirs take them out. That is better than the usual rules where a trust is used. The usual rules find *someone* to tax on the trust's income: the beneficiary (in this case, you in your capacity as employee); the person who created the trust, usually called the grantor (you again, this time in your capacity as employer); or the trust itself.

4. Amounts you collect at retirement or that your heirs collect after your death can qualify for reduced tax liability (compared to the usual rules), as discussed later. No tax is imposed on anyone else.

"IF I HAVE A KEOGH, WILL THE IRS AUDIT ME?"

Maybe, but not just because you have a Keogh. There's nothing sinister or suspicious about a Keogh, no taint of illegality or corner cutting. State your income and deductions openly, without fear.

WHAT YOUR KEOGH PLAN WILL SAY

Your Keogh is a kind of contract. The key provisions are *how much* and *when*.

How much. With one type of Keogh, your plan will say how much is to be put in for you each year. For example, you might say that 20 percent of your self-employment earnings is paid in for you each year.

If you choose another type of Keogh, it will say, more or less, how much you will collect each year when you retire. For example,

---

[3] Remember, from page 9 ("Who's Involved in Your Keogh?") that your Keogh contributions go into a trust or insurance company. If it's a trust, you can be trustee and have direct personal control of your investments. The postponement of tax described here, which assumes you use a trust, also applies if you use an insurance company instead.

your plan might say that at retirement you would collect an annuity equal to what your average self-employment income was during some period of years you select.

When. With either type, your plan will say *when* you get to enjoy those benefits. With one type of Keogh, it will be when you reach a certain age. With another type of Keogh, you can enjoy the benefits starting two years after you put funds in.

HOW TO *BECOME* QUALIFIED FOR A KEOGH

It takes only two things to qualify: You must be *self-employed,* and self-employment must be *profitable.*

If you're not self-employed now and want a Keogh, you'll have to start some self-employment activity. Easier said than done, of course. You'll need to choose an activity, gain a clientele, and operate in a businesslike fashion. That's a broader subject than this book can handle. But there are many books to be found in bookstores and libraries that can help you.

Some people hesitate to start a sideline because they fear that taxes will eat up their profits. Keoghs help a lot in such cases. Keogh tax benefits offset much of the tax burden on self-employment profits.

You may have a sideline already but work at it as an *employee,* so you're not *self*-employed. You might convert that to a self-employment activity and qualify for a Keogh. But be careful of possible extra costs. As an employee, you may receive certain fringe benefits, such as participation in a company health care plan or workers' compensation in the event of job-connected injury. Just possibly, you might be included in the company pension plan. If you have such benefits now, you'll lose them if you become self-employed. Also, the tax you must pay toward your social security benefits may go up.

And you'll have to behave differently to become really self-employed. If your sideline had you working on the premises of the company that paid you, you now should furnish your own workplace somewhere else—say, in an office or studio or at home. If you worked for one person only, you should widen your clientele.

Going self-employed can be worthwhile despite all the costs

and trouble. But be sure you've calculated both sides of the equation.

Despite all I've said on this topic, I don't feel I've been of much help to anyone thinking of becoming self-employed. I can do even less for the self-employed person who's losing money in self-employment. At this distance from any reader, nothing I could advise would be worth much in helping turn the activity around.

Except this: Suppose you have two different self-employment activities. One is profitable; the other is losing today but you hope to make it profitable soon. You can set up a Keogh for the profitable activity. The losses from the loser don't hurt the Keogh, even if its losses exceed your profits from the other activity. If the loser becomes profitable later, you could set up a second Keogh or maybe combine the two activities for your Keogh.

WHICH TYPE OF KEOGH PLAN?

"My company has a defined-benefit pension plan," Harold says, "and I've heard of other types of retirement plan. Where my wife, Judy, works, they have something they call a 401(k) plan, though she can't join it. These are *company* plans, though. What kind of plan could I have with a Keogh?"

You have several choices. You may adopt either a pension plan or a profit-sharing plan. You may choose between two types of pension plan. You may even adopt two different types of Keogh plan.

A pension plan is always a *retirement* plan. That means it sets limits on how early you can take funds out for personal, family, or business use. The general idea is that you take funds out only when you retire. That doesn't mean you can't get at your funds until retirement, but you may have to terminate the plan to do so, unless you have reached your plan's retirement *age*.

Even if you have a retirement plan, the investment characteristics predominate over the retirement part. You are free to sell, switch, and move your investments as you see fit. There's no penalty on that, and no one will interfere with anything you do, as long as you don't take funds out of investment and distribute them to yourself or others.

A profit-sharing plan does not have to be a retirement plan. Funds you put in the plan must stay in for at least two years before you withdraw them. Apart from that restriction, you're allowed to withdraw at any age, for any reason. But there's usually an extra tax to pay if you withdraw before you reach age 59½.

You could adopt a profit-sharing plan and make it a retirement plan. That might be advisable if you had employees. Otherwise don't do it.

A *profit-sharing plan* is the simplest type of plan. It involves the least commitment of any Keogh plan—and offers the smallest benefit to you. This is no criticism of profit-sharing plans or those who use them. Many self-employed persons have such plans and are satisfied with their performance. But you should be aware that profit-sharing alone is not the route to the *maximum* Keogh benefit.

A *money-purchase pension plan* (sometimes called a defined-contribution pension plan) also is a simple plan, but it involves a greater commitment on your part than profit-sharing. Depending on your age when you enter, a money-purchase plan can produce the largest benefit.

The *defined-benefit pension plan* (sometimes called a regular pension plan) is the other type of pension plan. It is a complex arrangement, involving a major commitment on your part. Depending on your age when you enter, a defined-benefit plan can produce the largest benefit.

For the next three chapters we will consider what the various types of Keogh plan might do for Elaine, Harold, and Peter and what they might do for you. I recommend that you select the plan that suits your situation and temperament. If you want to feel free to contribute something in some years and nothing in others, answerable to no one when you choose to contribute nothing, select a profit-sharing plan. If you are willing to commit what it takes to build up the largest possible pension benefit, despite some inconvenience, you will choose a money-purchase plan, a defined-benefit plan, or both. As you read on, you will find the principles to govern your choice of plan.

CHAPTER 2

KEOGH MONEY-PURCHASE PENSION PLAN

A money-purchase pension plan may be right for both Peter and Elaine. It's too early to be sure, but it's a good place to start. With a money-purchase plan, each year you put in a specific percentage of your self-employment earnings.

"Are you stuck in future years with the percentage you began with?" Peter asks.

Not really. You're allowed to increase or reduce the percentage. If you reduce it, you're supposed to give written notice of the reduction—to yourself—at least 15 days before the reduction takes effect. Personally, I prefer not to tinker much with the percentages. It's best to choose the largest percentage you can afford—20 percent of your moonlighting earnings, if possible—and stick with it as long as you can.

Those who want year-to-year flexibility in the percentages they use would do better to choose profit-sharing plans or profit-sharing combined with money-purchase plans (see Chapter 5).

When you start a money-purchase plan, you can't be sure how much your Keogh will grow to. Some might find this a problem, though I don't. Money-purchase plan amounts can't be known in advance for two reasons:

1. With a money-purchase plan you contribute a different amount to your Keogh each year. The amounts will vary, even though you contribute the same *percentage* of self-employment earnings, because the amount of earnings varies.

2. Your earnings on your Keogh investment also vary each year. This will happen with virtually any investment you make. Even if you don't sell or switch any investment once you've made it (and selling or switching will sometimes be the best move), each year you have a new Keogh contribution to invest, and each year's investment climate is different from the year before.

When you retire, you'll be entitled to collect everything you put in, plus everything you have earned by investing those amounts. But you can't know when you start how much you'll invest in the future. Nor can you know what you'll earn on these amounts. So you can't know at the start what you'll have when you stop.

Pension professionals tend to think of retirement plans in terms of the annuity paid when a person retires. Thus, a defined-benefit plan (discussed in Chapter 3) pays an annuity specified, or defined, in advance. They contrast this with a money-purchase plan. The latter doesn't pay an annuity defined in advance. It pays whatever annuity the funds you have at retirement will buy—in other words, what your money will purchase.

This old-fashioned language is still used for the pension plan we're considering here. But no one who goes into a money-purchase plan *has to* use his or her funds to buy an annuity at retirement. You will have several other options for those funds. See the discussion on this in Chapter 12.

That is how money-purchase plans work. Now for how they can pay off.

As before, let's assume Peter set up a money-purchase plan and contributed $6,000 (20 percent of earnings) to it each year. And let's say that now, at age 65, he wants to use his Keogh funds to buy an annuity. How big an annuity can he get? In pension lingo, how much will his money purchase?

We know Peter had $530,983 before paying any tax on it (see page 10). If he buys an annuity with this money, he won't have to pay any tax until he starts collecting the annuity. So he can spend the full amount on the annuity. If the annuity is based on an 8 percent interest rate, $530,983 will buy Peter an annuity of $54,081 a year for life.

Even if we use the more conservative 6.5 percent interest rate, $530,983 buys Peter a $48,187-a-year annuity. That is a comfortable retirement pension by any standard. I hope mine can be as good.

Shouldn't Peter be worried that 24 years from now $530,983 will be worth less than it is today because of inflation? Sure he should. So am I. But inflation also will increase the amount he earns each year and the amount he can put into his Keogh plan. And it may well increase his return on his Keogh investments.

So it's true that $530,983 won't be worth as much when Peter retires as it is today. But if there *is* inflation, Peter will have much more than $530,983. And it *could* be (no guarantees, of course) that what he'll have then will be at least equal in value to what $530,983 will buy today.

We'll consider the defined-benefit type of pension plan in the next chapter. That type of plan can come closer to inflation-proofing your retirement arrangement than money-purchase can.

CHAPTER 3

KEOGH DEFINED-BENEFIT PENSION PLAN

A defined-benefit pension plan is more complicated than other Keogh plans, more complicated because it is potentially the richest plan, especially for older moonlighters. I think Harold should adopt such a plan.

"Why should I want a defined-benefit plan?" Harold asks. "Peter can get a pension of at least $48,187 with his money-purchase plan. That's plenty good enough for me. Are you saying I can get *more* than that with a defined-benefit plan?"

No, I'm not. Harold couldn't get a larger Keogh pension. His pension will be much smaller. Even so, the defined-benefit type of Keogh is the best choice for him.

Peter will get more because he will have more in his Keogh. He will be contributing and investing, contributing and investing, for 24 years. Harold, if he means to retire at 65, has only 11 years of contribution and investment ahead.

Peter would be contributing 20 percent of his moonlighting earnings to his money-purchase plan. In Peter's case this is 20 percent of $30,000, or $6,000 a year. After 11 years of this, with investments earning at 10 percent, Peter would have $111,186.

Put Harold in a money-purchase plan and he could contribute no more than 20 percent of *his* moonlighting income each year. In his case, that would be 20 percent of $7,000, or $1,400 a year. After 11 years in a money-purchase plan earning at 10 percent, Harold would have $25,943 in his Keogh at retirement. That would buy him a Keogh pension of $2,642 a year at retirement (assuming an 8 percent rate). Much better than without any Keogh, and better than with a Keogh profit-sharing plan, but not good enough. Harold could have more, of course, if he moonlighted longer and retired later. Some might want to do that; Harold doesn't. Harold would rather build a larger retirement fund by contributing more than a money-purchase plan allows.

A *defined-benefit* plan will let him do this. He could put in enough each year to buy a pension of $10,000 a year when he retires. Depending on certain assumptions that I'll get to soon, this could mean a Keogh fund of $98,181 by age 65. That is 278 percent more than he could have with a money-purchase plan.

But remember: You don't have to spend your retirement funds on a pension when you reach retirement age. You are free to use those funds in other ways if you choose. Keogh rules are concerned with how big a pension you *could* buy with the funds you have available. No one except you and your family cares whether you actually buy one.

With a defined-benefit plan, you select the amount of pension you want at retirement. Then you work back to figure the amount you'd need to buy such an annuity from an insurance company on the basis of your life expectancy.

The richest plan you're allowed to have will pay you each year about as much as you made in any year from your moonlighting work. Specifically, you can collect each year what your moonlighting earned income averaged in the three consecutive years in which income was the highest.

For example, suppose you conducted a self-employment business as a sideline for 15 years before retirement in 1993, with earned income as follows:

1979	$ 4,000	1987	$ 6,000
1980	(1,200)*	1988	8,700
1981	6,500	1989	10,800
1982	5,400	1990	12,000
1983	3,800	1991	11,600
1984	12,000	1992	10,700
1985	8,100	1993	9,000
1986	5,800		

* Loss.

The average of your high three years (1989–1991) is $11,467. So you could establish a plan to pay you that much each year for life after retirement.

In private industry a pension that's equal to your salary is almost unbelievably generous. With a Keogh, charity begins at home. A pension equal to your earned income (the *average* earned income, that is) is entirely up to you.

You could set some lower pension if you want to—say, 60 percent of your average high three years. But most people would like the largest possible Keogh fund. If you are such a person, you should go after the highest pension you're allowed.

To reach the Keogh fund you've set for yourself, you will make a Keogh contribution each year, or most years, and take a tax deduction for it. And you'll get only the Keogh fund you pay for. You may have a fund of $250,000 in mind. But if what you put in, plus what you make investing it, adds up to only $160,000, then $160,000 is what you get.

Let's say Harold's moonlighting earned income averages $10,000 a year, or averages that much for his best three consecutive years. (Yes, I know Harold hasn't actually made this much. We'll deal with that shortly. Meanwhile, let's assume.) So he can pay himself a $10,000-a-year pension. Or put another way, he can build a Keogh retirement fund of $98,181, which (assuming an 8 percent interest rate) will buy a $10,000-a-year lifetime pension at age 65.

Harold could reach this amount by putting in $5,898 a year for the 11 years before he retires. This assumes he invests the money at 8 percent a year. He has other contribution options as well. We'll consider those shortly.

THE $10,000-A-YEAR SAFETY NET

Harold's moonlighting earnings average $7,000 a year, but he can have a pension as large as $10,000 a year if he wants to.

I've mentioned the *basic* limit on the size of your defined-benefit pension: your annual pension can go as high as the average of your earned income for your best three consecutive years. So you may be wondering why I've seemed to promise Harold a pension larger than this. It's because there's an exception to the basic limit that fits Harold perfectly, and I advise him to grab it.

You can have an annual pension in any amount you want up to $10,000 even though your average high three years is less than that amount. To qualify for this exception, you can't have had a profit-sharing or money-purchase plan for your moonlighting business, and you must have been in your defined-benefit plan at least 10 years before you retire.[1] Harold will meet both requirements.

Of course, you get only what you pay for. You will collect $10,000 a year only if what you put in, plus the earnings thereon, will buy that much at retirement. And tax deductions for your contributions can't exceed your self-employment earnings. So if your targeted $10,000 pension calls for you to put $4,000 into your fund this year, but you earned only $1,800, the most you can deduct is $1,800 even if you actually put in $4,000 by drawing on other funds.

RETIREMENT AGE—ANOTHER TOOL TO BUILD YOUR KEOGH FUND

Your first bit of defined-benefit planning is to decide on the amount of pension you want when you retire. Your second step is to decide *when* you want to retire. You must decide on both before you can know how big a Keogh investment fund you'll need.

"Decisions, decisions," Harold sighed. "This is all pretty complicated, you know." Sure it is. It's the price of taking your retirement future into your own hands.

Let's say you know how much of a Keogh pension you want. And let's say that's $10,000 a year for life.

Do you want to retire "early"? Let's consider the economic consequences of such a decision. If you retire early, you'll collect your pension for a longer period. That means you'll collect more

[1] If you're in for less than 10 years, your pension must be proportionately reduced, as described on page 26.

than if you retire later. To collect more, you'll need a larger Keogh fund than if you retire later.

But that's only part of the story. When you select your plan's retirement age, you are setting the period of time over which you will put money into your plan. The closer you are now to that retirement age, the more you'll have to put in each year.

Assuming the same amount of pension, the earlier you retire, the more you collect. And the earlier you plan to retire, the less time you have now to fund toward that larger amount. So with an early retirement you must build a large Keogh faster.

For example, suppose your pension is to be $10,000 a year. If you have a 20-year life expectancy when you retire at age 65, you'll collect $200,000 if you live to be 85. If you retire at 60 with a 24-year expectancy, you'll collect $240,000 by age 84.

Of course, an annuity to pay $10,000 a year over 24 years (a 24-year expectancy) costs more than one paying $10,000 a year over a 20-year expectancy—say, $105,288 for 24 years compared to $98,181 for 20 years (assuming an 8 percent interest rate). And you have a shorter time to build to that larger fund. At age 48 you'd have 12 years to accumulate $105,288, compared to 17 years to accumulate $98,181. It costs $2,655 a year to build $98,181 in 17 years at 8 percent. It costs $5,228 a year to build $105,288 in 12 years, again at 8 percent. In each case, costs are tax-deductible.

For most Keogh investors there's only one legal limitation to consider here: your pension may have to be reduced if you had your business for less than 10 years when you retire.

The largest retirement pension you're allowed under the standard rules is 100 percent of your average high three consecutive years' earned income. The percentage allowed if you're in business less than 10 years before retirement is 100 percent times the number of years in business, divided by 10.

Example.   Say you start a sideline business and set up a pension plan at age 53. You adopt age 60 as your retirement age. Your average high three years earned income is $10,000. Your pension at retirement can't be more than $7,000 a year; that is, $10,000 times 70 percent (100% × 7 ÷ 10).

More complex rules apply to persons with very large self-employment earnings who plan early retirement. They would apply, for example, if you planned to retire with $98,064 a year before age 65. Those rules are a bit too complex for discussion here.

"Retirement Age" Doesn't Have to Be the Age You Retire

I've been talking about retirement age in your Keogh as though it had no connection with your retirement from any regular job you may have. Well, there *is* no connection unless you want to make one.

You can make your Keogh retirement age the same as that for your regular employment. Or you can make it earlier or later. Knowing this, you might tend to select a Keogh retirement age that fits with when you intend to stop moonlighting.

Very reasonable and perfectly legal. But it's smarter to use your Keogh retirement age as a tool to build your Keogh fund. Remember retirement-age economics. The earlier your retirement age, the more you'll put in each year and the more you'll have in your retirement fund. So you maximize your Keogh fund if you adopt a relatively young Keogh retirement age.

"Are you saying you don't have to retire from self-employment when you reach your Keogh retirement age?" Elaine wants to know. "That you can pick an arbitrary retirement age, build up a Keogh investment based on that age, and then forget about retirement when you actually reach that age?"

"Well, yes," I answer. "More or less. *Arbitrary* is a heavy word. It sounds like *unreasonable*. You shouldn't do anything unreasonable or arbitrary with your plan. Pick the earliest age at which someone in your line of moonlighting work might *reasonably* decide to retire. If you're 41, like Peter, you're not likely to plan retirement at age 50. But you might consider age 60 or 62."

And it's reasonable only if you can afford it. You should aim to make your contributions fully tax-deductible. That means you shouldn't shoot for a Keogh fund so large that your annual contributions average more than your moonlighting income.

"But isn't there something wrong here?" Elaine asks. "Aren't you building a larger retirement fund than you're allowed? If you paid in toward retirement at age 60, and then you actually retire at, say, 68, won't you have too much?"

Yes, usually, though that's not the problem you might think it is. Let's take Elaine's example. You're set up to retire at age 60 with $15,000 a year for life from your Keogh. You'll need $188,255 for that at age 60 (assuming a 24-year life expectancy and an annuity earning 6 percent). Assume that when you reach age 60, you have $188,255 in your Keogh. That's OK even if you decide not to retire then. But you normally won't be allowed to make any further deductible contributions to your defined-benefit Keogh.

But even if you can't put more into your Keogh, your Keogh fund will still increase: you can continue to invest and reinvest your Keogh plan earnings. Thus (to continue Elaine's example), if $188,255 was frozen in the plan from age 60 to age 68, Elaine's "late retiree" would have $318,053 at his actual retirement, assuming funds earned at 6 percent over that period.

At retirement the late retiree would have $155,639 more than the $162,414 he needs to buy a $15,000-a-year life annuity (assuming an 18-year life expectancy and an annuity at 6 percent) from age 68. What happens to the "extra" $155,639? Forfeited to the IRS? Not at all. It belongs to the retiree. He'll pay a heavy tax on this portion (see Chapter 14) but the "young retirement" may still, on the whole, be a smart move.

Your plan need not provide specifically for two ages, one for normal retirement and another for early retirement. That is common in private industry, but for you, it's not necessary. It's your plan, and you can retire when you please. You'll usually pay a tax penalty on amounts you take out before age 59½, barring death or disability (see page 131). But that happens whether or not the plan specifically provides for two retirement ages.

HOW YOUR OWN INTEREST RATE FORECASTS HELP BUILD YOUR KEOGH FUND

Harold has noticed my repeated reference to interest rates. He's heard me say that an investment of so much will buy a pension of so many dollars, "assuming an 8 percent interest rate," or a 6 percent rate, or whatever. And that Keogh contributions of so many dollars a year will build to a Keogh fund of such-and-such size, assuming, say, an 8 percent rate.

"These are all *projections*," Harold notes. "We're just guesstimating what interest rates may be in the future. Since we can't be sure what rate to use, shouldn't we be conservative? Shouldn't we assume lower rates rather than higher?

"And by the way, do you really mean interest in the technical sense, like interest on a bond or bank deposit? Shouldn't we include any kind of profit on investment, be it dividends or rents, as well as interest?"

Harold is right about the meaning of *interest*. Pension professionals speak of "interest rate" because in the old days pension funds were usually invested in interest-paying bonds. "Rate of return on investment" is a more accurate term in these days of more free-wheeling investment. Still, in most cases I'll stick with the term *interest rate*.

And he's right too that it can be better to assume lower interest rates than higher rates. But the conservative interest rate assumptions that I advise have nothing to do with conservative *investment policy*. Conservative interest rate forecasts work for you whether your investment strategy is conservative or aggressive.

Your goal is the largest Keogh fund you can accumulate. The lower the rate you use, the larger your Keogh fund can be. To see how this works, imagine you're going to buy your pension as an annuity for your life from an insurance company. You tell the company how much it must pay you every year. Say that's $12,000. And it knows, sort of, how many years it must pay this amount. That is, it knows how old you are and can calculate your life expectancy. Say that will be 15 years at the time the annuity is to start.

So knowing how much and how long it has to pay, its next question is what to charge you for the annuity. Here's where its interest rate (investment return) projections come in. It will take your money and invest it. The more the insurance company expects to make on your money, the less of your money it will need. So the higher the rate it expects to get, the less your annuity will cost you.

Insurance companies will quote you the interest rate they use in calculating the annuity's cost to you. That is the rate after the company's cost and profit. Like interest rates quoted on bank deposits, it's the rate to the customer, not the rate the company earns. But rates to customers rise and fall to follow the company's own projected rate of return.

If the customer rate is 8 percent, you'll need $102,714 to buy a $12,000 annuity. If the rate is 6 percent, you'll need $116,546—13 percent ($13,832) more. You will buy your annuity many years hence, when you retire. You'll have to decide *now* how much you will need *then*. Interest rate projections are essential to that decision. So you, or someone you get to advise you, will make some kind of forecast now of the interest rate prevailing when you reach your retirement age.

You make further interest rate assumptions when figuring the amounts you will put into your Keogh investment fund. And here, too, conservative assumptions pay off. The lower your assumed interest rate, the more you put in each year. For example, you would put in $4,279 in each of 16 years to get to $110,000 if you assume your contributions earn 6 percent. But you put in only $3,619 if you assume an 8 percent return.

Conservative interest projections don't commit you to conservative investments. And if you do better on your investments than your conservative projections, that's good news, not bad: your money is going further.

Your conservative assumptions put more money in the fund sooner, giving you more money working for you in the early years. If you use conservative assumptions, you may arrive at retirement with more money than you need for the richest pension you're allowed. That could happen because you earned more on your investment than you assumed you would. Or the pension might cost less than you assumed because a higher interest rate applies at your retirement time. In either case you're overfunded. But don't worry. The excess funds belong to *you*. Your conservative assumptions still pay off.

For example, assume that at retirement you have $116,546, but your annuity costs only $102,714. The extra $13,832 is still your money, but this extra amount will bear a heavy tax, with none of the tax relief or postponement that could apply to the rest.

NO, YOU'RE NOT LOCKED IN

"Brrr," Harold said, with a mock shiver. "I said this sounded complicated, and that was half an hour ago, before I'd heard all of it. Look at what you're having me do:

"First, I'm picking a pension amount I'm supposed to pay for out of my future income. Then I pick the age at which I expect to retire. Then I make some forecast of how much I'll make investing the money I'll be putting in and what the pension will cost when I retire.

"How can I be sure of all of this now? In fact, how can I be sure of *any* of this now?"

Harold should take it easy. Of course he can't be sure. No one expects certainty, and no one punishes mistakes. You're not locked in.

A Keogh plan isn't a snapshot. It's a motion picture. Make your best guess, or the guess that does the best for you, then change whatever doesn't work out as you planned.

You aim for a pension based on the income you make or the income you expect to make. You can change the pension amount if things work out differently.

You assume or forecast a certain rate of return on investments. But in fact, what you earn varies from year to year. So you change your forecasts and what you do about them to fit your actual experience. You also may be forecasting what a pension will cost in the future. As you get closer to the time you'll buy it, you'll get a more reliable idea of its true cost and change your funding target accordingly.

You choose a retirement age. We've already covered what happens if you decide to retire later (very little). If you decide to retire earlier, this too can be accommodated.

What matters to most people is how changes in assumptions change the amounts they pay into the plan each year. The short answer is, you can put in more if your income rises, or you retire sooner, or your investment earnings are less than you figured. You usually will reduce your contributions if the reverse happens. But in any case you have wide latitude in what you must put in from year to year for any given pension.

If you choose a pension plan, you have a commitment to make regular contributions to it. But it's not quite like a duty to pay rent or taxes: your contributions can fluctuate. And if your pension is fully funded—if you already have as much as will be needed at retirement—you *can't* contribute or deduct any more.

But suppose you had self-employment income this year but want or need it for something other than a Keogh contribution.

Or suppose this year you had no, or negligible, self-employment income. Must you contribute anyway?

No. You can claim a hardship exemption so you won't have to contribute this year. You can skip one year or even more. You are expected to catch up later, but the requirements are not severe. There's no need to go into details here. If you're serious about your Keogh plan, it will be in your interest to pay in every year you can or to catch up quickly if you miss. If that becomes impossible, you can always terminate the plan and distribute all of the funds to yourself.

JOINT-AND-SURVIVOR ANNUITIES

Keogh *joint-and-survivor annuities* provide a pension for the moon-lighter and then another pension after the moonlighter's death, usually to the moonlighter's spouse. These two pensions cost more than one paying the same amount, and they are worth more. If you include a joint-and-survivor annuity in your Keogh planning, you can build a still larger Keogh fund. The many considerations in-volved in planning for joint-and-survivor annuities are explored in Chapter 12, "Cashing In: Collecting Your Keogh Wealth."

AN INFLATION-PROOF RETIREMENT FUND?

"Inflation-proof" is a tall order. But a defined-benefit plan can deliver more protection than other plans can, thanks to the feature that lets you increase your retirement pension as your income rises. If your average earned income in your three best moonlighting years is $11,000, you can have an $11,000 pension. If the average rises to $15,000, you can have a $15,000 pension. Pension experts and U.S. government officials consider that this power to increase the pension amount fosters retirement security and provides a mea-sure of protection against inflation.

But we shouldn't exaggerate this. It doesn't matter *why* your income has risen. You can have the larger pension whether your income went up because of inflation or because you increased your fees or took on more work.

And nowhere is it written that your moonlighting income has to rise just because inflation is at hand. You might have reduced your moonlighting activity as you neared retirement. So your moonlighting income might stay the same or even drop. You wouldn't have to reduce your pension amount because your income dropped. But the pension you collect, calculated in preinflation dollars, will be worth less when collected in inflationary times.

But assume the usual case; your income rises and you want a correspondingly larger pension. The larger pension will cost you more. To pay for it, you will have to pay into your Keogh a larger *proportion* of your moonlighting earnings than before.

No Keogh plan can offer you inflation protection *after* you retire from your moonlighting business.

Here we're considering inflation-protection features in the type of Keogh *plan* you choose. You can always decide to invest your Keogh funds, from whatever type of plan, in ways that offer a measure of inflation protection. For investment options, see Chapters 8 and 9.

CHAPTER 4

SHOULD YOUR KEOGH BE MONEY-PURCHASE OR DEFINED-BENEFIT?

I've been pretty emphatic that Harold should adopt a *defined-benefit* Keogh. And it seems clear that a *money-purchase* plan will be the richest for Peter. I think I know what to advise Elaine as well. But before we get to that, let's look at the considerations that should govern *your* choice.

A defined-benefit pension plan is more complicated and expensive to set up and administer than a money-purchase pension plan. It costs more to set up because it offers more options: a greater variety of goals and ways to reach them. It costs more to administer because you need to recalculate each year the return on investment and the minimum amount to be put in for that year. An actuary must make or approve these amounts and must sign the tax reporting form.

Cost aside, which type of plan is best for you depends on the interplay, in your own case, of these factors:

- Your age when you start the plan.
- The age you expect to retire.
- The expected rate of return on investment of Keogh contributions.
- The self-employment income you expect to earn in the years until retirement.

FACTORS FAVORING MONEY-PURCHASE PENSION PLANS

Your age when the plan is established. Assuming retirement at age 65, consider money-purchase if you are relatively young—your early 40s or younger.

Reason: Your Keogh contributions are made and invested over a longer period, so they can grow to a larger sum than the same (or even somewhat higher) contributions over a shorter period. Thus, $2,500 a year invested at 10 percent over 25 years will add up to much more than $5,000 a year at 10 percent for 10 years ($245,867 versus $79,687).

Expected investment return. Money-purchase is favored if you expect a comparatively high return on your investment.

Reason: With a money-purchase plan you're entitled to the total of your contributions plus all of the earnings thereon, however much they may be. There's a limit on the amount you can put in but not on the amount you can *collect.*

With a defined-benefit pension plan you're entitled to a specific amount of pension. This amount *can be* increased, but the amount of increase will depend on your self-employment income, not your investment earnings. Here there's a limit on the amount you can *collect* but not on the amount you can put in.

To sum up (and oversimplify a bit), high investment earnings in a money-purchase plan increase your Keogh fund but don't affect the amount you pay in. High earnings in a defined-benefit plan reduce the amount you pay in but don't greatly affect your Keogh fund.

FACTORS FAVORING DEFINED-BENEFIT PENSION PLANS

Your age when the plan is established. Defined-benefit pension plans are advisable when the Keogh investor is somewhat older.

Reason: With a defined-benefit pension plan you can contribute more over a shorter period than with a money-purchase plan.

Clearly, if you are 50 and plan to retire at 65, you will have more at retirement with a $5,000 annual contribution than with a $2,500 annual contribution, assuming the contributions earn at the same rate.

Of course, what matters is not your actual age when you set up the plan but the number of years between then and retirement. A relatively short period (say, less than 20 years) tends to favor defined-benefit pensions.

We saw (page 23) that a defined-benefit plan was better for Harold than a money-purchase plan because he's so close to retirement (11 years away).

Peter's distance from retirement—24 years, if he retires at 65—makes money-purchase much richer for him than defined-benefit.

Based on what we know of Peter's income, the largest pension he could receive on retirement is $30,000 a year if he chose a defined-benefit plan. (For technical reasons, discussed on page 98, it could be somewhat less than $30,000, but $30,000 a year makes my point.) To pay $30,000 a year from age 65, assuming a 20-year life expectancy, he'd need a Keogh fund of $344,098 (at 6 percent interest) or $294,541 (at 8 percent interest).

This compares badly with the $530,983 Keogh fund we figured he could have in money-purchase and with the $54,081 pension that money could buy (at 8 percent interest; a $46,294 pension at 6 percent interest).

Expected investment return. In a money-purchase plan a low investment return means a smaller Keogh fund than you hope for. With a defined-benefit pension plan low investment return means you have to pay in more. Your costs would be higher, but you'd still get the Keogh fund you're aiming for.

Example. $2,000 put into a money-purchase Keogh each year reaches $91,524 in 20 years if it earns at 8 percent. It reaches only $66,132 if it earns at 5 percent.

If you had a defined-benefit Keogh and wanted a $91,524 Keogh fund, you could still get there, even though your investment earned only 5 percent. You'd do this by contributing more each year. You'd put in a tax-deductible $764 more each year—$15,280 more in all over 20 years.

Changes in self-employment earnings. These affect money-purchase plans and defined-benefit plans in different ways. But they usually favor the person who adopts a defined-benefit plan.

If earnings fall below expectations, the amount you pay into a money-purchase plan (which is proportionate to earnings) must fall as well. Thus, you have less money working for you. In a defined-benefit plan, the amount you pay in *does not drop*. If your income is reduced, you may of course find it harder to make your required contributions. But you are not *obliged* to reduce your contributions as you are with a money-purchase plan. So you don't have to suffer a cut in your Keogh fund or your targeted pension. You can have as much money working for you as you planned and therefore can collect more than the money-purchase investor.

Example.   Moonlighting is bringing in $10,000 a year when you set up your Keogh. On that basis you can put $2,000 into a money-purchase Keogh. Let's say you'd put the same amount into a defined-benefit Keogh.

Suppose you continue to make $10,000 a year for the next four years and put $2,000 a year into your Keogh. Then, for the next five years you make only $4,000 a year. In a money-purchase plan you'd have to cut your contributions during the five lean years to $800 a year. In a defined-benefit plan you could continue to put in your $2,000 a year.

Of course, it's harder to part with $2,000 when you're making only $4,000 than it is when you're making $10,000. But you're *allowed* to continue to put in $2,000 a year in defined-benefit. With money-purchase you can't.

Suppose self-employment earnings rise. In a money-purchase plan what you put in goes up as your earnings go up. This gives you more money working, a larger Keogh fund, and a larger pension. But a defined-benefit plan uses more leverage. Three or four good years in a defined-benefit plan can greatly increase the Keogh you're allowed and therefore the pension amount. The contrast between money-purchase and defined-benefit can be dramatic.

Example.   Let's imagine two moonlighters, Steven and Ruth. They're unrelated to each other except in their desire to build wealth through the Keogh technique. We'll assume that each earns about $15,000 a year in a self-employment sideline.

Steve picks a money-purchase plan. Ruth adopts a defined-benefit plan. Twenty years later Steve will get what the $2,500 a year he puts in for 20 years (plus earnings thereon) will amount to. That is, he'll get $50,000 plus earnings. Ruth will have $10,000 a year for life.

Now assume that in 4 of those 20 years Steve and Ruth each earns not $15,000 but $30,000. This will let Steve increase the amount he puts in to $5,000 in each of those four years. His total contribution will go up. At the end of the 20-year period during which he operates his Keogh he'll have $60,000 plus earnings. But Ruth is now allowed a fund big enough to pay her $20,000 a year for life—100 percent more than before, not just 20 percent more.

This example oversimplifies. We don't know how much Steve will actually have 20 years from now nor what Ruth's pension will cost her until we know what each makes by investing the Keogh contributions.

But this much is clear: Decreases in self-employment income tend to cut into money-purchase Keogh funds but not defined-benefit Keogh funds. Increases in self-employment earnings help both funds but often help defined-benefit funds more.

The $10,000-a-year pension safety net. You'll recall that with a defined-benefit plan Harold is allowed to build a Keogh fund large enough to pay him $10,000 a year (see page 24). This opportunity is very important to Harold's Keogh planning. It's an added attraction defined-benefit plans offer persons with relatively low moonlighting incomes who are *fairly* close to retirement. There's nothing like that with money-purchase plans.

MONEY-PURCHASE FOR ELAINE?

Should Elaine adopt a money-purchase plan? The obvious economic considerations seem to point that way. She's young, with many years ahead to build a large fund through repeated contributions, investments, and reinvestments. She has no need for the $10,000-a-year safety net; she makes more than that anyway. On the purely economic terms we know about, Elaine seems an even better candidate for money-purchase than Peter is.

Personal and family considerations suggest the same answer. She's not her family's primary source of income. She might decide to give up her moonlighting business or just retire from it early, which I guess is the same thing. The less predictable her moonlighting future is, the simpler her plan should be. That indicates a money-purchase plan. She can fund it as heavily as the law allows while her moonlighting business is in operation. If she ends the business, she stops paying in. But she can continue to build her Keogh fund through reinvesting investment earnings.

For someone in Elaine's situation, and maybe for Elaine herself—we'll see—a profit-sharing Keogh might be better, or even a profit-sharing Keogh that's married to a money-purchase plan.

We'll explore these opportunities in the next chapter.

CHAPTER 5

KEOGH PROFIT-SHARING PLANS

If you aim to build the largest Keogh fund possible in your case, a profit-sharing plan is not for you. Or to be more accurate, you can't *stop* with a profit-sharing plan. You get bigger tax deductions with pension plans than with profit-sharing plans. Therefore, since less of your income goes to taxes, you'll have more funds available for investment.

Still, profit-sharing plans have several attractive features. They are more flexible than pension plans. Unlike pension plans, they don't have to be retirement plans. You're allowed to take out your contributions and the earnings thereon *before* you retire. At least two years must elapse between the time you put in a contribution and the time you take it out. The two-year period can be shortened in case of hardship. But hardship means *hardship:* "present or impending financial ruin, want or privation." Anyone in straits this dire probably will have to terminate the plan anyway.

Profit-sharing plans are closer in concept to money-purchase plans than to defined-benefit plans. You don't target a specific retirement pension. Instead, you make periodic contributions and invest and reinvest what they earn. You don't know when you start out what your fund will grow to or how much "retirement" it will buy when you come to draw your funds out.

Like money-purchase plans, profit-sharing plans perform best for those a long way from retirement, though profit-sharing typically does less well because less money goes into the plan.

Profit-sharing means you make Keogh contributions out of your profits—that is, your self-employment earnings. It may provide that contributions will be made only if profits exceed some particular figure. It may choose any percentage of profits, and the percentage may vary from year to year. You are allowed to skip contributions even though you have profits, and you don't have to make up the shortfall in a later year. However, you don't have a valid Keogh plan unless you expect to make substantial contributions over a number of years. A plan that is set up to make a contribution in one year and never again would not qualify.

These options are available to any moonlighter. But they matter most to employers with good-size businesses. There, the options are used as incentives to improve employee performance. Contributions are varied or suspended to fit current business needs. The various options matter little to moonlighters, who are eager to build up the largest Keogh investment fund possible and who have no one but themselves and their families to consider. Such people should be funding their Keoghs to the limit. The profit-sharing limit isn't high enough.

Let's show this with an experiment involving Elaine. Elaine is uncertain about her future as a moonlighter. She might want something more flexible than a money-purchase pension plan. Let's see if profit-sharing is better for her by assuming she'll stop moonlighting five years from now, when her younger child no longer needs his mother at home when he returns from school. And let's assume that during those five years she continues to make $15,000 a year from her indexing.

With a money-purchase plan she could put in $3,000 a year and deduct all of it from her taxes. Assuming she could make 9 percent on her money, she'd have a Keogh fund of $17,954 at the end of five years; $15,000 of this she contributed herself.

If instead she had adopted a profit-sharing plan, her tax-deductible contribution each year would be $1,956. Five years later she'd have a Keogh fund of $11,706; $9,780 of it from her own contributions.

Obviously, money-purchase gives Elaine more. She put $5,220 less in profit-sharing than she put in money-purchase. So choosing profit-sharing instead of money-purchase made her the poorer by the taxes she paid on the $5,220 she failed to contribute to her Keogh and whatever she could have made by investing that tax money.

That's what profit-sharing *costs* her. In exchange she got the right to withdraw from her Keogh fund before retiring.

We'd all like the freedom to tap into our Keoghs for personal reasons whenever we think we might need money. That is somewhat easier to do with profit-sharing plans than with pension plans. But even with profit-sharing there's a cost. In most cases you will pay an extra tax on amounts you take out of your Keogh before you reach age 59½.

If you *really* need money in a pension plan, you can get at it by terminating the plan. You'll still pay the extra tax, but more money will come to you because you'll have more in the plan than if you'd just used a profit-sharing plan.

If only you could combine profit-sharing *flexibility* with pension *fundability*—the power in a pension plan to put more money in and have more money invested than in a profit-sharing plan.

You can. That comes next.

MONEY-PURCHASE PLUS PROFIT-SHARING

We've seen that for some moonlighters a money-purchase plan is better than a defined-benefit plan. We showed that in Peter's case, for example, where his Keogh fund was about $200,000 more with a money-purchase plan than with a defined-benefit plan.

You don't have to choose between money-purchase and profit-sharing. For maximum benefit you can combine features of each. But first a warning: Having two plans doesn't mean you can put in and deduct the maximum for a money-purchase plan and, on top of that, the maximum for a profit-sharing plan. You can't put in and deduct more with these two plans than you could with money-purchase alone.

The two plans together are richer than profit-sharing alone and more flexible than money-purchase alone. You can set up a profit-sharing plan that will let you withdraw amounts from your plan before you retire. That's a real advantage, which is lacking in money-purchase plans. And your plan would let you vary the percentage of self-employment earnings you put in each year if you want to. Because I believe moonlighters should always fund profit-sharing and money-purchase to the limit, I don't think much of this option. But having it does no harm.

With a profit-sharing plan you could put in and deduct up to 13.043 percent of your self-employment earnings. That's significantly less—6.957 percentage points less—than the 20 percent of net earnings you could put in and deduct if you had a money-purchase plan.

So you set up a money-purchase plan to pick up the extra 6.957 percentage points. For technical reasons you get to your 20 percent target by putting 12 percent (not 13.043 percent) of self-employment net earnings into profit-sharing and 8 percent (not 6.957 percent) in money-purchase.

If Elaine were to do this, $1,800 each year would go into profit-sharing and $1,200 each year into money-purchase. In Peter's case it would be $3,600 into profit-sharing and $2,400 into money-purchase.

The percentage of income you put into the profit-sharing can vary each year. It can be anywhere from 12 percent down to zero, as you please. But you are *committed,* in a money-purchase plan, to put in the same percentage each year. You should not reduce that percentage except in a case of economic hardship or unless you formally change your plan to substitute a new percentage.

"The way you describe them, having two plans sounds fine to me," Elaine said, "and I can see that Peter is interested, too. Are there any special problems in having two plans?"

Yes, some. It costs more to set up two plans than to set up one. But both types of plans are simple enough, so the cost and trouble shouldn't be great. I'll have more to say on this in Chapter 15, "How to Get Started."

Also there's the trouble—trouble more than cost—of *running* two plans. Two plans are a greater nuisance than one, but the added bother isn't serious. Probably the most important point is to keep your profit-sharing investments separate from your money-purchase investments.

To sum up, if money-purchase is good for you, money-purchase and profit-sharing *could* be better. But money-purchase alone will do if you know you're in for the long haul; that is, you won't want to take funds out before you retire except by terminating the plan. And money-purchase alone is best if you don't want to incur the expense and nuisance of a second plan; for example, if your moonlighting earnings are relatively small—say, less than $5,000 a year.

For Elaine, money-purchase plus profit-sharing seems a good idea, at least based on what we know now. After five years she'd have $10,772 in her profit-sharing plan and $7,182 in money-purchase.

WHAT'S ALL THIS ABOUT 401(k) PLANS?

I've been trying to keep pension industry jargon out of this book. But I make an exception here to introduce you to what pension professionals call the 401(k) plan.

These are plans that give employees the option to take all of their salary in cash or have the employer put part of it (called the deferred amount) into a retirement plan. Up to certain limits the deferred amount is tax-free to the employee. It becomes taxable only when the employee takes it out.

To encourage employees to save for retirement, employers sometimes put in additional amounts to match those an employee chooses to defer. Matching might be in a ratio such as 50 cents for every dollar the employee defers.

For example, an employee earning $30,000 might have the option to defer, say, 10 percent of his salary. If he chose to defer that much, his company would pay him $27,000 and put $3,000 into the retirement plan for him. If the company also matched deferred amounts at 50 cents on the dollar, it would put an additional $1,500 into the plan for the employee, who would then have $4,500 in the plan and would pay tax on $27,000.

Moonlighters can use 401(k)s. As the business owner, you'll be both "employer" and "employee," as you are in any other Keogh plan.

A 401(k) plan is a special type of profit-sharing plan. With a 401(k) you face the same limits on tax deductibility that apply to profit-sharing plans. The deferred amount plus any "employer" matching contributions count as your profit-sharing contributions.

Your tax deduction for the sum of these amounts can't exceed 13.043 percent of your self-employment earnings.

There's nothing to keep you from having a money-purchase plan as well as a 401(k). Even so, you won't be able to put in or deduct more than if you had a regular, or non-401(k), profit-sharing plan coupled with a money-purchase plan, or if you had a money-purchase plan only. Thus, you can't make your 401(k) plan richer than any other plan you might have chosen.

Example.   Again we're planning for Elaine and her $15,000 a year of self-employment earnings. She could set up a 401(k) and put in the same amount as with a regular profit-sharing plan. This means $1,956 a year into her 401(k). She could put in $1,304 of this as a deferred amount and $652 as a matching contribution, but there's no point in being so fancy. It's the same $1,956 total, however she slices it. So she might just as well put the whole thing in at once. If she also adopted a money-purchase plan, it would be $1,800 each year into 401(k) and $1,200 into money-purchase.

After five years, she'd get to the same total Keogh fund as if she'd used regular profit-sharing instead of 401(k): $10,772 in the 401(k) plus $7,182 in the money-purchase plan.

Summing up: 401(k)s are popular with employees, but they're not right for a moonlighting business. A 401(k) Keogh offers the moonlighter no more than he or she would get with a regular profit-sharing plan, and it is more trouble. True, employees like 401(k) because they pay no federal income tax on amounts they direct their employers to put into the plan. But this doesn't apply to moonlighters' 401(k)s. Moonlighters are taxed on their entire profit, less the deductible amount they put into their Keoghs. This is no greater deduction than if they had a non-401(k) profit-sharing plan.

A 401(k) is technically harder to start up, which means it costs more to start. Also, for firms with employees, it's harder to operate, though there's no such problem for firms without employees.

A Keogh Scorecard

Pension (defined-benefit)	Pension (money-purchase)	Profit-sharing
Retirement oriented (p. 18)	Retirement oriented (p. 18)	Investment oriented (p. 18)
But need not be used for pension or annuity (p. 23)	But need not be used for pension or annuity (p. 20)	But can be used for pension or annuity (p. 40)
Preferred for those nearer retirement (p. 35)	Preferred for those farther from retirement (p. 35)	Preferred for those farther from retirement (p. 40)
Provides a specific retirement benefit (p. 23)	No predetermined retirement benefit (p. 20)	No predetermined fund or benefit (p. 40)
Annual contribution generally required (p. 31)	Annual contribution generally required (p. 19)	No annual contribution requirement (p. 41)
Contribution not directly tied to earnings; can vary from year to year (p. 31)	Contribution is a fixed percentage of earnings (p. 19)	Contribution is a percentage of earnings; percentage can vary each year (p. 41)
Offers some protection against inflation (p. 32)	Less inflation protection (p. 21)	Less inflation protection (p. 32)
Investment results affect cost more than size of fund (p. 36)	Investment results important to size of fund (p. 35)	Investment results important to size of fund (p. 40)
Has several options for increasing size of fund (and cost)	Options not available or do not increase size of fund	Options not available or do not increase size of fund
Use conservative investment projections (p. 28)	Not available	Not available
Select early retirement age (p. 25)	Does not increase size of fund	Does not increase size of fund
Select joint-and-survivor annuity (p. 32)	Does not affect size of fund	Does not affect size of fund
$10,000-a-year minimum (safety net) pension (p. 24)	Not available	Not available
Life insurance in plan does not affect size of fund (p. 85)	Life insurance in plan reduces size of fund (p. 85)	Life insurance in plan reduces size of fund (p. 85)
Comparatively high start-up costs and operating burdens (pp. 151–53; 163)	Lower start-up costs and operating burdens (pp. 151–52; 163)	Lowest start-up costs and operating burdens (pp. 151–52; 163)

CHAPTER 6

BUILDING YOUR KEOGH—
WHAT YOU PUT IN EACH YEAR

Your Keogh wealth comes from the money you put into your Keogh and the money you make investing it. This chapter looks at techniques for putting money into your Keogh—how you plant your seed money.

HOW MONEY GETS INTO YOUR KEOGH

Your Keogh contribution usually is a check, drawn by you. Some people are moved to make a Keogh contribution when they collect a fee or other payment from a client or customer. As we'll soon see, it's smarter not to wait until then, but many do.

You may belong to a Keogh *master plan* (see Chapter 15), in which you make your Keogh contribution by sending your master plan a check for the amount you want to put in. You would probably include a deposit slip or coupon, provided by the master plan, that says your money goes into a particular type of investment fund run by the plan. Your check would be payable to the plan or the fund.

If you have an *insured* Keogh (see Chapter 9), your check will be going to an insurance company to pay the premium on an annuity. Here, too, you would include some kind of slip or coupon that shows what your payment is for. Your check might be payable to a particular insurance company fund. Normally, in a master or insured plan, your check alone is the Keogh contribution even if you forget to include any deposit slip or coupon, as long as the payee will know what it's for.

If you're the trustee of your own Keogh, your contribution occurs when you make an investment or deposit *as trustee*. For example: You buy a bank CD as trustee. Your check to the bank is your contribution. Likewise, if you open or already have a brokerage account as trustee, your check to the broker is your contribution. Or if you have a money market fund account or other mutual fund account as trustee, your check to the fund is your contribution. Similarly, if you have a bank account—savings or NOW account or no-interest checking account—as trustee, your check to the bank for this account is your contribution even if the money is there only temporarily while you are considering a permanent investment.

No matter what the investment vehicle, the check can be drawn on your personal account or on any separate account you may have for your moonlighting business. Though it's usual to contribute via a check, there's no magic about checks. You might contribute in cash, via an electronic funds transfer, or in any other way that works.

CONTRIBUTE EARLY IN THE YEAR

You will put money into your Keogh each year. Put the money in as early in the year as you can afford to. Get it in and get it invested and earning income as soon as possible.

Investment earnings on funds *you* hold are subject to tax while you hold them, unless they are in tax-exempt securities or certain other low-yielding investments. Earnings on funds in the plan are tax-free while there, whatever the funds are invested in. The sooner you put your funds in your Keogh, the more you have working for you tax-free.

Contribute early? Okay, but how much? "I can see how your advice works for defined-benefit plans," Peter says. "But I'll be in a money-purchase plan. What I put in this year depends on how much I make by the end of the year. I won't know what that is until the year is over. So how can I put in at the *start* of the year?"

Make a guess. No one expects you to know at the beginning of the year what your net earnings will be at the end. Make an estimate and contribute on that basis. If you underestimated, you can make it

up later, within the deadline. If you overestimated, you can take out
the excess, within the deadline.

Exactly the same considerations apply for profit-sharing plans.
That is, the amount you can put in for any year depends on your
earnings for that year. As with money-purchase plans, you would
make an estimate of your earnings, contribute based on that estimate, and then adjust any undercontribution or overcontribution
later, within the stipulated deadline.

What's the deadline? The deadline is when the tax return is due
for the year in which you want to take your tax deduction. This
deadline applies whether you're making a single contribution for
that year, making a series of installment payments, or adjusting for a
previous underestimate. And you have until this date to take back
erroneous overcontributions.

Usually, your return is due April 15. If you got a filing extension
to August 15 or October 15, then August 15 (October 15) becomes
your deadline.

> **Example.**   In January 1991 you figure your 1991 net profit will be $40,000,
> and you contribute 20 percent of $40,000, or $8,000. Then, recalculat-
> ing in August, you decide 1991 earnings will be $50,000, so you
> contribute a further $2,000. As you make your final calculation of
> 1991 earnings when working on your 1991 tax return in March 1992,
> you find your earnings are $52,000. You contribute a further $400.
> The entire $10,400 is deductible on your 1991 return. If you contrib-
> uted a total of $11,000, then $600 would be an overcontribution.

You can take a tax deduction for a Keogh contribution only if
the Keogh is in existence by December 31 of the year for which the
deduction is claimed. Thus, to take a deduction for 1992 for
amounts put in in March 1991, a valid Keogh must exist in 1991.

Does when you contribute affect your Keogh deduction? Not if
you contribute on time. You can contribute any time from the first
day of the year to the tax return deadline (April 15, or August 15, or
October 15 of the following year). That's a spread of 15½ to 19½ or
21½ months. How much you deduct is not affected in the slightest
by when, during that period, you make your contribution. An early
contribution increases your tax shelter, not your tax deduction.

Quarterly minimums. You can make your full contribution on

January 1 if you want to. If later in the year is more convenient, that's OK, though certain minimum installment payments are required for defined-benefit or money-purchase plans.

To get the longest postponement without violating the law, you must make quarterly installment payments, starting in the second quarter of each year, of a certain percentage of the total contributions you owe. For most moonlighters, this means payments April 15, July 15, October 15, and January 15 of the following year. The percentage for each installment depends on the year involved. For 1991 the percentage is 18.75 percent. For 1992 and after the percentage is 25 percent.

HOW ABOUT CONTRIBUTING PROPERTY INSTEAD OF CASH?

You don't have to put *cash* into your Keogh. You may contribute property instead of cash, or contribute partly in cash and partly in property.

What kind of property? Property you put in should be property that produces income, such as stock or bonds. Don't try it with personal possessions, such as a vacation home or artworks. Also, don't contribute mortgaged property. Your Keogh can't take over your mortgage.

You'll have to transfer title, from yourself as individual owner to yourself (or whomever you've named) as trustee of your Keogh. This can be a nuisance.

What happens to my taxes if I contribute property? The mere act of contributing property often increases your taxable income. This somewhat undercuts the value of your Keogh tax deduction.

When you put property into your Keogh, you take a tax deduction for the property's worth or "fair market value." The amount you're allowed to deduct for a Keogh contribution is the same whether you're contributing cash or property. If your property's value exactly equals the Keogh deduction you're allowed, then that's what you deduct. If it's worth less, you deduct only what it's worth. You can, however, put in cash or more property to make up the shortfall and deduct that. It's unwise to contribute property worth *more* than you're allowed to deduct. The excess can be deducted in a later year, but you will owe a tax penalty of 10 percent of that nondeductible excess.

A property contribution is technically a sale of the property. So you have taxable income if you have a "paper profit" on it when you contribute it. By "paper profit" tax and investment experts mean property you currently own that's worth more than it cost you. You pay the same tax on your paper profit that you would on an actual sale of the property.

Example.   Peter can put $6,000 into his Keogh money-purchase plan this year. Peter, as we know, is an active investor. Among his other stock holdings, he owns 100 shares of stock that he bought at $35 a share and that are now worth $60 a share.

He *could* meet his commitment to put in $6,000 this year by contributing the stock. And he could take a $6,000 tax deduction for this contribution, just as he could be contributing cash. But he also has $2,500 of taxable income from this "sale" of the stock. This is his paper profit: the $6,000 the stock is worth minus his $3,500 cost. No taxable income would arise from a *cash* contribution.

The "sales" income that arises when you contribute property doesn't increase the amount you're allowed to contribute. You contribute based on your income from your moonlighting business. Income from contributed property is investment income, not business income.

Suppose your property happens to be worth *less* than it cost you. Say it's stock that has fallen in value, so you have a paper loss. You should not contribute such property to your Keogh. That would cost you a tax deduction for your loss. To salvage *that* deduction you would actually have to sell the property and contribute the proceeds to your Keogh. If you just contributed the *property,* you would deduct only its present worth.

Example.   We're back with Peter, and again he's committed to put $6,000 into his Keogh money-purchase plan. This time he has shares of stock he bought at $60 a share that are now worth $35 a share.

If he contributed the stock to his Keogh, he would have a tax deduction of $3,500, period. But if he sold the stock for what it was worth—$3,500, ignoring any selling expenses—and contributed the money to his Keogh, he'd have *two* tax deductions, totaling $6,000: the $3,500 deduction for the Keogh contribution and a $2,500 deduction for the loss on the stock sale.

As you noticed, this put only $3,500 (property value) into the Keogh. Peter is entitled to put in $6,000 and is committed to do so. He can contribute the $2,500 balance, in cash or property, and deduct that as well.

If you contribute two or more items of property, you can't net profits against losses. Each item of profit is separately taxable; losses are not deductible.

What's good about property contributions? Why should anyone who knows these rules want to contribute property? You might contribute property in cases where you've put your money into your business, investments, or personal assets, and therefore lack ready cash. So you contribute some of your investments to your Keogh. If you sold the investments to raise money for a cash contribution, you would pay the same tax as if you contributed the investments themselves. So *assuming you're without cash,* it costs you nothing to contribute investments. And contributing an investment, instead of selling it and contributing the proceeds, saves on selling expenses such as brokers' commissions.[1]

Any item you contribute to your Keogh becomes one more investment asset of your Keogh fund. Any income it generates can be invested and reinvested tax-free and you can sell it any time, also tax-free.

BORROWING FOR YOUR
KEOGH CONTRIBUTION

It's time for your Keogh contribution, and you're short of cash. You don't want the headaches that come with contributing property. What now? You can borrow what you need.

I keep saying you should put as much into your Keogh as you can afford, up to the legal limit. If you're in good financial shape overall, temporary cash shortage shouldn't delay your Keogh con-

---

[1] Ignore the ocasional stockbroker who says that contributions of securities aren't allowed. They're perfectly legal, and may be right for you, if you report any income that may arise, and if you aren't contributing securities subject to debt.

tribution. The economics favor borrowing now, contributing now, and repaying later out of future moonlighting earnings. You can take tax deductions for the interest on your borrowings, and there's no tax on what your Keogh investments earn.

Example.   Peter's situation illustrates the idea well. Peter tries to keep fully invested and is usually cash poor, except when he's just sold an investment or collected a fee.

On January 2 he figures moonlighting will bring him $30,000 this year, though he won't collect it until late in the year. On this basis he's allowed to put $6,000 into his Keogh and deduct it all. But he has only a few hundred in his checking account, and it's not the right time to sell any of his investments.

So he takes out a short-term loan for $6,000, using some of his personal investments as collateral. He'll repay this later, when he collects his fee.

He puts the $6,000 into his Keogh and invests it immediately in an investment that pays 10 percent a year. Peter collects his $30,000 fee in December and repays the $6,000 loan December 31. The loan bore interest at 12 percent a year.

How come the economics favor *borrowing to contribute to the Keogh?* Wouldn't it be better for Peter to wait until he collected his fee before contributing?

Harold, Peter, and Elaine now know too much about Keoghs to ask this question. But it's a reasonable enough question from someone who hasn't studied Keoghs.

The *tax* economics are what makes borrowing a good idea. Peter pays $720 interest on the $6,000 he borrowed, while his Keogh makes $600 on that sum. *Before tax* Peter and his Keogh lose $120. But Peter takes a tax deduction for the interest, so borrowing costs him, say, $468 *after tax.* And the Keogh's income is tax-free. So after-tax, Peter and his Keogh are $132 ahead ($600 minus $468). He made $132 on this with no out-of-pocket investment whatsoever.

Accountant Harold would point out that Peter would have made more, $468 more, if he hadn't had to borrow. Borrowing to contribute is $132 better than postponing the contribution. Early contribution without borrowing is $468 better still.

You can't borrow *from* your own Keogh to make a Keogh contribution.

MORE CONTRIBUTION TECHNIQUES FOR DEFINED-BENEFIT KEOGHS

You can choose among several additional contribution techniques for building your Keogh if it's a defined-benefit plan. They build up your Keogh slowly, somewhat faster, or high speed. The techniques considered here will give full, immediate tax deduction for what's put in. I suspect most moonlighters would like the high speed buildup if they could afford it, but each technique will fit someone.

When you put in money for a Keogh pension, you can take a tax deduction only for the pension you have already earned through work you have already done. Take Harold's case. Harold is 54 and wants to retire at age 65. He can't deduct for the years between 55 and 65 even if he put in money for those years today. He hasn't earned any pension for those years yet because he hasn't worked those years yet.

With 11 years to go to retirement, you could say Harold earns one eleventh of his pension each year. Taking his approach, how much more does he put in this year?

Method 1. Harold puts in the amount he needs to pay for the pension he has earned this year. He has earned one eleventh of a $10,000 annual pension, or $909 a year starting at retirement, for the work he did this year (year 1). Using a 7 percent rate, a $909 annual pension will cost $9,630 for someone with Harold's life expectancy when he reaches age 65. To get to $9,630 at age 65 using a 7 percent rate, Harold must put in $4,575 this year.

Next year, year 2, Harold will earn another $909 a year pension, payable from age 65. But next year retirement is 10 years away, not 11. So next year it will cost $4,875 to provide a $909 pension starting at age 65. And in year 3 it will cost $5,238. Method 1 starts small and increases every year.

Method 2. With this method, Harold figures the total he needs at retirement to buy a $10,000-a-year pension. And then he puts in a level amount each year to build to that sum. Using 7 percent, he would need $105,940 to buy a $10,000 pension at age 65. To reach this sum through level contributions he would put in $6,711 each year.

So with method 2 more goes in during the early years, and the Keogh builds faster than it would with method 1. Method 2 puts

$2,136 more into the Keogh in the first year and $3,952 more in the first two years. So we'll call method 1 the slow way—it costs less and you have less. Method 2 is somewhat faster.

You can't contribute for years you haven't yet worked. But you *can* contribute for *past* work. You can use past service to build your Keogh investment faster. Past service is work in the business before the pension plan went into effect.

Methods 1 and 2 show Harold contributing for the years he works between now and retirement. But Harold has had a moonlighting business from age 45—for nine years previously. To build his Keogh faster he can have his plan recognize his nine years' past service.

Whether you include or ignore past service, you will need the same amount at retirement to buy the retirement pension you want. If you cover past service, the amount you put into your Keogh each year will consist of two parts: (1) what you need to buy the pension you earn this year (called normal cost) and (2) an amount toward providing for the benefits earned in all the years before the plan began (called past-service cost).

You can figure normal cost this way: Harold is covering 20 years of service. He will need $105,940 at age 65 to buy his $10,000-a-year pension. To reach $105,940 in level payments over 20 years (at 7 percent) Harold would have to put in $2,584 a year. So normal cost is $2,584, and Harold should put in that much for *this year's* service.

But Harold is nine years in the hole for his past nine years of service. He put nothing into the plan for these years because he had no plan then, and now he must catch up. He's in the hole by $31,274, which is what $2,584 in each of nine years would have grown to by now at 7 percent.

Any moonlighter in this position *could* put in the full $31,274. But that's not a great idea. Many couldn't afford it. Harold couldn't. And no one could deduct it all at once; part of the tax deduction would have to be postponed.

So it's best to spread the catch-up payments out over a period that suits your finances and Keogh objectives. Spread over what period? It can't be longer than 30 years and it can't be shorter than 10 years. Any period within that range is OK.

Your payments are amortizations, like the payments on a home mortgage, except that unlike mortgage payments they are deductible in full. To amortize $31,274 over 10 years, Harold would pay $4,452 a year. So when he adds his normal cost of $2,584 and his past service cost of $4,452, he's putting in $7,036 a year from now on. Call this method 3.

To amortize $31,274 over 30 years, Harold would put in $2,520 a year. That plus his normal cost of $2,584 adds up to $5,104 a year. Call this method 4.

To continue the speed metaphor, method 3—past service amortized over 10 years—is high speed. Method 1 is still the slow way, with the others falling in between. That is how these methods usually finish, though the distances between them will vary with the interest rate, length of time to retirement, and length of past service to be covered.

The 10-year amortization of method 3 is the way to front-load contributions if you have past service. Harold, who wants the fastest possible buildup of Keogh funds, should choose that method.

Of course, there's something not quite right in the 30-year amortization option here. I guess you noticed. A person's Keogh fund at retirement is what he has contributed plus what the contributions have earned. The less you put in overall, the less you will have at retirement. So if Harold adopts 30-year amortization but retires in 11 years, his past service will not be fully funded at retirement. To have the funds he wants at retirement, he must at some point start putting in more than 30-year amortization calls for. This means he will come to pay in as much as he would under method 1.

CONTRIBUTING THE MINIMUM

In your defined-benefit plan you have made a legal commitment—to yourself—to provide a certain pension. To meet that commitment you generally must make certain *minimum* contributions to your plan. If your plan does not recognize past service, you must contribute at least the amount required in method 1. If it *does* recognize past service, you should contribute the amount in method 4.

You are excused from the need to make a minimum contribution in the following cases:

a. If your plan already has more than the minimum it needs at this point in its lifespan to provide the pension earned so far. For example, you may have put in more than the minimum in a past year. Or your Keogh fund may have grown faster than you projected. If either or both of these events have built your fund beyond minimum size requirements this year, you can skip this year's contribution.

> *Example.*   Say that you have $11,864 in your Keogh as you start year 3 of your plan. Using method 1, you must have a minimum of $12,609 in your Keogh at the end of year 3. But with earnings projected to be 10 percent you reach $13,051 at year's end, more than the needed minimum, with *no* contribution in year 3.

On the other hand, if you made all of the required contributions but had investment reverses, you will need to make up the shortfall through an *extra* contribution.

> *Example.*   You contributed in years 1 and 2, as required under method 1. But you lost money on your investments and have only $8,000 at the start of year 3. You must contribute enough to bring your Keogh to $12,609 by the end of the year.

b. If it would be an economic hardship to make the required minimum contribution. At your request, the IRS will let you postpone your contribution for one or more years. You eventually must make up the contribution itself and what it would have earned if contributed on time.

c. If you modify your plan to reduce the size of your pension. This will let you reduce future contributions, since your reduced pension will cost less.

d. If you terminate the plan.

CHECKLIST OF CONTRIBUTION TECHNIQUES

1. *How does money get into your Keogh?* Simple. Usually you just write a check.
2. *When should you contribute?* Contribute early in the year for more tax-free buildup.

3. *What if you are short of cash?* You can contribute investment property you already own. This can trigger a tax that
   somewhat offsets your Keogh deduction, but it can save
   selling expenses such as brokers' commissions. Or you can
   borrow and contribute the loan proceeds. No tax or penalty
   in that case.
4. *What special options for defined-benefit plans?* You can
   front-load your contributions to build your Keogh fund
   faster. Or you can spread them out to fit the funds you have
   in hand.

CHAPTER 7

CONTRIBUTING AS "EMPLOYEE": MORE ENRICHMENT FOR YOUR KEOGH

To your Keogh you are both employer and employee: the person who provides the benefits and the person who enjoys them. The Keogh contributions considered up to now are contributions you make as *employer* and take a tax deduction for. Now consider what you can put in as an *employee* and why you might want to do that.

WHY CONTRIBUTE AS EMPLOYEE?

For more Keogh wealth. Through your added contributions as employee you build an even larger Keogh fund, enriched with additional tax benefits.

As you'll recall, employer Keogh contributions enjoy three different tax benefits: (1) a tax deduction when money goes in, (2) no tax on investment earnings while the funds are in the Keogh, and (3) limited tax relief when funds are withdrawn from Keogh investment.

Two of these tax benefits—(2) and (3)—also are available for employee Keogh contributions. You get no deductions for your employee contributions. But investment earnings are tax-free until withdrawn, and the same limited tax relief is available when withdrawal occurs.

And there's another advantage denied to all *employer* contributions. You can take your *employee* contributions out when you feel like it.

I keep saying you should put as much in your Keogh as the law allows, so you can be sure I advocate making *employee* contributions.

HOW MUCH CAN YOU PUT IN?

There is no official ceiling. I believe you would be safe with an employee contribution equal to 10 percent of your self-employment earned income. You can count all the earned income you've made to date in your current self-employment business, even though you had no Keogh plan at the time.

Example.   You set up a defined benefit Keogh plan this year. Over all the years you have been moonlighting, including this year, your earned income totals $110,000. You can put $11,000 (10 percent of $110,000) into your Keogh as an *employee* contribution. You take a tax deduction for your contribution as employer, whatever it is, but not the added $11,000. But you pay no tax on the income the Keogh earns on either sum. And you can take the $11,000 back when you want.

Plans to which employees contribute are called contributory plans. Contributions may be either mandatory—the employee *must* contribute if he wants to participate in the plan—or voluntary.

Mandatory or voluntary contribution amounts are reduced if your contribution as employer to a money-purchase or profit-sharing plan are at or near the ceiling, or you had one of these plans once and now have a defined-benefit plan.

A mandatory arrangement may be desirable if you have employees. Otherwise, the mandatory feature does nothing for you. If you choose not to contribute this year, you can always make a catch-up contribution next year or in some later year.

WHAT'S THE PAYOFF FROM
EMPLOYEE CONTRIBUTIONS?

It's a somewhat richer Keogh, with no investment risk you wouldn't run outside the Keogh. Nothing spectacular, just another step toward prosperity.

Example.   Assume you are able to invest $500 a year in addition to your Keogh contributions as an employer. You could put this amount directly into fixed-income securities. Or you could invest the same amount in the same securities, as employee Keogh contributions. Assume in either case that you invest $500 a year over 20 years ($10,000 in all) at 10 percent and that your tax rate over that period is 30 percent. Twenty years hence you could have $20,498 after taxes if you invested directly and $25,842 after taxes[1] if you invested through your Keogh plan.

The law limits the size of a Keogh defined-benefit pension. This limit applies only to pensions paid for by *deductible employer* contributions and earnings. There is no limit on your pension or other Keogh wealth traceable to contributions as employee. Investment earnings on contributions are tax-free, so you should contribute as early in the year as possible.

CAN YOU BORROW TO MAKE YOUR
EMPLOYEE CONTRIBUTIONS?

You can. You would expect to repay any loan out of future moonlighting earnings. But you *could* repay by withdrawing from your Keogh the amount you contributed.

Since part of what you withdraw is taxable (see Chapter 14), you should withdraw only where absolutely necessary. Interest you pay on your loan may not be fully tax deductible. The deduction rules treat this as interest paid on an investment. You can deduct investment interest only up to the amount of investment earnings.

---

[1] No one can be certain what tax rates may apply many years hence. The tax liability shown here is based on realistic assumptions.

For example, say you paid $800 in interest on your personal borrowings for investment, and made $650 in dividends, interest, and so on from your investments. You could deduct $650 of interest; the $150 balance would carry over for deduction next year subject to the same tests. When figuring your investment earnings, don't count any *Keogh* earnings, even earnings on your employee contributions.

CAN YOU CONTRIBUTE PROPERTY?

The IRS has no official public position on employee contributions of property. Unofficially, some in the IRS say you must pay tax on the paper profit when you contribute property to a *defined-benefit plan*. This is the same rule that applies to employer property contributions to any type of plan. Also, some in the IRS are said to think there's no tax on employee property contributions to money-purchase or profit-sharing plans if the Keogh trustee has no right to sell that property.

I'm not convinced that an employee contribution of property to a defined-benefit plan is taxable, but it's not worth arguing about with the IRS. My advice is, *don't* make employee contributions in property.

TRACK YOUR EMPLOYEE CONTRIBUTIONS

Say you make your regular Keogh contributions (as employer) and also contribute as employee. It's OK to pool the money you put in, in a single investment fund. You can use the sum of what you put in to buy whatever investments you please. Or you can put employer contributions in one account and employee contributions in another account. Or you can invest employer and employee contributions in different ways.

In any case, you should know exactly how much your employee contributions were, when you made them, and what you made on them. If you keep all employee contributions in a separate account, it's not hard to know what you made on them. It's what you have in the account minus what you put in.

Nor is it hard to know what you made if you invest employee contributions and employer contributions in different ways. For example, suppose employee contributions go only into bank certificates of deposit, whereas employer contributions go into stocks or bonds but never into bank CDs. What you make on employee contributions is what you make on the CDs. Be sure your own records show which investments are made as employee.

If you pool employee and employer contributions, what you make on employee contributions is their proportionate share of the earnings in the pool for the period they are in the pool.

EMPLOYEE CONTRIBUTIONS—
YOUR PRIVATE BANK

You might want to think of the fund you build up with employee contributions as your private bank or war chest. You can tap into it when you need funds for any personal or business purpose.

For example, you might make a withdrawal when you need cash to make an *employer* contribution to your Keogh. Another reason might be to make a down payment on a home or vacation home.

You will owe tax on part of your withdrawal, the part considered to represent investment earnings. See Chapter 14 for details. So you shouldn't withdraw unless you need the money.

If you *expect* to have to withdraw an employee contribution, you might want to invest the money in some more liquid form than you do your employer contributions: in Treasury bills, short-term CDs, or money market funds, for example.

CHECKLIST FOR EMPLOYEE CONTRIBUTIONS

1. *Why contribute as employee?* Gives you a bigger Keogh fund with more money working for you tax-free.
2. *How much can you contribute?* Unofficially, up to 10 percent, depending, of *all* of your earned income from the business.
3. *When can you take out contributions?* Your plan can be

written to let you withdraw whenever you want. Part of what you withdraw is taxable.
4. *What about borrowing to contribute?* No legal problem.
5. *What about contributing property?* Some legal uncertainties here. Best not to do it.

CHAPTER 8

INVESTING YOUR
KEOGH FUNDS

Chapters 6 and 7 covered your Keogh contributions—planting your seed money. Now for how to make it grow through investment.

Most successful investors have an investment philosophy. Here are the basic principles I have developed for the Keogh investor:

First: Make investments you feel comfortable with. You can be as active as you please, moving in and out of whatever you like. Or you can invest for the long-term. You can be in stocks, bonds, mutual funds, money market funds, real estate mortgages, or anything else. The only legal limitation is that your Keogh can't invest in collectibles: paintings, antiques, postage stamps, and the like. Small loss, this. There's no place for collectibles in a tax-exempt portfolio.

Second: Always keep in mind just how important it will be to you to have these funds available at retirement. Maybe your retirement needs are well covered in other ways, through a generous company pension plan, for example. If so, you can treat this as a pure investment account and take any flier that seems promising. Otherwise, if you're like most Keogh investors, safety and steady appreciation will be your goal.

Third: Forget about tax-favored investments, such as tax-exempt bonds or tax shelters. Keoghs are completely exempt from tax. Any and all income is tax-free, and no one gets any benefit from tax deductions or losses. That means you need not hesitate to sell profitable assets when the price is right. There's no tax on either short-term or long-term profits. Invest, sell, and reinvest for the maximum return consistent with your investment objectives, and ignore taxes entirely.

Fourth: Be scrupulous about your status as trustee, if you are your own trustee. Keogh investments should be made *as trustee*—for example, John Jones, Trustee of [the John Jones Defined-Benefit Plan]. And of course, when selling, the sale is by John Jones, Trustee.

DIVERSIFYING YOUR INVESTMENT PORTFOLIO

Investment advisors always urge investors to diversify their investments. Investors, they say, should own a variety of common stocks (equities), a variety of bonds or other interest-paying debt instruments (securities),[1] and maybe other investments (gold, collectibles, preferred stocks) as well. Diversifying your investments will give you income, growth of capital, and safety.

It's not easy to diversify a Keogh portfolio in the early years. But it's not necessary to diversify your *Keogh* investments if you diversify your entire portfolio, Keogh and personal investments combined. You could, for example, make your more secure and conservative investments in your Keogh plan and your more aggressive and growth-oriented investments personally. Conservative investments produce a steady income stream that is fully taxable each year if received personally. Making such investments via the Keogh postpones the tax and increases your after-tax return. Most of the income from growth-oriented investments tends to be taxed only when the investments are sold. This is another form of tax postponement. Tax-sheltered investments and real estate rental properties should be owned personally.

---

[1] The term *securities* is often used for stocks as well as for bonds and other debt instruments and is generally so used in this book.

THE NEW HERESY: HIGH-RISK
KEOGH INVESTMENTS

Make high-risk investments or play it safe? It's up to you, depending on your wealth and your temperament. But if you intend to make high-risk investments anyway, and have a defined-benefit Keogh plan, consider the following argument for making your riskier investments through your Keogh: If your high-risk investment pays off with a big return, your Keogh pays no tax on it. If it's a loser, you may be able to make up your losses through *fully tax-deductible* Keogh contributions. That beats what happens in a personal portfolio, where windfall income is fully taxed, losses get only a limited deduction, and make-up investments aren't deductible at all.

We already know that *good* investments do better inside the Keogh tax shelter than outside it. And you *can* do better investing through a Keogh even if the investment goes bad. Thanks to the full Keogh deduction, you can get back to where you started, you can make up your losses, with fewer dollars in a Keogh than outside it.

So is there a good logical argument for making a high-risk investment through a Keogh if such an investment would be made anyway? There is. And do I therefore expect the world of Keogh investors to run out and make high-risk investments through their Keoghs? I do not.

Logic doesn't count for much among investors who rely on Keoghs for their retirement security. They insist on playing it safe with their Keogh money, whatever risks they may run with their personal portfolios. And even for those more inclined to gamble, the argument weakens as retirement approaches. Near retirement, you are playing for higher stakes, since you have less time to make up an investment shortfall with new contributions.

WHERE TO PUT YOUR MONEY

The following types of investments are in widest use in Keogh plans.

Common Stocks

Since World War II, investments in publicly traded common stocks have earned a higher return than have investments in the interest-bearing securities available at that time. The rate of return combines dividend income and profits (less losses) on sales of stock. Rate of return also is measured by the increase (or decrease) in a stock's market value since it was purchased, even though it has not yet been sold. Common stocks are among the more volatile of the investments chosen for Keogh plans. Prices fluctuate more widely than with the other investments, so gains—and losses—tend to be proportionately greater.

Of course, how much can be made on money invested in any particular stock depends on the characteristics of that stock; there's no guarantee against picking losers. Many investors seek to spread the risk of picking a loser by diversifying, investing in many stocks. But diversification is not easy for Keogh plans in the early years, when relatively little has been contributed to the plan. Common stocks are typically sold in hundred-share lots. Brokers' commissions are higher on "odd lot" purchases (fewer than 100 shares). Thus, wide diversification in hundred-share lots is financially difficult in the early years. You can diversify in odd lots, but that is wasteful because of uneconomically high purchase costs in the form of brokers' commissions.

One approach is to buy one or a few safe stocks in the early years. As investment funds build up over several years of contributions and earnings, you can then diversify your common stock holdings. A similar approach is to build funds through investment in income-producing securities and then diversify in stocks. Or you can, in effect, diversify by investing in common stock mutual funds (see below).

Common stocks are usually bought and sold through securities dealers.

Preferred Stocks

Preferred stocks usually pay a fixed dividend out of profits. They are "preferred" over common stock of the same company because they have the first claim on dividends and on the assets of the company at liquidation, but they are subordinate to the company's bonds. Preferred stock ordinarily does not vote or participate in company earnings after the fixed dividend.

Yields on preferred stocks generally are higher than on common stocks, and price fluctuations are less (except for convertible preferred stock; see below).

Preferred stock isn't often found in Keogh portfolios; bonds are safer and yield about as much.

Preferred stock is bought and sold in the same way as common stock.

Bonds

Corporate and U.S. Treasury bonds are often used in Keogh plans because of their safety. Usually they are long-term investments whose yields, over the period until withdrawal, can be higher than other interest-paying investments.

Bonds usually are bought and sold through securities dealers. New issues of Treasury bonds also can be bought through Federal Reserve banks and commercial banks. The coupon interest rate of a bond usually depends on the going rate of interest when the bond was issued; the rate is fixed for the life of the bond. A few pay a floating rate, recalculated periodically to reflect current interest rates, such as those payable on U.S. Treasury bills. The sale or purchase price of the bond after issue rises as interest rates fall below the rate prevailing when it was issued; the bond's price falls as interest rates rise above that rate.

A bond's *coupon rate* is the interest it pays expressed as a percentage of the bond's face amount. The face amount is what the investor gets when the bond is redeemed at maturity. A bond's *yield* is the money the investor collects expressed as a percentage of the price he or she pays for the bond. Depending on context, yield may refer only to the current coupon paid or may also include the difference between the amount to be received at redemption and the price paid for it. The bondholder would have a gain or a loss if he or she sold the bond before maturity.

Example. A bond was issued for $1,000 and paid a semiannual interest coupon of $35. The coupon rate is 7 percent ($70 ÷ $1,000). Five years later, when interest rates have risen well above 7 percent, an investor buys the bond for $800. The investor's *current yield* is 8.8 percent ($70 ÷ $800). The *yield to maturity* is higher; it reflects current yield plus the fact that at maturity the investor will collect a $200 profit ($1,000, whereas he paid only $800). The exact amount of that yield to maturity depends on the length of time to maturity.

Bond price movements are less drastic than those of stocks. That is welcome in the less volatile atmosphere of Keogh plans, especially defined-benefit plans, where predictability of long-term results can be important.

Most bonds are in face amounts of $1,000 or $5,000. Therefore, a Keogh plan in its early years may not be able to afford bonds (see "Mutual Funds" below).

Zero coupon bonds. With zero coupon bonds, interest is compounded until maturity and can be withdrawn only when the bond is redeemed.

Zero coupon bonds are issued by corporations; the U.S. Treasury also has a version of such bonds. They are popular with pension plans, which invest for the long term and may have little need for current income. In 1985 General Electric bought $824 million U.S. Treasury zero coupon bonds for its pension plan.

Zero coupon bonds carry a long-term commitment to pay a particular interest rate, which is true for any bond of comparable duration. But in addition, zero coupon bonds promise that income also will be *compounded* at that rate. For example, an ordinary coupon bond may pay interest at 10 percent. But the cashed-in coupon interest, when reinvested, will earn at the current rate, which may be less than 10 percent. With a 10 percent zero coupon bond, the interest is reinvested at 10 percent.

Zero coupon bonds produce no income until maturity, but they can be sold like any other bonds. Zero coupon bond prices fluctuate widely.

Example.   A 10-year zero coupon bond that yields 12 percent costs $1,160 when issued and $5,000 at maturity 10 years later. If you sold it after six years, you would get about $3,180 if interest rates on four-year debt were 12 percent at that time. You would get less if rates were higher and more if they were less.

At this writing, interest paid on long-term investments is greater than on short-term investments. This can be seen as good for Keoghs, which invest for the long term. Defined-benefit Keoghs are especially attracted by favorable rates for long-term investment. The higher the rate of investment return, the less the Keogh pension will cost.

Bank CDs (Certificates of Deposit)

Bank CDs are bank time deposits for fixed periods of from six months to five years. The amount you must deposit depends on the bank and the deposit period, but in many cases there is a $500 minimum. The interest rate you get is higher than passbook savings pays and normally rises as the period of time on deposit increases. Usually the rates are fixed: for example, 9 percent over the period. With some banks you can get a guaranteed minimum rate that is increased to follow some market rate, such as the yields of certain Treasury debt instruments.

For practical purposes, there is no market for your bank CD investment. You can only redeem it; you can't sell it. You will pay a penalty if you redeem (withdraw principal) before the end of the period you selected. The penalty is loss of part of the interest otherwise earned. Apart from this, federal law guarantees your account against loss up to $100,000. Unlike investments in bonds, for example, you are sure to recover the cash you put in.

CDs are simple, conservative investments, requiring little attention. In most CDs interest compounds automatically. Investors should keep track of when their CDs mature so they can reinvest promptly (in CDs or something else) without loss of income after maturity.

Mutual Funds

There are mutual funds of stocks, bonds, and various kinds of short-term debt. Within these larger categories—bond mutual funds, for example—there are subcategories: mutual funds of tax-exempt municipal bonds (issued by a particular state) or mutual funds of high-risk corporate bonds. Money market funds (see page 73) are mutual funds invested in short-term debt.

Mutual funds have two special attractions for the Keogh investor or other investor, compared to buying stocks, bonds, or other items directly. First, the mutual fund is a diversified portfolio of the items within the category, so the investor spreads the risk. He or she can't be wiped out by a disaster in one stock. On the other hand, the investor bears a part of any loss resulting from the downfall of an item that the investor would not have bought but that was in the fund's portfolio. Also, there are mutual funds dedicated to making risky investments—in start-up companies, for example. Investment in such funds, even though diversified, can be riskier than investment in a single stock with characteristics of safety.

Second, it's usually possible to buy into a mutual fund for less than the typical transaction cost in a direct ownership investment. That makes it easier to get started in stock or bond investment. For example, a money market fund might buy short-term debt instruments costing a minimum of $100,000. You could buy a share in such a fund for, say, $500 or $1,000.

The term *income fund* is used for mutual funds investing in stocks for safety and current dividend income with modest growth. The term *growth fund* is used for mutual funds investing in stocks for future appreciation in asset values and stock prices. These funds are thought of as riskier than income funds. The term *balanced fund* is used for mutual funds investing in both stocks and bonds, balancing income and safety (from the bonds) with hoped-for appreciation (in the stocks). Funds like these do, with varying degrees of success, what an individual might do by investing in two different funds.

One mutual fund is preferable to another of the same type (investing in the same category or subcategory of investment) depending on its investment results. But all mutual funds, regardless of their success, charge for their service one way or another. Those charges reduce return on investment. Thus, investors who are confident of their own judgment may pull out of mutual funds and invest on their own once they have enough funds for diversified investment.

Some mutual funds are sold through securities dealers or agents; for others, the investor deals with the mutual fund directly.

Some mutual funds are specifically designed for Keoghs. Since Keoghs aren't taxed, the fund managers are expected to disregard the tax consequences of their transactions. Supposedly, the fund that feels free to ignore tax considerations on its trades tends to do better than tax-conscious funds investing in the same type of securities. That is an attempt to offer through the mutual fund device the freedom you would enjoy in your direct Keogh investments.

Money Market Funds

Money market funds are mutual funds that invest in short-term securities, such as Treasury bills, large-denomination bank CDs, and large-denomination corporate debt. Money market yields vary from week to week and from one fund to another. Banks offer them too, sometimes calling them market rate accounts.

Money market funds are often used as places to park funds between investments or while suitable new investment is being investigated.

Real Estate Investment Trusts (REITs)

REITs are like mutual funds. Some invest directly in real estate as owners and landlords of shopping centers, hotels, and so on. Some invest as lenders on or holders of real estate mortgages. As with mutual funds, particularly common stock mutual funds, REIT investments grow through dividends and profits on sale of the REIT asset. REIT shares are bought and sold through securities dealers.

GNMAs and Other Mortgage-Backed Securities and Securities Funds

Government National Mortgage Association securities (GNMAs or Ginnie Maes) are the most widely held form of mortgage-backed security. These securities represent investments in FHA- or VA-insured mortgages and are guaranteed by the federal government. Yields are high and are paid monthly. Safety is assured by the government guarantee.

They are often advertised as "recommended for IRA or Keogh plans" because of their safety and high yield. But because they are *mortgage* securities, each monthly payment represents both interest and principal. So the investor's capital investment in the GNMA certificate drops with each payment he or she collects. To stay fully invested, the investor must find a new investment for each payment he or she collects. That is also true for any bond interest or cash dividend the investor gets. But it matters more with GNMAs because payments are made more often (monthly), and they are larger in proportion to the sums invested because they include principal as well as income.

GNMA certificates have a face amount of $25,000 or more. For those unable or unwilling to invest that much, there are GNMA mutual funds that accept investments of much smaller amounts. Such funds may arrange to reinvest the monthly payments of principal and interest you collect. Reinvestment is at the rate prevailing at the time reinvestment is made, not the rate of the original investment. A commission is charged on entering the fund and also may be charged as collections are reinvested.

There is a variety of other mortgage-backed securities sold by private agencies. They are often considered safe investments, though they lack the GNMA guarantee, and their yields are higher. There are also mutual funds investing in such securities.

Mortgage-backed securities are generally bought and sold through securities dealers.

Convertible Securities

Convertible securities combine characteristics of safety and current income on the one hand with the opportunity for capital appreciation on the other.

A convertible bond is a corporate bond, paying interest currently, with a bond's usual degree of safety. The bond may be traded in to the corporation (converted) for a predetermined number of its shares of stock. This benefits the bondholder when the stock shares he or she gets in exchange are worth more than the bond is. For example, if a bond worth $1,000 could be converted into five shares of stock, the investor would convert when the stock share market price went above $200.

The investor would have bought the bond when the stock price was below $200. So buying convertible bonds can be seen as a speculation but with a hedge against your speculative risk. That is, you bet or speculate that the stock price will rise. But if it doesn't rise, you still have the bond, a secure, income-producing investment.

Every opportunity and every protection has its price. You will pay a higher price for a convertible bond than for a similar *non*convertible one, or you will get a lower rate of interest, which in economic terms is about the same thing.

Convertible bond prices fluctuate with interest rates (rising as rates fall, falling as rates rise). Prices also fluctuate to some degree with the prices of the stock into which they are converted (rising with stock price rises, falling with stock price declines).

Convertible bonds are sometimes called convertible debentures.

Convertible preferred stock is the same idea. Convertible preferred, less safe than a bond but maybe paying a higher rate of return, is convertible into a certain number of shares of common stock of the same company.

Life Insurance Investment Products and Programs

These life insurance industry offerings are important to the retirement-minded investor:

Annuities, including variable annuities.
Guaranteed investment contracts.
Life insurance.

These investments are considered in Chapter 9, with further analysis of annuity investments in Chapter 12.

Insurance Funding

Insurance companies are best known for selling life insurance policies and annuities (see Chapter 9). But they are now financial supermarkets, where you can also shop among investment opportunities like those offered by securities dealers. You can now invest periodically in one or another insurance company fund that invests in bonds, mortgages, common stocks, money market instruments, and so on. At retirement you can use your assets in an insurance company to buy an annuity from the company, but that is not required. You could instead just withdraw the cash in a lump sum.

You can switch from one fund to another as you please, but the insurance company may impose a fee on withdrawal in the early years.

DIRECT INVESTMENT

The investments described above are typically made through an institution or agent—bank, insurance company, securities dealer, and so on. But you are free to invest your Keogh funds directly. For example, your Keogh could lend money on a real estate mortgage. Other forms of direct investment—venture capital investments in start-up companies or ownership of rental real estate—also are permitted but not ideal for Keogh plans. As noted on pages 65–66, the tax advantages that make such investments appealing are meaningless in a Keogh portfolio. If you want such investments, make them personally.

INVESTMENT EXPENSES

Brokers' commissions and other investment expenses should be paid out of Keogh fund assets or income. These are fund expenses, not your expenses as employer; you will not be allowed a personal tax deduction for these expenses if you pay them.

A MODEL KEOGH PORTFOLIO?

There's no such thing. But if you're relatively close to retirement, you might favor safety with relatively high income: mortgage-backed securities or bonds, including zero coupon bonds. Such investments, with predictable long-term rates of return, are especially good for those starting defined-benefit plans—Harold, for example.

If retirement is farther away, investments offering long-term appreciation will look good: common stocks generally and growth mutual funds. That is where Peter can be expected to put most of his money, though, as you may remember, we projected no extraordinary investment results for him, no extraordinary growth. These investments will predominate in money-purchase plans and profit-sharing plans until the Keogh investor approaches retirement. At that point, safety with high income tends to take over.

Elaine, with relatively little to invest at first, might opt for a stock mutual fund or, more conservatively, a money market fund or bank CD. Until she develops a long-term investment philosophy, or knows whether she will keep on moonlighting, those are the best alternatives.

CHAPTER 9

INSURANCE OPTIONS AND OPPORTUNITIES

For much of this century insurance companies have played a central role in America's private pension system. They have been less conspicuous in the Keogh environment. Sometimes they have priced themselves out of consideration by many Keogh investors. But many of today's insurance companies mean to compete with other institutions that might attract your Keogh dollars. Insurance products or programs may belong in your Keogh planning.

INSURED KEOGH PLANS

Insured Keogh plans are retirement plans in which the Keogh funds consist primarily of annuity contracts. The basic idea of the insured plan is that your Keogh buys annuities for you, year by year, while you're still working. They are called deferred annuities because you start to collect them in the future.

Insured plans are to be contrasted with plans in which the moonlighter controls his or her own investments; the latter are called trusteed plans, though insured plans may use trustees too. The Keogh rules and Keogh opportunities we've considered in earlier pages apply to insured plans as well. You can have insured defined-benefit plans, insured money-purchase plans, and insured profit-sharing plans. But insured Keoghs have a few unique features.

TWO TYPES OF INSURED PLAN

You can choose either retirement annuity contracts or retirement income contracts. You could even have some of each, though there's not much reason to do this intentionally. Sometimes a person might start out buying income contracts and then later buy annuity contracts.

Retirement annuity contracts are annuities with no life insurance features. Retirement annuity contracts are written to pay $10 a month (or multiples thereof) for life, starting at a specified retirement age. For an extra charge, they will carry a guarantee to pay for not less than, say, 10 years, even if the participant dies within 10 years after retirement. The premiums you pay the insurance company each year are your Keogh contributions.

In selecting an insurance company from which to buy, these factors are important:

- Interest rates. The higher the rate used, the better, other things being equal.
- Quality or safety of the company itself. Insurance companies are rated by A. M. Best Company.
- Charges. Insurance companies often impose front-end charges, which go largely for agents' commissions and related sales expenses. Charges vary from company to company. Whatever you pay reduces the amount you have working for you. Some companies impose an exit charge if you withdraw from the plan. The charge may drop with the length of time you are in the plan. Many companies impose administrative fees. And many pass along state insurance premium taxes to customers, directly or indirectly.
- The company's investment policies. You may be able to get a statement of what the company invests in.

Depending on the insurance company you are dealing with, you can buy annuities in either of two ways. One way is through level premiums each year—in effect, buying the annuity on the installment plan. This approach should suit a defined-benefit plan. The company will guarantee the interest rate to be earned on the premiums and also guarantee the rate to be used in the annuity itself (called the settlement option). These guarantees are minimums. Actual rates may be higher.

Example.   The insurance company guarantees that a minimum of 5 percent a year will be paid on Keogh annuity premiums of $2,200 a year for 21 years. And it guarantees that the accumulated funds can convert to a pension at a minimum 5 percent. Assuming a 15-year life expectancy at retirement, this represents a pension of $7,567 a year.

   If the company actually credits 7 percent a year and uses 7 percent when the accumulated funds convert to a pension, the pension will be $10,837 a year.

The other way is to buy a separate annuity contract each year for the pension earned that year. At retirement, you collect the sum of the annuities bought each year. This kind of arrangement suits money-purchase or profit-sharing plans.

Example.   You will use each year's money-purchase Keogh contribution to buy retirement annuity contracts. Annuity payout will start at retirement, when you will have a 15-year life expectancy. You make $14,000 moonlighting your first year, when you're 21 years from retirement, and $10,000 your second year. You put in $2,800 in year 1 and $2,000 in year 2.

   Say that at retirement the $2,800 from year 1 has grown to an amount that would buy you an annuity of $1,449 a year. And that the $2,000 from year 2 would buy you an annuity of $962. When you retire, you get the sum of these amounts each year, plus any annuities paid for out of any future contributions you make.

Some defined benefit plans can use this approach.

Example.   Your plan provides a pension equal to 8 percent of pay for each year of service.

   You make $15,000 this year and buy a retirement annuity contract that will pay you $1,200 a year at retirement, say 12 years hence. This might cost you $5,645. Next year, year 2, you make $18,000. It might cost you $7,248 for an annuity contract to pay $1,440 a year at retirement (which next year is 11 years away). As in the preceding example, when you retire you will get the sum of $1,200 and $1,440 a year, plus any annuities bought with any future contributions.

For the moonlighter who wants to include "death benefits" (this is the pension industry's way of saying "life insurance") in his or her plan, a *retirement income policy or contract* may be used. Such a policy typically provides $1,000 of life insurance for every $10 of monthly annuity payment.

A retirement income policy is like a retirement annuity except that it costs more than a retirement annuity providing the same monthly payment at retirement because life insurance is added.

Since the investor is paying for both an annuity and life insurance, after a time the "cash value of the contract" (the insurance industry's way of saying "the amount in the annuity account") can be more than the face amount of the life insurance policy. In that case, the amount payable at death (before retirement) is the higher amount: the cash value.

Example.   A moonlighter buys $12,000 a year in annuities together with $100,000 of life insurance. If his annuity account has reached, say, $107,000 when he dies, before retirement, his beneficiary will get $107,000, not $100,000.

WHAT'S GOOD ABOUT INSURED PLANS?

Safety. Insurance companies guarantee the interest rate to be earned on future investments. And they guarantee that the annuity you've paid for, through payment of premiums, will be there at retirement. No such guarantees can be made by trusteed plans.

WHAT'S NOT SO GOOD ABOUT INSURED PLANS?

Two things: (1) investment return is relatively low on insured plans, and (2) they aren't very flexible.

The rate of return on investment in insurance company products such as annuities is often lower than that generally available through other investments. Partly, this results from the greater security of insurance company investments. And partly it results from the sales and administrative charges the investor must pay. Of course, some persons in trusteed plans do worse than they would in an insured plan.

A lower investment return than you can get elsewhere means you pay more for the same benefit.

Example.   You want a $12,000-a-year annuity over an 18-year life expectancy. This would cost $112,462 at 8 percent; $129,931 at 6 percent. Retirement is 15 years away, and you will pay for this in equal installments over the 15-year period. If your investment return is 8 percent, you put in $4,139 a year (to reach $112,462). If it's 6 percent, you put in $4,836 a year (again to reach $112,462). Over the 15 years the lower return costs you $10,455 more ($697 × 15).

Your payments are tax deductible. Even so, the lower rate of return costs you $6,796 more after tax if you're in the 35 percent tax bracket. (See Chapter 19 for the use of a 35 percent tax bracket.)

Also, there's little flexibility with insured defined-benefit plans. The way moonlighting income fluctuates, it's not always easy to fit the funds you have available around a particular annuity contract.

As we know from earlier pages on retirement plans using trustees, you don't *have to* convert your Keogh fund into an annuity. You could, for example, withdraw your Keogh fund all at once.

The same is true for insured Keoghs. You could withdraw your annuity account all at once. Few do. Most of those who go into insured plans do so for the annuity feature and the guaranteed annuity purchase rate.

It's not as easy with insured defined-benefit plans as with trusteed plans to increase your retirement pension to match future increases in self-employment earnings.

Insured plans have advantages and disadvantages; trusteed plans aren't right for everyone. But insured plans aren't used much now in moonlighter Keoghs. All plans discussed elsewhere in these pages are trusteed plans. My own plan is trusteed.

THE "SEMI-INSURED" KEOGH

Please indulge my shorthand way of describing the immediate participation guarantee contract. Here you invest your Keogh funds with the insurance company, generally until retirement. You share in the company's investment results (minus a little off the top as its profit). So your investment return is not insured, or guaranteed. But the company guarantees the rate or price at which the annuity can be purchased.

The company may offer you the chance to invest in a pool of common stocks, bonds, or other assets (for more on this, see Chapter 8). Normally your investment return will be based on the yields of assets acquired in the year your money went in and not the totality of such assets owned by the company.

GUARANTEED INVESTMENT CONTRACTS (GICS)

The plain-vanilla GIC has a fixed interest rate, a future maturity date, with interest compounded internally to maturity, like a zero coupon bond. A variation pays fixed interest periodically, like a regular bond.

Further variations allow a form of installment purchase, offer multiple maturity dates, offer floating rates with a guaranteed minimum, or offer an indexed rate tied, for example, to the prime rate.

They are unmarketable, illiquid, and you may be hit with a substantial penalty if you cash one in before maturity.

These contracts have no annuity features but can be used to buy annuities at rates prevailing at maturity.

Those I know of are pricey for Keoghs: $100,000 and up for the plain vanillas, more for the exotic flavors. But you may find one in your price range. If interested, ask.

VARIABLE ANNUITIES

When you buy an annuity, you are relying on the insurance company's guarantee that you will collect throughout your lifetime. But

> With these contracts, every payment is fixed; each monthly check is for the same amount. During inflationary periods, fixed payments produce steadily diminishing purchasing power. This undesirable

circumstance can be dealt with using the *variable annuity*. With a variable annuity, the insurer makes no promise regarding the size of each annuity payment. The amount received by the annuitant is a function of the performance of an underlying portfolio of common stocks. The theory is that the same forces that drive up consumer prices will also drive up the dividends and market prices of the underlying portfolio, allowing the insurer to deliver an increasing stream of income to the annuitant. Variable annuities are always purchased on a deferred basis and can be purchased with period certain, joint-and-last-survivor, or refund guarantees.[1]

You might follow a program of investing each year in securities, equities, and so on, but every few years convert some of these pension assets into variable annuities.

WHAT'S "SPLIT FUNDING"?

You may hear the term *split funding* from an insurance agent. It usually means putting part of your Keogh money in a retirement annuity or retirement income contract and the rest in other, trusteed investment. It can be a response to year-to-year fluctuations in moonlighting incomes. If your Keogh contributions might vary from say, $1,500 to $4,000 a year, you might commit to pay $1,500 a year toward a retirement annuity and put any excess into your trusteed Keogh portfolio.

DOES LIFE INSURANCE BELONG IN YOUR PLAN?

The law allows you to include a limited life insurance benefit in your plan. In a defined-benefit plan, that amount can be as high as 100 times your monthly retirement annuity. Thus, if your monthly annuity is $800, your plan can include insurance coverage of $80,000. You would, of course, have to pay for this coverage at insurance company rates.

---

[1] Taken from Mark Dorfman and Saul Adelman, *The Dow Jones-Irwin Guide to Life Insurance* (Homewood, Ill.: Dow Jones-Irwin, 1988). Reproduced with permission. Period certain, joint-and-last-survivor, and refund guarantees are explained in Chapter 12.

In a money-purchase or profit-sharing plan, up to 50 percent of your Keogh contribution can go for whole life insurance or up to 25 percent if it's term insurance or universal life.

Do you want life insurance in your Keogh? That depends first on whether you need insurance. An insurance agent would urge you to look at it this way: Your Keogh is building a nest egg for retirement. If you should die before you retire, your Keogh may not have reached the financial goal you set for it. Of course, you won't need a *retirement* nest egg if you don't live to retire. But suppose your Keogh wealth was to help support family members when you stopped working. You might then want to consider a life insurance arrangement to cover any shortfall in Keogh wealth that might be caused by your premature death.

Some of the country's wealthier professionals and business owners buy life insurance to pay the various taxes imposed on their pension assets at their deaths. May you be one of the few to amass such Keogh wealth as to have to worry about this problem, discussed in Chapter 14.

You can spend part of your Keogh plan contribution on life insurance; that's one way to buy it through the plan. Another way is to use Keogh plan earnings to buy the insurance.

Let's consider the first way. If you have a money-purchase or profit-sharing Keogh, whatever you spend on insurance in your Keogh reduces, dollar for dollar, what you can put to work for your retirement. With $15,000 of self-employment net earnings, you could put $3,000 into a money-purchase Keogh. If you spend $600 of that money on insurance, only $2,400 is directly invested toward your retirement.

This limitation doesn't apply with defined benefit. It's OK to make the *retirement* contribution your plan calls for and *in addition* pay for allowable insurance. Thus, assuming $3,000 was the right retirement amount, you could put in $3,600, with $600 going for insurance.

What you pay in for insurance isn't tax deductible. Thus, in the money-purchase Keogh in our example you would deduct $2,400; in the defined-benefit plan you'd deduct $3,000. So in a defined-benefit plan your tax treatment is the same as if you had bought the insurance personally, outside the Keogh.

Now for the second way: buying insurance out of Keogh plan

earnings. You can't deduct here either. It's not even your money; it's the Keogh trust's money. But part of the amount spent on life insurance premiums is taxable income to you, computed under a complex formula that I'll assume you don't feel need to learn at this point.

Life insurance agents are used to selling insurance through the plan because corporate business owners often get their insurance that way. (The corporation gets a tax deduction for the premium, which generates a modicum of taxable income to the business owner.) In a Keogh environment, there's no strong reason to buy through the Keogh rather than personally.

However, you *may* be able to get insurance more easily, or at slightly lower cost, through your Keogh. Some companies don't require "evidence of insurability" for insurance bought through an insured plan. "Evidence of insurability" is the insurance industry's way of saying it finds you in good health after a medical examination.

So if you're already a customer of the insurance company because you're buying an annuity, your life insurance may come cheaper. If your health is somewhat below par, you may get insurance, or lower-cost insurance, if the company waives evidence of insurability.

YOU DON'T NEED AN INSURED PLAN TO HAVE A RETIREMENT ANNUITY

In preceding chapters, we talked of buying an annuity from an insurance company. We were *not* considering *insured plans*. In the trusteed plans of earlier chapters moonlighters invest their money as they please, and then, if they want an annuity, they use the Keogh fund to buy it from the insurance company when they retire. It's your money, and you are at risk until you buy the annuity. If I wanted an annuity, I would buy it at retirement.

CHAPTER 10

AN IRA WITH YOUR KEOGH?

"IRAs for everyone." This sweeping slogan announced one of the blessings of the 1981 Reagan Revolution. Five years later, "IRAs for everyone" was the big casualty of President Reagan's Tax Reform. From 1982 through 1986, almost everyone who worked could invest 2,000 tax-deductible dollars (sometimes up to 2,250) in an account that earned tax-deferred income. Deduction plus tax deferral are key parts of the Keogh concept, too, though Keoghs offer more. Tax deduction rules for IRAs (individual retirement accounts) today are less appealing. IRAs no longer suit everyone.

Today's rules let some individuals deduct all or part of their IRA contributions. For others, IRA contributions are permitted, but only out of after-tax dollars, with no tax deductions.

WHO CAN DEDUCT?

Give me a moment on that question. It's easier to say first who *can't* deduct.

You can't deduct if your income exceeds a certain level *and* you or your spouse is covered by a company or a Keogh plan. It's a two-pronged test. It's one strike against deduction if you or your spouse is in any kind of company plan—defined-benefit, money-purchase, profit-sharing, stock bonus, ESOP (employee stock ownership plan), annuity, thrift, or savings plan—or any kind of Keogh plan. But even if in a plan, you can get full deduction where your income is below $25,000 if single or $40,000 for a married couple filing a joint return.

At incomes between $25,000 and $35,000 if single or $40,000

and $50,000 on a joint return, a partial deduction, explained later, is allowed. So the second and final strike against deduction is your income level: Your income exceeds $35,000 if single or $50,000 on a joint return.

You get full IRA deduction if you work and neither you nor your spouse is in a company or Keogh plan. "So some people must choose between a deductible IRA and a Keogh?" This is from Elaine, who doesn't miss much.

Yes, *some* must choose. Not Harold, Peter, or Elaine, though. They have no choice. Even without counting Keoghs, *they* can't deduct for IRAs. Peter is in a company—the university—plan. Harold is in a company plan and exceeds the $50,000 ceiling on his joint return with Judy. Elaine is considered in a company plan through her husband, Frank; adding his income to hers on their joint return puts them over the income ceiling.

NONDEDUCTIBLE IRAS, ANYONE?

Earnings on all IRA investments are tax-deferred until withdrawn. Tax reform didn't change that. So other things being equal, IRAs, deductible or not, have the edge over normal, taxable investments.

Example.   Say you contribute $2,000 a year for 15 years to an IRA that earns at the rate of 7.75 percent. If you withdraw it, you'd have $53,259 before tax and about $45,100 after tax ($30,000 of the $53,259 comes back tax-free). An investment whose earnings are taxable each year would build to about $43,150 after tax.

A $1,950 edge over 15 years—6.5 percent of the total amount invested—won't make your fortune. And remember I said "other things being equal." They aren't quite equal. For one thing, with IRAs you don't have the same wide spectrum of investment opportunities as with normal investments—or with Keoghs. This won't matter to you if you will invest in fairly conventional ways, such as mutual funds, common stocks, bonds, or CDs.

More important are the tax penalties on premature withdrawal. The law grants IRA tax relief to induce people to put money aside for *retirement*. The law punishes those who withdraw these retirement funds for personal use too early. There's a 10 percent tax penalty, in addition to the regular tax, on premature withdrawals. That is, you compute the regular tax on withdrawal, add a 10 percent penalty, and pay the IRS the total. For more on the regular tax and the penalty, see Chapter 14.

Your withdrawal is considered premature if it happens before you reach age 59½, unless you have become disabled or are taking the money out in the form of a lifetime annuity.

Example.   Return to the previous example and assume the IRA withdrawal is premature. The tax penalty cuts the after-tax fund to about $42,775, which puts it *behind* normal investment.

These examples oversimplify. You could get a different answer using a higher investment yield, or a longer investment buildup, or different tax rates over the investment period or when withdrawal occurs.

The point is that a nondeductible IRA can be right for you and wrong for someone who might need the money for a business or personal purpose before retirement. While many might benefit from a nondeductible IRA, they're best for those who have reached 59½ and those nearing that age.

IRA CONTRIBUTION CEILINGS

As we've seen, even nondeductible IRAs offer tax benefits. So Congress has set a ceiling on what you can contribute to your IRA. It's the same amount whether deduction is allowed or not.

IRA contributions can be put in and deducted up to a total of $2,000 per year per worker ($2,250 for a married couple where only one earns income from personal services). Where husband and wife both work, *each* can put in and deduct up to $2,000. This will give them a combined deduction of $4,000 on a joint tax return. Contributions beyond these limits are not allowed and are penalized, even if no deduction is claimed for the excess.

If your self-employment earnings together with any earnings you have as an employee total less than $2,000, that total is all you can contribute. This limit mostly affects homemakers.

Peter and Harold have had IRAs since 1982. That was the first year persons already in a pension or profit-sharing plan were allowed to have an IRA as well. Elaine, who has never been in any company plan, has had an IRA since she started moonlighting six years ago.

Harold's wife, Judy, also has had an IRA since 1982. As a part-time employee, she's not in a company plan. Judy could have got into IRAs sooner. But she didn't become convinced IRAs were a good idea until her accountant husband started one of his own.

CHOOSING A DEDUCTIBLE IRA

You must know by now whether you can have a Keogh. If you can have a Keogh, you can have an IRA—at least the nondeductible kind. A few readers may face a choice between a Keogh and a deductible IRA. You are among them if neither you nor your spouse is in a company or Keogh plan now. Setting up a Keogh plan will kill your IRA deduction for each year your income exceeds $35,000 if single ($50,000 on a joint return) and will reduce that deduction if your income is between $25,000 and $35,000 (between $40,000 and $50,000 on a joint return). Adopting a Keogh plan for yourself will kill or cut your spouse's IRA deduction under the same rules.

Normally, a Keogh is preferable to a deductible IRA if your Keogh deduction will exceed your IRA deduction. This happens in a money-purchase Keogh where self-employment earnings exceed $10,000 and with lower earnings in a defined-benefit Keogh. But for each year your Keogh is in existence, you have killed your chance (and your spouse's chance) to deduct IRA contributions unless income that year falls below $35,000 if single ($50,000 on a joint return).

If self-employment earnings will be modest, and you can fully deduct IRA contributions now, you might be better off forgoing Keoghs.

PARTIAL IRA DEDUCTIONS

These are allowed when income is between $25,000 and $35,000 if single or between $40,000 and $50,000 on a joint return.

Say you fit one of these categories and contribute $2,000 to your IRA. The general rule is that your deduction for $2,000 is reduced by 20 percent of the amount by which your income exceeds $25,000 (or $40,000). Put another way, deduction is reduced $1 for every $5 of income over $25,000 (or $40,000).

But an exception to this rule guarantees at least $200 of deduction if income is below $35,000 ($50,000 on a joint return).

Example.   Herb makes $35,000 a year and is in his company's plan. His wife, Winnie, earns $8,000 a year from part-time work in a store. Each has an IRA; each contributes $2,000. They file a joint return; their combined income is $43,000. Each can deduct $1,400, or a total of $2,800. That's $2,000 for each, less $600 for each (20 percent of $3,000, the amount over $40,000).

   If their joint return income were $49,800, they could each deduct $200. Under the *general* rule, deduction would be only $40 each—that is, $2,000 less $1,960 (20 percent of $9,800). But they can deduct $200 under the exception that guarantees the $200 deduction.

If joint return income exceeds $50,000, no IRA deduction—not even the $200 guarantee—is allowed.

The income test is applied to adjusted gross income. This is the income figure on your tax return before you take your itemized or standard deduction. On the sample income tax return in Chapter 16, it's the amount on line 31.

Peter, Elaine, and Judy *won't* contribute to their IRAs this year. Tax deferral isn't worth the restrictions and penalties, they feel, now that their tax deduction has been taken away. But they'll continue active management of their previous IRA investments.

Harold *will* make a $2,000 nondeductible contribution this year. He values the tax-deferral more than his Keogh colleagues do, and he's closer to the age when withdrawal is no longer premature.

I have no advice to offer on nondeductible IRA contributions. It's a close call, and at today's tax rates not much rides on it either way.

OTHER IRA CONSIDERATIONS

You must begin to withdraw from your IRA not later than April 1 following the year in which you reach age 70½. Unlike the case with Keoghs, you can't make deductible contributions to your IRA after that age. But if you wish, you can spread out your IRA withdrawals over a fairly long period. There's an economic advantage in this, discussed on page 121.

The Keogh investor should treat his or her IRA as one more tax-favored investment portfolio. The Keogh investment opportunities outlined in Chapter 8 are available for IRAs as well.

WHAT'S DIFFERENT ABOUT IRAS?

1. Your Keogh and your IRA are separate funds. You can't have a single fund of your own that combines both your Keogh and your IRA funds. You can, however, have your Keogh and your IRA in the same common investment fund, such as the same mutual fund. For example, you are free to invest both your Keogh money and your IRA money in the Calvin Bullock Aggressive Growth Fund.[1]

2. You can't be trustee of your IRA, as you can of your Keogh. Although it's up to you to decide where to put your IRA money, your investments must be made through an authorized independent trustee or custodian—bank, brokerage house, mutual fund, insurance company. You pay for this service, of course. You pay management fees or commissions on transactions or both. You could avoid or reduce those costs if you were in sole charge. The added expense is seldom a major consideration, and Keogh investments of the same amount through the same institution would incur the same costs. But since your IRA *must* work through an institution, you won't find it easy to make a direct investment— for example, in a real estate mortgage.

3. Because contributions to IRAs can't exceed $2,000 a year, your IRA will often be less richly funded than your Keogh. So your IRA may be unable to afford certain investments and may be less able to diversify investments than your Keogh is. But you can achieve the effect of diversification by holding some assets in your IRA and others in your Keogh and personally.

---

[1] This fund name is used for illustrative purposes only. No endorsement or other opinion is intended.

4. The spouse of an IRA investor need not be offered a share of the IRA fund. Also, there is no special tax relief for lump-sum IRA withdrawals.

5. It's easier to set up an IRA than a *pension* plan, and there's no obligation to contribute next year (or any other year) just because you contributed this year. There's no such thing as a defined-benefit IRA.

You will have seen the argument for making your more conservative investments through your Keogh (pages 65–66). On this point there need be no distinction between IRAs and Keoghs. Investments held in IRAs need be no more or less conservative than those held in Keoghs.

Persons who withdraw from a pension or profit-sharing plan sometimes put their money into an IRA. This move, made only for tax reasons, is considered in Chapter 14. Movements of funds from a pension or profit-sharing plan to an IRA, between pension or profit-sharing plans, or between IRAs are called rollovers and are tax-free. Rollover *from* an IRA *to* a pension or profit-sharing plan is not permitted.

How IRAs and Keoghs Differ

IRA	Keogh
Contribution limited to $2,000 a year	Contribution limit depends on type of plan, but all types allow contributions much larger than $2,000
No tax benefits on withdrawal	Limited tax benefits on withdrawal
Tax deduction limited or barred if IRA investor or spouse participates in company plan or Keogh	Tax deduction generally unaffected by participation in IRA, company plan, or another Keogh. Spouse's plan participation is irrelevant
Contributions not allowed beyond $2,000 limit, whether deducted or not	Extra nondeductible contributions allowed
Deductible contributions not allowed after age 70½	Deductible contributions allowed after age 70½
Must invest through an institution	Can invest through an institution or directly
Spouse of IRA owner has no right to share in the IRA fund	Spouse of Keogh participant generally must be offered a share in the Keogh fund

SIMPLIFIED EMPLOYEE PLAN

A simplified employee plan (SEP) (sometimes called a SEP-IRA) is not technically a Keogh plan but is much like a Keogh profit-sharing plan. With a SEP, the idea is that the employee sets up his or her own retirement plan—an IRA—to which both employee and employer contribute.

The SEP concept can extend to moonlighters, who, as with Keogh plans, are both employer and employee. As a moonlighter, you set up an IRA, contributing up to the $2,000 IRA ceiling. Then, in your capacity as employer, you can make a further contribution to the IRA of up to 13.043 percent of your self-employment net earnings. This additional employer SEP contribution is the same as would be allowed under a Keogh profit-sharing plan and is tax-deductible. Tax deduction for the IRA contribution must pass the deduction tests described earlier in this chapter; treat a SEP as a company plan or a Keogh when figuring your tax deduction. You would not segregate your regular IRA contributions from your employer SEP contributions. It's all one pool of IRA investments.

Who Wants a SEP?

As the name suggests, a SEP is a *simplified* plan. Little is required in the way of formal reporting to government agencies, no trustee is involved, and plan investments are handled as with any other IRA.

Simplicity is the SEP's chief attraction, but it has another: It offers a one-time opportunity to cure a failure to set up your Keogh by the deadline. For example, suppose moonlighting nets you $20,000 in 1989. If you want to make a deductible Keogh contribution for 1989, you must set up your Keogh by December 31, 1989. You have through April 15, 1990 (August 15, 1990, if you get an extension to file your tax return) to make a deductible contribution, but the plan must be in existence during 1989.

But an IRA (and hence a SEP) is different. An IRA effective for 1989 can be set up as late as April 15, 1990. The deductible SEP contribution for 1989 can be made anytime during 1989. It also can be made from January 1 to April 15, 1990, inclusive, whether or not the SEP was in existence in 1989. So if you missed the December 31 deadline for setting up a Keogh, you have an additional 3½ months to salvage a Keogh-like benefit: Set up your SEP by the following April 15 and put up to 13.043 percent of your self-employment earnings into your IRA. This would be in addition to the IRA contribution you made (or make at this time). If you have no IRA, set up the IRA and make your IRA contribution when you set up your SEP.

With a SEP, the moonlighter's spouse need not be offered a share of the fund. That is because a SEP is an enriched IRA, and IRAs need not be shared with spouses.

Can You Have a SEP and a Keogh?

Yes. If you have a Keogh plan of any kind and a SEP as well, the SEP is treated as a profit-sharing plan. The limits on contributions and deductions that apply where a profit-sharing plan is present (see Chapter 5) apply if a SEP is involved. That means, for example, that tax-deductible employer contributions to your Keogh and your SEP generally can't total more than 13.043 percent of your self-employment earnings. Your IRA contribution and any *employee* Keogh contributions you make aren't counted in this 13.043 percent figure.

If you have both a SEP and a Keogh, you have lost the benefit of a *simplified* plan. A SEP plus a Keogh is more complicated than either plan alone and not much less complicated than two Keoghs.

In my opinion, money-purchase and profit-sharing Keoghs are easy enough to establish and operate, especially if a master plan is used. (For master plans, see Chapter 15.) There's no reason for a moonlighter to turn from Keogh to SEP because of the SEP's greater simplicity. I can recommend a SEP to salvage a deduction for a year in which you have substantial self-employment earnings but no Keogh plan. Once that deduction is obtained, you should set up the appropriate Keogh and forget about further SEP contributions. SEP contributions you make one year don't commit you to make SEP contributions in future years. But since your SEP contribution was part of your IRA, you would go on investing it along with any other IRA funds.

To get started with a SEP the simplest way, you file IRS Form

5305-SEP. A sample filled-in Form 5305-SEP appears on page 97. You can't use this form if you already have a Keogh—but then, in my opinion, you should use a SEP only to salvage a deductible contribution where you have no Keogh.

Elaine, Peter, and Harold are all getting their Keogh advice before December 31 and will set up their Keoghs by then. They have no need for, and don't adopt, SEPs.

Form **5305-SEP**

(Rev. June 1991)

Department of the Treasury
Internal Revenue Service

Simplified Employee Pension-Individual
Retirement Accounts Contribution Agreement

(Under Section 408(k) of the Internal Revenue Code)

Joan Powell
(Business name—employer)

makes the following agreement under the terms of section 408(k) of the Internal Revenue Code and the instructions to this form.

The employer agrees to provide for discretionary contributions in each calendar year to the Individual Retirement Accounts or Individual Annuities (IRA's) of all eligible employees who are at least __21__ years old (not over 21 years old) (see instruction "Who May Participate") and worked in at least __1__ years (enter 1, 2, or 3 years) of the immediately preceding 5 years (see instruction "Who May Participate"). This ☐ includes ☒ does not include employees covered under a collective bargaining agreement and ☐ includes ☒ does not include employees whose total compensation during the year is less than $363*.

The employer agrees that contributions made on behalf of each eligible employee will:

- Be made only on the first $222,220* of compensation.
- Be made in an amount that is the same percentage of total compensation for every employee.
- Be limited to the smaller of $30,000 or 15% of compensation.
- Be paid to the employee's IRA trustee, custodian, or insurance company (for an annuity contract).

Joan Powell
Signature of employer

By _____

_3/17/91_
Date

97

CHAPTER 11

OTHER KEOGH CONSIDERATIONS

By now I think you will have decided whether Keoghs are for you. So at this point I feel comfortable about introducing some of what may seem to be technical matters. I won't be offended if you skip this chapter. But the matters raised here are part of the complete picture of Keogh considerations:

HOW YOUR "EARNED INCOME" DETERMINES YOUR KEOGH WEALTH

"Earned income," usually in the phrase "self-employment earned income," will appear in the language of your Keogh plan. The amount you put in a money-purchase or profit-sharing Keogh and take a tax deduction for is technically a percentage of your self-employment *earned income*.

If you adopt a defined-benefit plan, the largest pension you're entitled to is a percentage (100 percent) of self-employment *earned income* averaged over a certain period.

"Earned Income" Can Set the Limit on Your Keogh Contribution

For persons not used to Keogh rules, earned income is sometimes a difficult concept to work with because it involves a circular computation. Earned income is the net earnings (the profit) from self-employment minus the tax deduction for your Keogh contribution. Expressed as an equation, it's

Earned income =
>Self-employment net earnings − Keogh deduction

The first step, net earnings from self-employment, is easy enough. It's the amount on line 31 of Schedule C of your federal tax Form 1040. There's an example of this on page 107. For those subject to self-employment tax, there's a second step after 1989: Reduce that Schedule C income by half the self-employment tax.

The next step, the amount of the deduction, is harder to figure for a money-purchase or profit-sharing plan. That's because the deduction is a percentage of earned income, the amount we're trying to compute.

Fortunately, for moonlighter money-purchase and profit-sharing Keogh plans, we already know the amount of deduction we want: the maximum. The maximum money-purchase deduction is 25 percent of earned income. Knowing this, we can find earned income using junior high school algebra.

x (that is, earned income) =
>self-employment net earnings − 25 percent x

In Elaine's case, with her net earnings of $15,000, the equation goes as follows:

$$x = \$15,000 - .25x$$
$$1.25x = \$15,000$$
$$x = \$12,000$$

So Elaine's earned income is $12,000, and she can put in and deduct $3,000 (25 percent of $12,000) under a money-purchase plan. She would then pay tax on earned income of $12,00. With a profit-sharing plan, the computation works the same way except that the most you can deduct is 15 percent of earned income.

$$x = \$15,000 - .15x$$
$$1.15x = \$15,000$$
$$x = \$13,043$$

So earned income is $13,043, and the deductible contribution is $1,957 (15 percent of $13,043). Elaine would pay tax on $13,043.

Elaine was considering combining a profit-sharing Keogh with a money-purchase Keogh. She could put 15 percent of earned income into profit-sharing and 10 percent into money-purchase.

(Other percentages are possible—such as 5 percent profit-sharing and 20 percent money-purchase—but would leave her with less flexibility.) The equation for this is practically the same as that for money-purchase alone:

$$x = \$15,000 - (.15x + .10x)$$
$$1.25x = \$15,000$$
$$x = \$12,000$$

Earned income is $12,000. The amount put into the profit-sharing Keogh is $1,800 (15 percent of $12,000). The amount put in the money-purchase Keogh is $1,200 (10 percent of $12,000).

Pension professionals have a shortcut through all of this. Instead of the circular computation to a percentage of *earned income,* they use the percentage of *net earnings* that yields the same result. Thus: 25 percent of earned income is 20 percent of net earnings (20 percent of $15,000 is $3,000); 15 percent of earned income is 13.043 percent of net earnings (13.043 percent of $15,000 is $1,957).

As you'll recall, I've always spoken of Elaine's *net earnings* and have used 20 percent of net earnings as the money-purchase ceiling, 13.043 percent as the profit-sharing ceiling, and 12 percent plus 8 percent where profit-sharing and money-purchase are combined. You may find it more convenient to use this valid shortcut in your projections, instead of the circular computation in the Keogh law.

Why Circular Computations Anyway?

The circular computation has a purpose: to bring Keogh rules into parity with those governing corporate pension plans. Suppose you were the only employee of a corporation that earned $10,000 after all expenses except your salary and pension contributions. The amount contributed for your pension will reduce what you can get as pay. If the corporation contributed $2,000 for your pension, and you got the $8,000 balance as salary, the $2,000 for your pension would be 25 percent of your salary.

In Keogh plans the yardstick used to measure the pension contribution for self-employed persons is not salary but self-employment earned income. But the approach is the same as with corporations. The amount contributed toward the pensions reduces your self-employment earned income—just as it would reduce your salary if you were incorporated.

When Earned Income Limits the Size of Your Pension

In money-purchase pension plans and profit-sharing plans the amount of your earned income sets the limit on how much you can put in your Keogh and how much you can deduct. The earned income concept doesn't mean quite so much in defined-benefit Keoghs.

True, your pension in a defined-benefit Keogh is based on your earned income. Your pension can't be more than your earned income for a specific period. Earned income here, as with other Keoghs, is self-employment net earnings minus the deduction for your Keogh contribution.

So if you had net earnings of $17,000 and put $5,500 in your Keogh, your earned income would be $11,500. Right?

Right.

And with earned income of $11,500, your pension can't be more than $11,500 a year. Right?

Not right. Your pension is based on *average* earned income amounts. If you want the largest pension possible, you'll pick the average for those three years in a row when earned income is highest. For example, if there were three years when you made about $17,000 a year and contributed about $2,500 a year, that would give you earned income of $14,500 (instead of $11,500). You could build a Keogh fund large enough to pay a pension of that amount—say, a Keogh fund of $166,313 assuming a 6 percent interest rate and a 20-year life expectancy at retirement.

When Earned Income *Doesn't* Limit the Size of Your Pension

Earned income, as you will have noticed, is the amount of your moonlighting earnings you pay tax on. It would be ideal if you could pay tax on a fairly low amount and then use a higher amount to figure your pension and your Keogh fund.

Well, that can be arranged. We know one way already. It's the $10,000-a-year safety-net pension Harold is building. Harold pays tax on his *real* earned income, which is his net earnings from moonlighting minus the deductible amount he puts in his Keogh. But he uses a higher amount ($10,000) as the basis for his Keogh pension.

Another way: Include your past service (see page 55). Your net earnings for those past years might in any case be higher than they are now. But even if they aren't—even if, for example, they're about the same—they won't be cut down by any Keogh deduction. With no Keogh deduction, net earnings and earned income are identical. So you have the result you seek: the earned income you use to build your Keogh fund is from a prior year and is a larger amount than you pay tax on now.

> *Example.*   You've been moonlighting for six years. You averaged $12,000 in your three best previous years. This year you expect $12,200. You want a pension of $12,000 a year and put $4,500 into your Keogh out of this year's earnings to provide that amount. You use $12,000 to build your Keogh fund but pay tax on only $7,700 (this year's $12,200 minus the deductible $4,500).

Some moonlighters who now want defined-benefit Keoghs had profit-sharing Keoghs once. If that's your case, your *earned income* in the past years won't be the same as your *net earnings* for those years. It will be lower, by the amount of tax deduction you took in those years (usually 15 percent of your *net earnings*). If in our example you had deducted an average $1,800 (15 percent of $12,000) in your best three previous years, $10,200 ($12,000 minus $1,800) would be the earned income amount you would use to build your Keogh. This year you would pay tax on $12,200 minus the amount you put in this year toward a Keogh fund that will provide a pension of $10,800 a year.

Some moonlighters in profit-sharing plans before 1984 switched to money-purchase plans thereafter because of the larger deductible contributions allowed in money-purchase plans. "Switched" is no overstatement here, if the moonlighter was in a profit-sharing master plan: Many master plan sponsors provided stroke-of-the-pen shifts from *their* profit-sharing plan to *their* money-purchase plan.

If you're in a money-purchase plan now and want defined-benefit, you would set up the defined-benefit and freeze the money-purchase. As with profit-sharing, there are some limits on your defined-benefit if you had another plan first. Your pension professional or actuary will explain these limits to you.

A few Keogh investors should go the other way—*from* defined-benefit *to* money-purchase. This can happen when you have funded the maximum dollar amount of defined-benefit the law allows[1] and are still making a large self-employment income. To find out more about this, see a pension professional; you can afford it.

DEFINED BENEFIT PLUS . . .

"You said that combining a money purchase plan with a profit-sharing plan might work for me." This is Peter, recalling our discussion in Chapter 5. "Wouldn't one of us do even better combining a *defined-benefit plan* with some other plan?"

Not really. You're allowed to *have* a defined-benefit plan plus a money-purchase plan, or defined-benefit plus profit-sharing. But there are limits on the *benefits and contributions* you're allowed with two such plans. And you can't deduct more than the maximum deductible if you had only one plan and funded it to the limit.

It's more trouble than it's worth to set up a defined-benefit plan and another plan at the same time.

"What do you mean, 'at the same time'? Why is that? Is there a reason to set them up at different times?"

Yes, if you don't try to run them simultaneously. Some moonlighters went into profit-sharing plans before 1984 because defined-benefit allowances were so stingy then. Many should now switch to today's richer defined-benefit plans. Actually, "switch" is an oversimplification. You would set up a new defined-benefit plan and freeze (stop contributing to) your profit-sharing plan. There are limits on just how rich your defined-benefit plan can be if you had another kind of plan first. These limits are relaxed through passage of time, once your defined-benefit plan becomes operative.

---

[1] This depends on your age when you retire. For retirees age 65 in 1991, the limit under any one plan is $108,963 of pension each year.

KEOGH PLANNING WITH TWO
MOONLIGHTING BUSINESSES

The more you make moonlighting, the more you can put into your Keogh and the bigger Keogh fund you'll have. So it's generally best to consider your various self-employment activities as a single business if this is reasonable under the circumstances. Writing and lecturing are examples of two activities that can be considered a single business. If you have two quite different activities—such as carpenter and musician—you should treat them separately, with a separate plan for each business.

If you have one profitable business and another business that's currently losing, set up the plan for the profitable business alone. Your plan will specify what your business is. Define that business clearly and narrowly so the tax authorities won't consider the losing business to be part of it.

"VESTED" AND "FORFEITED" KEOGH FUNDS

Funds "vest" for an employee when he or she becomes absolutely entitled to the funds, even if the employee should leave the job before reaching retirement age. Funds that aren't vested are "forfeited" back to the employer or to other employees.

If you have no employees, the terms *vested* and *forfeited* will have no practical significance. You could forfeit only by ceasing your business. Any amount you forfeit as an employee would come back to you as the employer.

But by law your plan must state when funds vest for employees. Since you collect as an *employee,* that means you must say when the funds vest for *you.* You have these two options: (a) Everything must vest within three years, meaning that you can postpone vesting to the end of the third year if you wish; (b) Vest 20 percent the second year and 20 percent each succeeding year (or some vesting ratio faster than that—for example, 25 percent the first year and 25 percent each succeeding year).

I have chosen (a). Why (a) rather than (b)? Because if I should hire an employee for my moonlighting business, funds for *him* wouldn't vest for three years. So if he should leave before then, he couldn't take with him the pension contributions I made for him;

they would come back to me as his employer. If I had chosen (b), he could take some of that money with him when he walked.

CHOOSING YOUR KEOGH TRUSTEE

Banks, investment institutions, lawyers, or other professionals, trusted friends or family—any of these can be trustee of your Keogh.

I recommend that you choose yourself to be your trustee. *You* direct the investments. You can delegate the paperwork, which in any case involves mostly reporting to yourself. But you should keep the ultimate control, as trustee.

And if you *are* the trustee, you should have the trust agreement exempt the trustee (you) from any liability for imprudent investment. Necessary? Not really. It's just protection against possibly overzealous state authorities. You don't have to worry about federal authorities here. Federal oversight of trustee behavior doesn't extend to Keoghs that cover only the owner.

You can be your own trustee even though you get professional investment advice. Anything you spend for investment advisory services will be offset, at least in part, by the trustee fees you save.

You might name a successor trustee, though—a person or institution who would step in should you die before you retire or terminate your plan. Since your business will end with you, your successor trustee will have no long-term duties except to sell off the Keogh's investments and pay them out to your spouse or other beneficiaries, as the plan specifies.

For this role you might want to name your spouse, some trusted friend or relative likely to outlive you, an attorney, or a trust company.

BORROW FROM YOUR KEOGH?
WELL, HARDLY EVER

In the fine print, the law grudgingly lets self-employed persons borrow from their Keoghs.

A loan from a Keogh to its owner is a "prohibited transaction," banned by federal labor laws. But the Department of Labor can waive this restriction upon due application by the Keogh owner.

I consider myself quite the wheeler-dealer when it comes to Keoghs, but I've never done a prohibited transaction exemption for a Keogh owner and have never seen one.

Keogh plans can be written to allow loans whenever exemption is obtained. I advise you to include such a clause in your plan: Many of us optimists think the Labor Department will one day make it easier to get an exemption.

Restrictions that apply to *corporate* pension plan loans to *employees* will apply to Keogh borrowings, should such things be permitted. Thus:

- The *most* you can borrow is $50,000; the amount usually is less.
- If you're married, your spouse usually must consent to the loan. This is because your spouse has a stake in your Keogh assets, as you'll see in Chapter 13.

  When you borrow, hard cash goes from the plan to your pocket, to be replaced by your IOU. Your spouse must OK this metamorphosis of his or her retirement security.
- You must pay interest on your loan at the standard rate, a rate a commercial lender would charge on a loan to the likes of you. Interest you pay, at whatever rate, goes to enrich your own plan; that's the good news. The bad news is that the interest is not tax deductible.

All things considered, you'll probably be happier getting a bank loan, if it's for an otherwise tax-deductible purpose such as a home or vacation home, use in a business, or, in some cases, a personal investment.

SCHEDULE C (Form 1040)	**Profit or Loss From Business** (Sole Proprietorship)	OMB No. 1545-0074
Department of the Treasury Internal Revenue Service	Partnerships, Joint Ventures, Etc., Must File Form 1065. ▶ Attach to Form 1040 or Form 1041. ▶ See Instructions for Schedule C (Form 1040).	**1990** Attachment Sequence No. **09**

Name of proprietor: **Harold Wolf**
Social security number (SSN): **010 00 1111**

A Principal business or profession, including product or service (see Instructions)
B Enter principal business code (from page 2) ▶

C Business name and address ▶ (include suite or room no.)
D Employer ID number (Not SSN): **13 987 6543**

E Accounting method: (1) ☒ Cash (2) ☐ Accrual (3) ☐ Other (specify) ▶

F Method(s) used to value closing inventory: (1) ☐ Cost (2) ☐ Lower of cost or market (3) ☐ Other (attach explanation) (4) ☐ Does not apply (if checked, go to line H)   Yes No

G Was there any change in determining quantities, costs, or valuations between opening and closing inventory? (If "Yes," attach explanation.)
H Are you deducting expenses for business use of your home? (If "Yes," see Instructions.) . . . .   ☒
I Did you "materially participate" in the operation of this business during 1990? (If "No," see Instructions for limitations on losses.) . . .   ☒
J If this is the first Schedule C filed for this business, check here . . . . ▶ ☐

Part I Income

1 Gross receipts or sales. *Caution: If this income was reported to you on Form W-2 and the "Statutory employee" box on that form was checked, see the Instructions and check here* . . . . ▶ ☐	1	**7,540**
2 Returns and allowances	2	
3 Subtract line 2 from line 1. Enter the result here	3	
4 Cost of goods sold (from line 38 on page 2)	4	
5 Subtract line 4 from line 3 and enter the **gross profit** here	5	
6 Other income, including Federal and state gasoline or fuel tax credit or refund (see Instructions)	6	
7 Add lines 5 and 6. This is your **gross income** . . . . ▶	7	

Part II Expenses

8 Advertising	8		21 Repairs and maintenance	21	
9 Bad debts from sales or services (see Instructions)	9		22 Supplies (not included in Part III)	22	
10 Car and truck expenses (attach Form 4562)	10		23 Taxes and licenses	23	
11 Commissions and fees	11		24 Travel, meals, and entertainment:		
12 Depletion	12		a Travel	24a	
13 Depreciation and section 179 expense deduction (not included in Part III) (see Instructions).	13		b Meals and entertainment		
14 Employee benefit programs (other than on line 19)	14		c Enter 20% of line 24b subject to limitations (see Instructions)		
15 Insurance (other than health)	15		d Subtract line 24c from line 24b	24d	
16 Interest:			25 Utilities	25	
a Mortgage (paid to banks, etc.)	16a		26 Wages (less jobs credit)	26	
b Other	16b		27 Other expenses (list type and amount):		
17 Legal and professional services	17		Professional Dues 120		
18 Office expense	18		Stationery 25		
19 Pension and profit-sharing plans	19		Business Cards 15		
20 Rent or lease (see Instructions):			Typing 150		
a Vehicles, machinery, and equip.	20a				
b Other business property	20b		27b Total other expenses	27b	**310**

28 Add amounts in columns for lines 8 through 27b. These are your **total expenses** . . . . ▶	28	**310**
29 Net profit or (loss). Subtract line 28 from line 7. If a profit, enter here and on Form 1040, line 12. Also enter the net profit on Schedule SE, line 2 (statutory employees, see Instructions). If a loss, you MUST go on to line 30 (fiduciaries, see Instructions).	29	**7,230**

30 If you have a loss, you MUST check the box that describes your investment in this activity (see Instructions). . . 30a ☐ All investment is at risk. 30b ☐ Some investment is not at risk.
If you checked 30a, enter the loss on Form 1040, line 12, and Schedule SE, line 2 (statutory employees, see Instructions). If you checked 30b, you MUST attach **Form 6198**.

For Paperwork Reduction Act Notice, see Form 1040 Instructions.   Schedule C (Form 1040) 1990

CHAPTER 12

CASHING IN: COLLECTING
YOUR KEOGH WEALTH

Every reader will arrive at this chapter with a lot of questions. Our group of moonlighters, Peter, Elaine, and Harold, are no exceptions:

"When can I take money out of my Keogh?"

"When *should* I take money out?"

"Can I have it all at once, or is it spread out?"

"How much of my Keogh will go for taxes when I withdraw?"

The short answer to all of these questions is "It depends." Well, would you expect a lawyer to say anything else? But there's a long answer to each of them, requiring your full attention, which I'll shortly proceed to give. That too is about what you would expect from a lawyer.

But to put some minds at rest before exploring all of the options, here are the basics:

First principle: You can *always* have *all* of your money, whenever you want it, because you're always free to terminate your plan. There can sometimes be an extra tax, sometimes called a tax penalty, if you withdraw too early. This is in addition to regular tax on your withdrawals. In many cases your Keogh move will still leave you ahead of the game, despite the penalty tax and the regular tax.

Second principle: Keoghs are tax shelters. The longer you can keep wealth in your Keogh, the faster it grows. You'll find this fact at war with any wish you might have to withdraw and start spending your Keogh wealth. It's the choice you've faced from childhood: Do you want to have your cake or eat it?

This chapter will cover the options Keogh investors have to

collect their Keogh wealth. Chapter 14 will cover the tax on whatever you collect. The way you're taxed may influence whether and how much you want to collect at any one time. We'll consider that too.

So now for the withdrawal options:

"I WANT WHAT I WANT WHEN I WANT IT"

This was the title of a song sung by the vigorous baritones of my childhood, in the Great Age of Radio. As a child I thought this made a lot of sense. But if it expresses your Keogh philosophy, you won't have a Keogh plan for very long.

You *are* allowed to take out all or any part of your Keogh, whenever you feel like it, if you're the only one in it. But you may have to terminate the plan to get the money.

You'll have to do this if your Keogh is a *retirement* plan and you want to withdraw before you reach retirement age (unless you are disabled). Every pension plan is a retirement plan. Also, a profit-sharing plan can be set up as a retirement plan. I don't recommend this, but a retirement plan will result for profit-sharing funds invested in the retirement insurance or annuity contracts of an insured plan (Chapter 9).

So if you want to withdraw from a retirement plan before reaching retirement age, you must terminate the plan (again, unless you are disabled). You may pay a high tax on this (see Chapter 14), but you *can* do it.

Termination can be a realistic or necessary withdrawal opportunity; it is considered at greater length later in this chapter. But if you mean to keep your pension tax shelter alive, the withdrawal options that matter most are those that come when you have reached the retirement age you put in your plan. At that point you have three choices:

1. You can stop work and collect on your Keogh in whatever way your plan allows. This is true retirement.

2. You can continue to work but start collecting your pension. Your Keogh tax shelter goes on for funds you leave in the plan and you can continue to put funds in and deduct them.

3. You can continue to work and put off collecting until a later date. *You* decide how much later, except that you must start to collect after you reach age 70½. Those who take this route are making the most of the Keogh's wealth-building and estate-building features.

We will explore all of these options.

TRUE RETIREMENT: YOU STOP WORK AND START COLLECTING YOUR KEOGH WEALTH

The scene is 11 years from today. Harold is 65, and he is about to retire from his regular job and from moonlighting. His Keogh holds investments worth $96,000, about what we predicted he'd have if he funded his plan to the full. His Keogh holds some stock shares, some bonds, and some bank CDs, all in his name as trustee.

Harold should close out his trust account. He will *sell* the investments as trustee and use the proceeds *as trustee* to buy an annuity for himself and his wife, Judy. That way he would escape tax until he starts to collect on the annuity.

Another person in Harold's position could choose to take what he got as trustee from selling his Keogh assets and write himself a check for that amount. He is now free as an individual to invest or spend his Keogh money as he pleases. He is subject to tax on this lump sum, as explained in Chapter 14, but tax is computed under favorable rules. Or while acting as trustee, he could put the money into an annuity on his life alone.

ABOUT KEOGH ANNUITIES

In Keogh planning there are two basic kinds of annuity. There's the *single life annuity,* which pays a specified amount, usually monthly, for the life of one person, the self-employed person. And there's the *joint-and-survivor annuity,* which pays a married self-employed person for life and then, if he or she is outlived by a spouse, for that spouse's remaining life.

In the standard annuity, you get a payment for life (or over joint and survivor lives) however long *or short* that may be. If a person's life expectancy is 15 years when the annuity starts but he lives for 22 years, he collects for 7 years at the insurance company's expense. He has paid the company for 15 years (plus the company's profit) and collects for 22; a windfall. If his life expectancy is 15 years but he lives for only 3, the company gets the windfall: it has collected for 15 years but paid out for 3. That kind of annuity is called a *straight life* annuity.

Some annuity customers don't like this gamble. They want a guaranteed minimum return, so they buy an annuity that will go on for life in all cases but for at least 10 years no matter how soon they may die. This is called 10-year certain, meaning that if the annuity customer (annuitant) lives for, say, 3 years, his heir will collect on the annuity for another 7 years. A variation of this is the annuity for life but with the insurance company's additional commitment to pay back (to the annuitant and his heirs) the initial cost of the annuity. This is called a "refund feature" and means that if the annuitant puts up $90,000 and collects, say, $30,000 before his death, his heir will collect $60,000.

These types of annuity cost more than do straight life annuities because they may pay more and therefore are worth more.

Your maximum pension in a defined-benefit plan is based on straight life, without any additional features such as 10-year certain or refund. Since these features increase the value of your pension, adding one will reduce the annual amount you collect on your pension. (In pension industry jargon, your guaranteed annuity will be reduced to the "actuarial equivalent" of the straight life version.) For example, if the maximum pension you could have under a straight life annuity is $12,000 a year, the maximum you could have with a guaranteed payment feature might be, say, $11,200 a year, depending on the guaranteed payment period you chose.

Joint-and-Survivor Annuities

A joint-and-survivor annuity usually goes into effect at the moonlighter's retirement. It pays a certain amount while the moonlighter is living, then the same or a different amount after his or her death to a surviving spouse for life.

A Keogh plan can give the survivor anywhere from 50 percent of the joint amount up to 100 percent of the joint amount. A joint-and-survivor annuity that pays the survivor half of the joint amount is called a *joint-and-50-percent-survivor annuity*.[1] One that pays the survivor 100 percent of the joint amount is called a *joint-and-100-percent-survivor annuity* (or a *joint-and-full-survivor annuity*). Should you be so inclined, you could have some oddity like a joint-and-75-percent-survivor annuity.

Take a joint-and-50-percent-survivor annuity paying, say, $10,000 a year for the life of the moonlighter, then $5,000 a year for the life of his or her surviving spouse. That is more valuable than a $10,000 straight single life annuity for the moonlighter alone. It is more valuable because the joint-and-survivor annuity is *certain* to pay *as much* as straight single life ($10,000 a year as long as the moonlighter lives), and there's a good chance it will pay more. If the moonlighter's spouse outlives the moonlighter, it will pay $5,000 a year more, for *the spouse's* life.

A joint-and-*full*-survivor annuity is worth even more. If the moonlighter's spouse outlives the moonlighter, the spouse will get $10,000 a year instead of $5,000. It's worth more and it costs more.

Joint-and-Survivor Annuities to Increase Keogh Wealth

In a defined-benefit Keogh you can have a pension equal to your average earned income for your best three consecutive years or a $10,000 safety-net pension if that will give you more. You can build your Keogh as high as necessary to pay a single life annuity of this amount. If joint-and-survivor annuities are part of your planning, you can build a Keogh to pay for the same amount for yourself for life and then anywhere from 50 percent to 100 percent of that for your spouse for life if he or she survives you. That program will allow a higher Keogh fund than if only a single life annuity is planned.

Harold will seize this Keogh-building opportunity. Harold can

---

[1] In Keogh and company plans the annuity drops only if the moonlighter's or employee's spouse is the survivor. Under joint-and-survivor annuities in other settings, the annuity drops no matter who survives.

have a $10,000 a year pension—in other words, a $10,000 straight single life annuity. That would mean a Keogh fund of $105,940 (assuming a 20-year life expectancy and a 7 percent interest rate). But suppose he makes this a joint-and-full-survivor annuity. That would then allow a Keogh fund of $119,062.

Technically, you can fund toward a joint-and-survivor annuity even though you're not married. But that has been criticized as an abuse; I'm not recommending that you do it.

Suppose you fund for a joint-and-survivor annuity but then you and your spouse decide you want the money in a lump sum instead or in some other nonannuity form. The most the two of you can collect *under your Keogh* is what you could have built up for a single life annuity. The balance would revert to you as owner on termination of the plan. It's your money, of course, but subject to higher taxes.

Example. Theodore builds to $236,516, the amount needed for a joint-and-full-survivor annuity paying $20,000 a year at retirement. But when Theodore comes to retire, he and his wife, Rose, decide they don't want an annuity. They want all the money at once to buy a retirement home. Theodore is trustee of his Keogh and must now enforce the law, against himself, sort of.

The most Theodore the trustee can pay out to Theodore the employee is $211,880, which is the lump sum equivalent of a single life annuity of $20,000 for Theodore's life expectancy. Theodore the trustee turns the $24,636 balance of the Keogh fund over to Theodore the employer. This is the amount left after the Keogh has discharged its lawful obligation to every employee. The $24,636 Theodore gets as employer is taxed at a higher rate than the other Keogh funds.

It's the same story if you build to a joint-and-survivor annuity and then have no spouse when you retire. The extra funds, over what's needed for a single life annuity, revert to you as employer at a higher tax. No, I don't give advice on marriage as a tax shelter.

You can buy refund or guarantee features in joint-and-survivor annuities, as you can in single life annuities. For example, you could buy a joint-and-50-percent-survivor annuity with a refund feature that would pay your heir what you paid for the annuity minus what you and your spouse collected under the annuity. As you might expect, the value of the refund feature reduces the amount you can collect under your joint-and-survivor annuity in a defined-benefit plan.

Example.   You are allowed a pension of $11,000, based on your self-employment earnings. You are married and want a joint-and-full-survivor annuity. Such an annuity will pay $11,000 for your joint lives and $11,000 for the life of your surviving spouse after your death. Say the cost of such an annuity is $120,000, and the cost of the same annuity but with a guarantee or refund feature is $128,000. The most you can build to in your Keogh is $120,000. At retirement, if you want the refund feature, you will get the annuity—with the refund feature—that $120,000 will buy. That might be $10,230 a year instead of $11,000.

Only in *defined-benefit* plans can you build a larger Keogh fund to pay a joint-and-survivor annuity. With a money-purchase plan or profit-sharing plan, your Keogh fund will be the same amount whether or not a joint-and-survivor annuity will be paid. You contribute to those plans based on your self-employment earnings, not what you might use the money for when you retire. So if your contributions and investment earnings thereon reach, say, $70,000, you can spend that money on a joint-and-survivor annuity if you want to, and many moonlighters will want to. But the amount the moonlighter collects under a joint-and-survivor annuity *must* be less than he or she would collect under a single life annuity costing the same amount.

Variable Annuities

We considered the variable annuity as an inflation-resistant investment. Variable annuities come in single life or joint-and-survivor forms and can be had with period certain and refund features. You could build your Keogh as high for a variable annuity as for the regular, fixed payment kind—as high, but no higher. For example, if you could build up $120,000 for a single-life fixed payment annuity, you could instead build to $120,000 for a variable annuity.

Joint-and-Survivor Annuities—or Else?

If you have a pension plan, you can give yourself a choice between lump sum and annuity. Or you can *require* an annuity. Of course, it makes more sense to offer yourself the choice.

A single person is free to take either lump sum or annuity. But every *married* participant must be offered a joint-and-survivor annuity. You and your spouse can decline joint-and-survivor in favor of an annuity for your life only or a lump sum. It takes *two* to decline a joint-and-survivor annuity—you *and* your spouse.

What Investment Advisors Say about Annuities

Maybe it's not fair to call Uncle Sam a Big Brother when it comes to annuities. You don't *have* to take an annuity. But there's no denying a governmental bias favoring annuities in pension plans, especially joint-and-survivor annuities.

Some investment advisors aren't quite so friendly toward annuities. They note that an annuity is a disappearing asset. When the annuitant dies, the asset is gone. Except for refund or term-certain features, the annuitant's heirs get nothing. Also, the interest insurance companies pay on annuities tends to be lower than you could get on other investments. Of course, a lifetime annuity guarantees that the annuitant will never outlive his or her retirement income. But, some advisors argue, the investor can come close to what you would get with an annuity, this way:

Take a lump-sum payout and use the after-tax funds to buy long-term bonds. Make sure they have a top safety rating and mature at some date well beyond your life expectancy. That way you can be certain, or almost certain, you won't outlive your assets. The periodic interest you get on the bonds may come fairly close to what you would collect on an annuity. But it will be less because the annuity is returning both interest and principal. At your death there will still be a valuable, income-producing asset for your heirs.

This argument will appeal to those who value Keogh estate-building opportunities. The thought is that you can leave more to your heirs and still get fair lifetime income from your Keogh assets.

Example. An annuity for a 15-year life expectancy that costs $100,000 and earns at a 7 percent rate pays the annuitant $10,979 a year. Bonds costing $85,000 (the amount left after tax on a $100,000 lump-sum payout) and yielding 8 percent pay their owner $6,800 a year, plus around $85,000 on maturity.

And some advisors suggest this way to beat the price on a

joint-and-survivor annuity, while reaching the same destination: Buy a single life annuity and use part of the annuity to buy insurance on your life, naming your spouse as beneficiary.

Example.   Suppose your Keogh fund will buy a single life annuity of $15,000, or a joint-and-survivor annuity of $13,000 for your joint lives and $6,500 for the life of your surviving spouse. The two of you could agree to take the $15,000 single life annuity but use part of it to buy an insurance policy that will buy your spouse a $6,500 annuity at your death. You save this way if the insurance premium is less than $2,000 a year. Even a premium of around $2,000 would be OK if the policy had a cash value you could borrow against.

Sometimes couples take a higher single life annuity in a gamble on their life expectancy. This way of avoiding the high cost of the survivorship element in a joint-and-survivor annuity is something Elaine and her husband, Frank, might consider. Say they are the same age and retire at the same time. Elaine might choose to rely on a sex-based life expectancy that says her life expectancy at age 65 is 3.2 years longer than Frank's. Elaine's Keogh nest egg will buy a larger annual payment as a single life annuity than as a joint-and-survivor annuity. So it might seem OK to take a single life annuity on Elaine's life alone. All the same, it *is* a gamble. The couple's joint-and-survivor life expectancy is 3.8 years longer than Elaine's alone. Still, they might decide to go for single life if Frank is adequately protected by his company pension should he outlive Elaine.

TAKING OUT A LUMP SUM

Withdrawing a lump sum means selling all of the assets as trustee and making out a check—to yourself individually—for what you got for them. If for any reason it's not a good time to sell or close out an investment—you hope for a market upswing on a stock, or you would forfeit interest on a bank CD that's not yet matured—you could transfer the investment from the trust to yourself.

You have the option to buy an annuity with part of your Keogh fund and pay over the rest of your Keogh fund to yourself in cash, in unsold investments, or both.

Lump-sum withdrawals are a standard form of cashing in a

profit-sharing plan. They are also fairly common in pension plans but should not happen before retirement, except where the plan is being terminated.

IRA ROLLOVER

This is a way to withdraw money or other assets from a plan. But it's not cashing in. It's moving your wealth from one sheltered environment to another, without paying tax on it *or getting the use of it*. Rollovers are explained in Chapter 14.

PARTIAL WITHDRAWALS

You can withdraw part of your Keogh fund and leave the balance. You might withdraw to get funds for some personal or investment purpose, such as a down payment on a second home. You would take part rather than all of it so what remains would continue to enjoy tax-free buildup in the Keogh tax shelter.

Partial withdrawals are allowed in profit-sharing plans if the funds have been in the plan at least two years. Pension plans don't permit partial withdrawals until you have reached retirement age. In either case, partial withdrawals are allowed whether you retire or keep working. You can make a partial withdrawal to buy an annuity.

DISABILITY RETIREMENT

A moonlighter who retires because of disability can take out his or her funds as for any other retirement. The considerations just described involving lump-sum withdrawals, single life annuities, and joint-and-survivor annuities apply to disability retirement.

Since disability retirement is likely to occur sooner than normal retirement, the Keogh fund at retirement may be less than the moonlighter expected to have when he or she retired.

"Disabled" means unable to engage in any substantial gainful activity. Moonlighters who retire for disability aren't subject to the penalty tax usually imposed on early Keogh withdrawals. But because of this tax relief it's government policy to check whether a moonlighter who drew out of his Keogh on a claim of disability is still working.

TERMINATING YOUR PLAN

You can cash in on your Keogh benefits by terminating your plan. It would be good if you had a *business reason* to terminate. Giving up your moonlighting business is one good reason. Another, even if you keep your business going, is that it's not as profitable as it was.

But government officials probably won't even ask you why you're terminating *if you have no employees*. Your plan should give you the right to terminate, leaving the reason for termination up to you.

It might be said that a Keogh terminates automatically when the business ends through the moonlighter's death or disability. I prefer to cover this specifically in the plan. The plan would say it terminates if the employer (moonlighter) ceases to exist. On the other hand, the plan would not terminate *automatically* if the moonlighter should become disabled. The moonlighter would decide whether he or she wants it terminated. Thus, the plan should allow *retirement* for disability but would not specifically require *termination* for disability.

If you should decide to terminate for any reason, the plan should allow you these options:

1. If your Keogh is a pension plan, it should let you sell the investments and use the proceeds to buy an annuity. That annuity would begin to pay at the retirement date you set in your plan. You would *not* collect on the annuity now. But you would collect more later than you could starting now, thanks to tax-free investment buildup in the interim. If you are married, the annuity will be of the joint-and-survivor type unless you and your spouse waive this when you reach retirement.

2. Whether you have a pension or a profit-sharing Keogh, you could sell the investments and pay the proceeds to yourself in a lump sum. In a plan *termination,* you don't *have to* offer annuities. Nor must you offer survivor benefits or a share in the Keogh fund to your spouse. One exception: If the Keogh is terminating because of the moonlighter's death, the surviving spouse gets the benefits provided for him or her as described in Chapter 13.

"FREEZING" YOUR PLAN

"Freezing" a plan is continuing it as before but putting no new money in it. I don't think of freezing as termination because you don't get at your assets that way; you don't cash in. But those who draw the legal language for pension plans put the right to freeze with the right to terminate. The right is well worth having in any plan, and including it with the termination clauses does no harm.

When you freeze, you would still pay out benefits when the plan requires that be done. But the benefits will be less than you figured on when you started because you stopped putting new money in.

Freezing is a reasonable step when you intend to start another Keogh of a different type or if you are continuing another Keogh. Many self-employed persons who had profit-sharing Keoghs before 1984 wisely froze them once they started defined-benefit Keoghs.

HOW DO YOU WANT YOUR MONEY?

Annuity or lump sum, now or later?

That is a hard question. I can't answer it for myself until I get to retirement age. *You* don't have to decide either, until *you* get there. You—and I—will have to deal with some heavy questions at that time. Like the following:

How are you feeling? It may be a grim fact, but if a person's health is poor, he's not likely to want an annuity. He'll take the lump sum. You buy an annuity when you're in the pink, to win the insurance gamble on your life expectancy.

What kind of person are you? If yours is a personality that prizes security, an annuity will look good. If it matters more to be free to move your money around or to spend it, you'll take a lump sum. How you see yourself *now* doesn't count. What matters is what you will be like at retirement.

What are you worth? Financially, that is, not morally. If you're well off and don't need the Keogh money to live on, there's a good case for taking *nothing* out: neither annuity nor lump sum. More on this shortly.

What's the best tax move? No, it's *not* saving the most taxes. Good tax planning means winding up richer after taxes, not just avoiding taxes. Here's an example of what I mean: You're due to get $10,000 this year when you're in the 35 percent tax bracket. (See Chapter 19 for the definition of tax bracket.) You put off collecting the money until you're in the 25 percent bracket, four years from now. That saves you $1,000 in tax. But if you could buy tax-exempt municipal bonds today paying 8 percent, you would have $1,343 more four years from now than by avoiding the tax: $8,843 versus $7,500.

But even good tax planning must yield to getting the outcome you really want. If you want your money to spend and enjoy now, no one should gainsay you because it might be a better *tax* move to take an annuity or leave it in the Keogh.

Will you be up to it? This question asks about mental powers and self-control after retirement. Will you be able to manage your investments and spend your money wisely as you get older and older? If you have doubts, you may choose to buy an annuity. That would be safer than taking out a lump sum, leaving the money in, or paying yourself an annuity out of your Keogh wealth. One alternative, which some might find embarrassing, would be to appoint a trustee who would manage your wealth and look after your needs if your powers seem to fail.

Based on what I know of them now, I'd guess that Elaine would take the lump sum, Harold would buy an annuity, and Peter would leave most of his money in the Keogh well beyond "retirement age." But their attitudes toward life may change between now and then; they could fool me. Elaine and Peter are both younger than I, so I may never know what they decide.

THINK—DO YOU REALLY NEED THAT MONEY NOW?

I'm now going to ask you to think about leaving your Keogh funds alone a while longer. You may think this a strange request in a chapter about cashing in on your Keogh wealth. But I want to impress you with the real value of the Keogh tax shelter.

Wealthy Keogh investors put off cashing in as long as they can. Since investment earnings build tax-free while in the plan, the longer you postpone your withdrawal, the more you will have when withdrawal occurs. If you don't need the funds to live on, why take them out? That is true even if you're not putting new money in. That is, the Keogh tax shelter keeps working for you even though you have stopped moonlighting, are making no new Keogh contributions, and are just investing earnings on your existing fund.

To prove this, consider the situation when Peter, our Keogh plutocrat-to-be, reaches age 65. He can expect a pension from his university of, say, $20,000 a year, including social security. He has investments outside his Keogh worth, say, $150,000. And he has his Keogh fund of about $531,000 if expectations are met.

If he retires now, he gets his university pension plus the income (after taxes) from his outside investments. If he wants more money this year, he could cash in some of those outside investments. That is a smarter move than cashing in his Keogh right now. If he can make 9 percent on his Keogh money this year, his Keogh will grow by $47,790 if he leaves it alone, even though he's putting no new money in.

You can put off taking anything out of your Keogh until you reach age 70½—or, to be technical, until April 1 of the year after the year you reach 70½. That means that most people—everyone whose birthday falls before October 1—will have passed their 71st birthday before they *have to* withdraw something.

You can put off retiring until that date and start your retirement and withdrawals at the same time. Or, like Peter, you can retire (stop moonlighting) earlier but put off withdrawals until that date. Or you could even go on working beyond that date, put new moonlighting earnings in, and take old Keogh money out.

Estate Building after 70

So now you're 70½. Now you *must* start withdrawing. But you don't have to take it out all at once. You can continue your Keogh shelter, for most of your Keogh wealth, for many years more.

At this point, an interruption from Elaine: "I know the tax shelter benefits. In fact, I'm up to here with tax benefits. But let's leave tax shelter aside for a minute and look at real life. What sort of person would want to postpone withdrawal at that point in life?"

The motive I see most often is the wish to leave a larger estate for one's children or grandchildren. Many who postpone withdrawal do so expecting they will never take out all of their Keogh assets. The balance, protected and increased thanks to years of, yes, tax sheltering, will go to their heirs.

Another reason, less popular but not unreasonable, is to maximize their retirement security by leaving their nest egg untouched as long as possible.

I doubt that those will be my goals at age 71. I think I will have started to enjoy my Keogh prosperity long before then. But if they're *your* goals, I have several suggestions for how to take out each year as little as the law allows.

First, you need an annuity. It's not an annuity you buy from an insurance company. The Keogh tax shelter ends on any money you pay the insurance company. It's an annuity you pay yourself, out of your Keogh fund.

We'll see this first with a single life annuity, on your life alone.[2] The amount you must withdraw this year is the amount you get by dividing your Keogh fund by your life expectancy.

Example.   Your Keogh fund is $250,000 at age 70. Your life expectancy at that age is 16 years (according to the IRS table). If you divide $250,000 by 16, you get $15,625. That is the amount you *must* withdraw the first year (you could take more). The $234,375 balance is still invested in your Keogh, tax-free.

Another technique is to recalculate your life expectancy each year. The gimmick here is that the longer anyone lives, the longer he or she is *expected* to live. For example, at age 65 a person's life expectancy under the IRS table is 20 years;[3] he or she is expected to live to age 85. But at age 85 the same person's life expectancy is 6.9 years; he or she is expected to live to age 92 (91.9). So by recalculating each year, you spread withdrawal over a greater number of years, as your expected life span grows.

---

[2] As covered on page 127, this means you are unmarried at this point or your spouse agrees.

[3] The figures depend on the life expectancy table you are using.

Example.   To continue from page 122, it's one year later and you are now
71. Assuming an 8 percent rate of return, the $234,375 balance from
last year has grown to $253,125. Your life expectancy is now 15.3
years. This year you must withdraw $16,544 ($253,125 ÷ 15.3). The
balance, $236,581, is still invested.

And the following year, you recompute. Last year's $236,581 is
now $255,507. At age 72 your life expectancy is 14.6 years. You
withdraw $17,501, leaving $238,006 invested tax-free. And so on.

Using this approach, the amount you withdraw and the balance
still invested tax-free varies from year to year but would almost
never entirely disappear. Not until age 106[3] would a living person
have a life expectancy of as little as one year. So not until that age
would he or she need to withdraw the entire balance.

You could, if you wished, compute only once, at age 70½, and
withdraw the same amount each year over what your life expectancy was at that age. Assuming you outlive that life expectancy
and have funds left, you would withdraw whatever amount you
pleased each succeeding year.

The same postponing techniques are available with joint-and-
survivor annuities with your spouse. You can use a long joint-and-
survivor life expectancy, and you can recalculate each year using
the new combined life expectancies at each later age.

Another option is a joint-and-survivor annuity with someone
other than your spouse. This option is available if you're unmarried
or your spouse waives his or her survivorship rights. The survivor
could be anyone you choose, however young, such as your child or
grandchild. Coupling your survivor's life expectancy with yours
would let you spread distribution over many decades. However, if
you recompute each year based on life expectancy, you can change
only for changes in your own life expectancy, not your co-
annuitant's.

Put In as You Take Out

If you continue your self-employment business, you can go on
contributing to your Keogh plan. You still get full tax deduction
against your self-employment earnings, and the Keogh tax shelter
continues for everything in the Keogh.

This is the last word in maximizing your Keogh benefits.

Though you must start withdrawing after age 70½, you make up for some of what you must take out by what you put in and what it earns.

A money-purchase pension plan is usually preferable at this point. A defined-benefit plan will be treated as fully funded—that is, the money in the Keogh is enough to pay the targeted pension. Where this is so, you would not be allowed to make further tax-deductible contributions.

WHEN TO WITHDRAW

I keep saying that the longer you keep funds in your Keogh, the more you will have, thanks to tax-free compounding. If you must withdraw during a year, make it as late in the year as possible. And you might fit the time you withdraw to some event in your investment portfolio—for example, the day a bank CD matures. If you withdraw at that point, you'll get full value and you won't have to hunt up a new investment.

LIFE INSURANCE POLICIES

Life insurance in a Keogh may require special handling.

Remember why you bought the insurance. Maybe it was to assure that the Keogh fund or its equivalent would be there if you should die before you reached retirement age. Well, you have lived to retirement age, and no longer need protection against premature death. So maybe it's time to stop paying premiums and collect the value of the insurance policy as one more Keogh plan asset. The Keogh can surrender the policy to the insurance company for its cash value and pay you the proceeds. Another option is for the Keogh to trade the policy for an annuity. Or, the Keogh can distribute the policy.

Other options let you collect *some* of the cash value and continue *some* insurance protection. For example, the Keogh trustee, who might be you, could take out a policy loan and buy you an annuity with the proceeds. The Keogh would then give you the policy. You could keep up the premiums or could convert it to a paid-up policy (with a lower death benefit). Or the Keogh could give you the policy, and *you* could take out the loan and keep up the premiums. In a policy with a "vanishing premium" feature, future premiums might be unnecessary.

SUMMARY OF THE WAYS YOU GET YOUR MONEY OUT OF YOUR KEOGH

As an annuity. An annuity can be only for the life of the annuitant (moonlighter) or can pay up to a guaranteed minimum after the annuitant's death.

Joint-and-survivor annuities continue to pay the moonlighter's surviving spouse after the moonlighter's death. The annual amount to the survivor may be from 50 percent to 100 percent of the payment to the moonlighter. Guaranteed minimums are available with joint-and-survivor also.

Annuities are more common in pension plans than in profit-sharing plans. Generally, they are available in pension plans only at or after retirement.

In a lump sum. Lump-sum withdrawal occurs more often in profit-sharing plans than in pension plans and more often in money-purchase plans than in defined-benefit plans. It is available in profit-sharing plans after two years and in pension plans at or after retirement. A lump-sum withdrawal may include an annuity.

A partial withdrawal. Partial withdrawal occurs more often in profit-sharing than in pension plans. It is available in profit-sharing plans after two years and in pension plans at or after retirement. A partial withdrawal may include an annuity.

CHAPTER 13

KEOGH FOR OTHERS: YOUR SPOUSE AND YOUR HEIRS

Harold will collect $10,000 a year under his joint-and-survivor annuity. It will cost more than a straight single life annuity for the same amount. The extra cost goes for what his wife, Judy, will collect after Harold's death.

"And well worth it, too," Harold says, and so will many another Keogh investor.

But suppose that, though married, you don't want a joint-and-survivor annuity. Maybe you don't think the joint-and-survivor type is a good investment. Maybe you're on the outs with your spouse and don't want the extra cost for something he or she alone will enjoy. Or maybe you don't want any kind of annuity.

Like it or not, many married Keogh investors are now stuck with joint-and-survivor annuities.

Under federal and state law your spouse has certain rights in your Keogh. The two of you can waive the *federal* rights; they are not, in that historic phrase, "inalienable rights." But unless they are waived, your spouse at some point can claim some part of your Keogh wealth. A spouse's federal rights must be stated in the Keogh plan. The rules are as follows:

Rights on divorce or separation. There is a general, and growing, tendency under state law to treat a worker's share of a pension or profit-sharing plan as an asset of the marriage. When marital property is divided or alimony is awarded in divorce or separation, one often sees part of the spouse's interest (say, a husband's interest) in a plan awarded to the other spouse (the wife). And even where this doesn't happen, one spouse (say, the wife) may have obtained some other marital asset by surrendering her claim against a pension.

Federal law does not *grant* one spouse an interest in the other's Keogh in divorce or separation. Rather, it will accept what state courts[1] have granted, up to a point.

Generally speaking, the moonlighter's spouse can't get any of the Keogh fund before the moonlighter could. However, the spouse *can* collect an annuity out of the Keogh fund, starting at the earliest date the plan lets the moonlighter withdraw retirement funds, whether he or she has retired or not.

Rights in your pension when you retire. Every married participant in a pension plan must be offered a joint-and-survivor annuity. You and your spouse may decline joint-and-survivor in favor of an annuity on your life alone, or a lump sum paid to you alone. But a married person in a pension plan must take joint-and-survivor benefits unless *the couple* decides on something else.

The time to decide is the 90-day period ending on the date the self-employed person retires. The couple could of course have agreed on the matter years before then. But only the paper—called a waiver or election—that they sign during this period counts if they want something other than a joint and survivor annuity.

Rights in your pension at your death. A pension plan generally must provide an annuity for your spouse if you should die before retirement. You and your spouse can agree to waive this requirement at any time after your 35th birthday. You can waive in order to give your spouse a lump sum or in order to give a lump sum or annuity to any other beneficiary you name. If there's no waiver, an annuity must be paid to the surviving spouse.

And how much does the surviving spouse get? If you wish, the plan could say that the *entire* Keogh fund must be used to buy an annuity for the surviving spouse. But you can leave less. In a money-purchase plan, half of the fund *must* go to buy an annuity for the surviving spouse; the rest can go to anyone else you name. In a defined-benefit plan, half of the fund goes toward an annuity for the spouse if the plan is building toward a joint-and-*50*-percent-survivor annuity; someone else can get the balance. If it's building

---

[1] A court also could tap into a Keogh fund to provide support for a moonlighter's child.

toward a joint-and-*full* survivor annuity, the entire Keogh fund goes for the spouse's annuity.

When does the surviving spouse start collecting? It's up to you. You could make it late. The plan can start the annuity as late as the first date the moonlighter could have retired had he or she lived.

Example.   A moonlighter might have set up a plan at age 50, with retirement funds payable starting at age 62, and then died at age 55. The plan could make his widow wait seven years to collect on the annuity. In this case, the Keogh fund and hence the annuity she gets will be larger.

Or you can make it sooner. You could have the plan start the annuity at some date close to your death. This way, your spouse can get some money right away, but the annuity would be less than if he or she waited.

Or you could put the late start date in the plan, but then you and your spouse could later waive an annuity if circumstances make this wise. With the waiver, your spouse could get at his or her share of the Keogh fund in a lump sum, immediately upon your death.

If the couple is collecting under a joint-and-survivor annuity at the moonlighter's death, the surviving spouse will thereafter collect the specified amount of the survivor's annuity.

Rights in your profit-sharing plan during your lifetime. If your profit-sharing plan is a retirement plan, your spouse has the same rights in it that he or she would have in a pension plan. If it's not a retirement plan, or one that pays you a lifetime annuity, federal law gives your spouse *no* rights in your plan during your lifetime. A moonlighter can take out any or all of the funds with no need to share any of it with his or her spouse. However, to avoid sharing, the plan must carry a provision for the spouse if the moonlighter should die before withdrawing all of his or her Keogh account. In that case, the plan must offer the surviving spouse the entire remaining Keogh fund in a lump sum. The spouse may waive this.

Rights in your profit-sharing plan at your death. All of your Keogh assets go to your surviving spouse unless the two of you waive this. Assuming no waiver, they go to your spouse as a lump sum or otherwise, whatever your spouse chooses.

If you are in a profit-sharing Keogh of the retirement type, your assets go the same way they would in a pension plan, just described. Retirement-type profit-sharing is not the usual form, and it's not something I would recommend to a moonlighter.

But not the first year. Your Keogh can be written to ignore your marriage and refuse anything to your spouse, if the two of you are married less than a year before your death (in the case of death benefits) or before your retirement or other benefits are scheduled to begin. But the plan must honor a state court award in the case of divorce or separation.

If your pension or profit-sharing plan includes life insurance, that money goes to the person you named as your beneficiary, whether that person is your surviving spouse or someone else. Federal law does not give a spouse any special rights in life insurance in a moonlighter's Keogh plan.

SUMMARY OF YOUR SPOUSE'S RIGHTS IN YOUR KEOGH

On divorce and separation. Your state decides your spouse's rights. Your Keogh must go along with any court award but need not pay out anything until you have a right to withdraw retirement funds.

During your lifetime. In a pension plan, a right to a joint-and-survivor annuity with you when you retire.

In a profit-sharing plan, no rights, unless the plan is of the retirement type. If it is, same rights as in a pension plan.

On plan termination, no rights.

On your death. Right to the survivor's share in a joint-and-survivor annuity, if the annuity has started. Otherwise,

- In a pension plan, a right to an annuity. At least half of the Keogh must be used for that annuity.
- In a profit-sharing plan, a right to the entire Keogh fund in a lump sum.
- As to life insurance, no rights under federal law.

A spouse may waive any of his or her federal rights.

KEOGH FOR YOUR HEIRS

Consider your Keogh as coming to an end at your death. Any funds still in your Keogh at your death will go to your heirs. As we have just seen, your surviving spouse is automatically an heir of *part* of the fund unless the two of you decide otherwise. Your Keogh plan should include a beneficiary designation, specifying who gets what portion of your Keogh fund. A sample beneficiary designation is on page 175.

If you should die before retirement. Your trustee (or if that was you, your successor trustee) will sell your Keogh investments and pay them out as the plan requires.

A beneficiary who is not a surviving spouse may be awarded an annuity or a share of the Keogh fund in cash. If your beneficiary is a child, an old person, or a disabled person, you may want to leave your money to a trustee, custodian, or guardian, who will care for the beneficiary. When an old or disabled person is involved, it's usual to provide for lifetime care. When a child is involved, it's usual to provide for care up to some age of maturity and at that point to give the child, or someone else, ownership of whatever is left in the fund.

Death after retirement. Here the typical situation is the Keogh investor who has bought a joint-and-survivor annuity with his spouse and dies before he or she does. The annuity continues for the survivor. If there is a guarantee or refund feature, any "unspent" portion of the guarantee or refund at the survivor's death would go to his or her heirs, usually in a lump sum. This is also the case if the investor has a joint-and-survivor annuity with someone other than his or her spouse.

The outcome is similar with a single life annuity. Any unspent portion of an annuity with a guarantee or refund feature goes to the investor's heirs. If there is no guarantee or refund feature, the heirs get nothing from the annuity.

If the Keogh investor dies after a withdrawal that wasn't for an annuity, the remaining Keogh funds will be paid out to those who would collect if he or she had died before retirement, under the rules just described.

Life insurance. If your plan includes life insurance, the insurance proceeds will go to the beneficiary named in your policy. Proceeds will be in a lump sum, installments, or as an annuity, as you specified in the policy's settlement option.

CHAPTER 14

YOUR KEOGH TAXES

It was a free ride, with tax relief stops along the way. But once you start to collect on your Keogh, you will have to share some of your Keogh wealth with Uncle Sam.

This chapter shows what your tax might be when you collect your Keogh wealth. Then it shows the tax your heirs might have to pay on any funds left in the Keogh at your death.

It's not hard to be specific about today's tax rules. They may be complicated—all right, they *are* complicated—but they're knowable. No one can be certain that today's rules will apply years or decades from now when you come to collect your Keogh wealth. But today's rules are our best guide to tomorrow's.

TAX PENALTY HITS MOST "EARLY" WITHDRAWALS

In many cases there is a special tax, sometimes called a tax penalty, on amounts you withdraw from your Keogh before you reach age 59½. It's on top of the regular income tax on your Keogh collections. Thus, if you withdraw $30,000 before age 59½, you must pay the IRS a tax penalty in addition to any income tax on your withdrawal.

The tax penalty isn't always the disaster it seems at first. Remember that you escaped tax on the funds you put in and on everything those funds have earned up to this point. So you can be ahead of the game despite the penalty.

I'm not trying to talk anyone into withdrawing early. Amounts you withdraw lose their tax shelter forever. But fear of the withdrawal penalty is no reason to stay out of the Keogh game. The penalty hurts you in your Keogh, but staying outside a Keogh can hurt more.

The penalty applies to amounts you collect even if you are terminating the plan. If you want to stop putting money into your Keogh but don't need to collect your Keogh wealth now, just freeze your plan, as explained on page 119. You're not cashing in on your plan this way, and you owe no tax penalty or regular tax.

There's no tax penalty on withdrawals from your Keogh in any of these cases:

- You are age 59½ or older.
- You are disabled.
- You have retired and are withdrawing funds in approximately equal installments over your life expectancy or a joint life expectancy with someone else.
- You have retired and are age 55 or older.

TAX ON ANNUITIES

Most Keogh investors get annuities by selling their Keogh assets and using the proceeds to buy the annuity from an insurance company. That is what Harold expects to do. He will pay no tax until he starts to collect on the annuity. So he and all others who buy annuities have thereby postponed tax on the moonlighting income put into their Keoghs until the annuities begin to pay off. The tax payments are then spread over the period they collect on the annuities, a further postponement.

Some Keogh investors with insured plans don't *buy* annuities at retirement. They have already bought individual annuity contracts each year. But that is the only difference. They too pay no tax until they start to collect on their annuities. Here, too, tax payments are spread over the period they collect.

Money you put into your Keogh *as employee* comes back to you tax-free out of your annuity. That is nothing but good news, of course, but it complicates the tax computation. So let's put that computation off and take the simpler situation first.

This is how you are taxed if you did *not* contribute to your Keogh fund as an employee: Everything you collect is fully taxable. Thus, if the pension is $800 a month, you report the full amount as income and pay regular income tax on that amount. So if you're in the 35 percent tax bracket that year, your tax is $3,360 (35 percent of $9,600), and you have $6,240 left. (See Chapter 19 for information on tax bracket and the use of 35 percent.)

The tax rule is identical for joint-and-survivor annuities. Harold, as we know, is building toward a joint-and-full-survivor annuity, to pay $10,000 a year ($833 a month) for his life, with the same amount going to Judy if she survives him. If Harold does indeed buy the $10,000 annuity and is in the 25 percent bracket when he collects it, his tax would be $2,500. The $10,000 Judy gets after Harold's death is also taxable, the same way. In the 25 percent bracket, she too would pay $2,500.

If Harold had bought a joint-and-50-percent-survivor annuity that paid $10,000 during his lifetime, Judy would get $5,000 a year after his death. If she is in the 25 percent bracket at that time, her tax would be $1,250.

If you did contribute as employee, some of what you collect will be tax-free. In most cases, you will pay tax on part and escape tax on part of each annuity payment received, for as long as the annuity is paid. You find the tax-exempt part by dividing your contributions as employee by the amount you expect to collect under the annuity. That is the amount you will receive each year multiplied by your life expectancy as predicted in IRS tables. So if you have a 20-year life expectancy when you retire, you contributed $22,000 (as employee), and the life annuity will pay $600 a month, then 15 percent ($22,000 ÷ [$600 × 12 ×20]) of each annuity payment is exempt from tax.

If a joint-and-survivor annuity is involved, you make the same calculation, except you use the total annuity to be collected over the lives of both recipients. For example, suppose your annuity will pay you $600 a month and the same amount to your spouse after your death. And suppose your joint-and-survivor life expectancy is 22 years. Assuming that you contributed $22,000 in your capacity as employee, then 14 percent ($22,000 ÷ [$600 × 12 × 22]) of each annuity payment is exempt. That percentage also is used by the survivor, so 14 percent of each $600 payment he or she collects is exempt.

Keogh investors expect to collect their annuities after retirement, when they have lower incomes and are in lower tax brackets. Some see this as a tax advantage because tax brackets (and taxes) would be higher if the fund were collected earlier.

I understand this attitude, but it's not part of my own tax or investment thinking. I would not postpone collection of funds for a long period in the hope that I might be poorer when I got them. The other tax-saving considerations in Keogh plans matter more to me than this does.

In a few cases, moonlighters 65 or over may be able to claim a modest tax credit against their retirement income.

TAX ON LUMP-SUM WITHDRAWALS

You are taxed on your Keogh money as you collect it. If you collect it all at once, you pay tax on it all at once. But the tax on *Keogh* income is less than it would be if you were collecting the same amount from some *non*-Keogh source.

You pay no tax when you take out money you put in in your capacity as employee. For example, if you made $40,000 of regular contributions plus a nondeductible $10,000 as an employee, and the whole pie grew to $120,000, you get your $10,000 back free of tax. Only the $110,000 balance is subject to tax.

The balance comes in for a tax benefit called forward averaging. Averaging reduces the tax below what would be due at regular rates.

Forward averaging doesn't mean your tax is spread over future years. Rather, you pay a tax in a single year that is figured as if you had collected your Keogh fund in equal installments over a number of years, usually five, instead of in a single lump sum. This puts you in a lower-than-normal tax bracket on the lump-sum amount.

For most Keogh investors, the chance to use forward averaging for a lump-sum withdrawal comes once in a lifetime. The tax will be calculated at rates in effect when withdrawal happens.

What's a Lump-Sum Withdrawal?

You make a lump-sum withdrawal when you take out everything *remaining* in your account—your entire account balance—in a single calendar year. You may have taken money or assets out over several years. That's OK, but they weren't lump-sum withdrawals because you left something in. Only what you take out in the year you empty the account counts as a lump sum.

A second condition: If you're withdrawing from a Keogh, you must be age 59½ or over or disabled.

Some may spend part of their account balance to buy an annuity and take the rest in cash. The lump-sum amount you pay tax on is the cash plus the purchase price of the annuity if you bought it in your individual capacity. But if you bought it *as trustee,* it is removed from the lump-sum amount in figuring your tax. Instead, you pay tax as you collect on the annuity, under the usual rules for annuities.

Noncash Assets

In your lump-sum withdrawal you may take plan assets other than cash. In most cases, you will figure your tax on the lump-sum withdrawal by adding together the *current value* of the noncash assets to the amount of any cash. But two types of plan assets get special treatment:
• Annuity contract. You pay no tax when the *contract* is transferred to you, only as you receive annuity payments.
• Insurance policy. This is taxable like any other plan asset, at its cash surrender value. But if you convert it within 60 days into an annuity contract, you are taxed only as you receive annuity payments.

Since any tax levied on noncash assets must be paid in cash, you will have to raise the tax money from other sources. (Remember, if you're your own trustee, it was *your* idea to distribute the asset rather than sell it and distribute cash.) You might raise the tax cash by selling the item as tax day draws near. Where the asset is an insurance policy, you might borrow out the tax money via a policy loan.

WITHDRAWAL FROM TWO PLANS

Many moonlighters will have two plans when they retire: their Keogh plus the plan where they work full time. That will be true for Harold. Some may have more than two—like Peter, with his university plan and his two Keoghs.

You compute your tax on lump-sum withdrawals the same way whether you are withdrawing from one plan, two plans, or more than two—*if all withdrawals happen the same year.* Simply combine the taxable portions of all plans.

You get forward averaging for only one year. So if you empty out one plan in one year and another plan the next year, you get forward averaging in either year you choose, but not both.

For best tax results when withdrawing in different years, claim forward averaging for the larger withdrawal. That *could* be your company plan rather than your Keogh.

You can take a lump sum from one plan and an annuity from another. Your company's plan may *require* you to take an annuity, as is true for Harold's company plan and Peter's university plan. If both plans permit lump-sum withdrawal, you can take the lump sum from one in one year and a large installment from the other in a later year. Since you get no tax benefit from a second lump-sum withdrawal, there's no *tax* incentive to withdraw everything from the second plan.

ROLLOVERS

You can take a lump-sum distribution from one plan and put it into another plan. This is called a rollover. You can take a lump sum from a company plan and put it into a Keogh or vice versa. Or you can take one from either or both types and put it or them into an IRA.

Take a lump sum from your company plan and put it into your Keogh when you have this option. That way you pass control of your company plan money from your boss's trustee to yourself. Or you might roll a lump sum from one Keogh into another, to combine them into a single investment pool. That is not a high-priority item, but some might like it.

All rollovers are tax-free, but a rollover from a Keogh to an IRA can cost you later on.

Amounts you withdraw from an IRA don't get the tax relief available for lump-sum withdrawals from Keogh plans (or company plans). It can be OK for employees *without Keoghs* to roll their company withdrawals into IRAs. They pay no tax on the rollover, and their tax shelter continues for what goes into the IRA for as long as it stays there.

But if you have a Keogh, you can do better, even if you already have an IRA. If you roll your company (or some other Keogh) withdrawals into your Keogh, you will get what an IRA gives you: continued tax shelter with no tax on the rollover. And these two benefits besides: (1) you can still get tax averaging on a future lump-sum withdrawal of the funds you rolled over, and (2) you will have direct control over your Keogh assets, not the more limited control an IRA gives you.

Amounts you contributed in your capacity as an employee can't be rolled over from any plan. But they come to you tax-free.

OTHER WITHDRAWALS

Suppose you take money out of your plan, and it's not as an annuity or a lump sum. Maybe you have a profit-sharing plan and withdraw money for a down payment on a second home, say, or because of financial hardship. Or say you are past retirement age. You don't want to empty out your account and lose the tax shelter for everything, nor do you want to tie up your Keogh funds in an annuity. But you want a sizable chunk of your money for some personal or investment reason.

In such situations, what you withdraw is taxed like any other income you may have. It's added to your income, and tax is computed in the usual way. If you are withdrawing before age 59½, you may owe a tax penalty as well (see page 131).

If you made contributions as employee, part of each withdrawal is tax-free. It's the percentage that employee contributions bear to the total Keogh fund.[1]

---

[1] Different rules apply if you were in a Keogh plan on May 5, 1986.

Example.   You contributed $10,000 as employee. When the total Keogh fund stands at $100,000, you withdraw $6,000. Of this, $5,400 is taxable and $600 is tax free. The tax-free portion is $6,000 times 10 percent ($10,000 employee contribution divided by $100,000 total Keogh fund).

"Extra" money returned to you as employer. Self-employed persons with defined benefit plans may arrive at retirement with more money than they need to buy the pension the plan has promised. This "overfunding" can happen when plan investments outperform expectations.

Some plans pay employees everything, overfunding and all. Other plans are written to pay the extra money—the money not needed for the promised annuity—to the *employer,* when the plan terminates.

There's a special, heavy tax—the complexities of which I won't go into—on money going back to the *employer.* If you are and expect to be your plan's only employee, you'll want the extra money to come out to you as *employee,* and should omit the plan provision that pays the money to you as *employer.*

TAXES YOUR HEIRS MUST PAY

Your heirs (the plan will call them beneficiaries) must pay tax on what they receive out of your Keogh fund or Keogh annuity. These are the rules:

No penalty taxes. The tax penalty on early withdrawals (page 131) does not apply to heirs. Withdrawal after death is never an early withdrawal.

Annuities. Beneficiaries are taxed on their annuities as the Keogh investor would be, with one modification: Remember the rule on page 133 about annuities in which the Keogh investor contributed to his fund as an employee. Such contributions reduce the taxable part of the annuity. If an *heir* gets an annuity out of a Keogh, he or she gets the same benefit. And more. Besides what the Keogh investor *actually* put in as an employee, the beneficiary can count an *additional* $5,000 as an employee contribution. That means an additional $5,000 of annuity collection is tax-free. If the Keogh investor put *nothing* in as employee, then $5,000 of annuity collections are tax-free.

Example.   Moonlighter contributed $22,000 as employee. Heir will get an annuity of $600 a month over 20 years. The heir escapes tax on 18.75 percent of the annuity, or $112.50 a month. That is $27,000 ÷ ($600 × 12 × 20). Moonlighter with the same annuity amount and a 20-year life expectancy would escape tax on only 15 percent, or $90 a month; that is, $22,000 ÷ ($600 × 12 × 20).

The tax-free $5,000 does not apply to what the heir receives as a survivor on a joint-and-survivor annuity with the deceased moonlighter.

No more than $5,000 in all is tax-free, even though the moonlighter leaves more than one annuity—for example, a Keogh annuity plus one under a company pension plan. The $5,000 tax exemption can be taken on either one or shared between the two. Also, the tax-free $5,000 must be shared among all of the moonlighter's heirs; it's not $5,000 for each heir.

Other payments. Here, too, beneficiaries are taxed on what they get from the Keogh just as the Keogh investor would be. For example, a beneficiary can get forward averaging on a lump-sum withdrawal, as the Keogh investor could have done. *In addition,* a beneficiary will escape tax on $5,000 that the Keogh investor would have been taxable on.

Example.   Moonlighter made regular contributions but no contributions as employee. His heir gets his entire Keogh fund, which is $100,000 at moonlighter's death. The taxable portion is $95,000. If the moonlighter had contributed $10,000 as employee, the taxable portion would be $85,000.

Again, the tax-free treatment for the $5,000 is shared among all heirs; it's not $5,000 each.

Life insurance. Life insurance proceeds paid in a lump sum are exempt from income tax. If the proceds are paid out in installments or as an annuity, interest earned on these postponed payments is taxable.

Federal estate tax. The federal estate tax is levied on the net worth you leave behind at your death. The tax is imposed on the privilege of transferring your wealth from the late you to your heirs (yes, tax experts think taxing such a "privilege" is funny, too). There's no tax on your estate for any amount you leave your spouse or charity. And there's no estate tax on assets you leave to others, such as your children, if the total worth of these assets is $600,000 or less. So if your net worth at death is, say, $2 million, and you leave $600,000 to your children and $1.4 million to your spouse, there's no estate tax on your estate. Your assets include what you hold in your Keogh at your death. In figuring the size of your estate, annuities payable to heirs are figured at their value on the date of your death. There's no tax, or tax exemption, specifically for Keogh assets.

TAXING KEOGH MILLIONAIRES

Since the early pages, I have tastefully refrained from talk of "Keogh millions." That would be hype, oversell, I thought. But now it's time to revisit that phrase, led on by our nation's lawmakers. They have chosen to levy a special tax on pension plan millionaires: those who have built up great wealth in Keogh or company plans, or both.

(Feel free to skip this part if you don't expect to become a pension millionaire.)

There's no tax on the wealth itself. The U.S. government isn't comfortable with a tax on capital. It's a tax on what you take out of the plan and is called a tax on "excess distributions." But remember you're *required* to take a significant portion out once you reach a certain age. Should you have the rudeness to die with a fortune still undistributed in your pension plan, the tax on excess distributions becomes an estate tax without the usual estate tax exemptions.

What you withdraw from your plan in any year is an "excess distribution" if it's more than $150,000[2] in that year. The tax is 15 percent of the amount over $150,000 and is on top of any other tax on the withdrawal.

---

[2] This amount may go higher in future years.

Example. Make the happy assumption that you have built up great wealth in your Keogh. You withdraw $180,000 this year. Assume your *regular* tax on this is $63,000. Your excess distribution is $30,000 ($180,000 minus $150,000); your tax on this is $4,500 (15 percent of $30,000). Total tax is $67,500 ($63,000 plus $4,500).

In calculating what's an *excess* distribution, you combine all withdrawals from company plans with all withdrawals from Keoghs and all withdrawals from IRAs. If an item is exempt from regular tax because it's a repayment of an employee contribution, it's exempt from the excess distribution tax also and is ignored in computing what's "excess."

Example. You withdraw $90,000 from a company plan, $70,000 from a Keogh, and $20,000 from an IRA in a single year. Your tax is $67,500, the same as in the last example. If $10,000 of your withdrawals were tax-free repayment of employee contributions, your total tax would be $62,500 ($59,500 regular tax and $3,000 excess).

You avoid the excess distributions tax by keeping annual withdrawals to $150,000 or less. At age 65, you could have a Keogh or other pension fund totaling $1,590,000 and still owe no excess distributions tax, by taking $150,000 annually over an assumed 20-year life expectancy and a 7 percent interest return.

You will have more than $1,590,000 when you're 65? Really? Then start withdrawing earlier—say at age 60. You avoid excess tax on an amount that would be $2,412,000 at age 65 if you withdraw $150,000 a year over your 24-year life expectancy at age 60 (assuming a 7 percent interest rate).

It's a fairly simple, and rigid, system. Take out over $150,000 this year: pay the excess tax. Take out $150,000 or less: no tax, and no credit against a withdrawal over $150,000 in some other year. For example, withdraw $110,000 in year 1 and $180,000 in year 2, and your tax is $4,500 (for year 2), not zero, even though your *average* withdrawal is less than $150,000.

Lump-sum withdrawals get special relief from regular tax and get special relief from the excess tax as well. On a lump-sum withdrawal, only an amount that exceeds $750,000 is an excess distribution. So if you withdraw $800,000, the excess tax is $7,500 (15 percent of $50,000).

A lump-sum withdrawal is one that empties your account. All withdrawals during a year are combined as a single lump sum if the last withdrawal empties the account.

Suppose someone takes out, say, $150,000 in each of years 1, 2, 3, 4, and 5, and $750,000 as a lump sum in year 6. This sidesteps the excess tax but is perfectly legal. The excess distributions tax means to penalize large distributions (over $150,000 or $750,000) during life and large accumulations at death. The authorities don't mind clever tax-avoiding withdrawals during life: The tax shelter ends for amounts withdrawn.

Excess pension wealth owed the participant at death is subject to a special estate tax, called a tax on "excess accumulations." The tax is on pension wealth that exceeds the present value of a $150,000 annuity over the participant's life expectancy. Yes, they really base the tax on the life expectancy of a dead person. Expressed more humanely, it's the life expectancy of the average person who was the participant's age when the participant died.

Example. Blanche withdrew $150,000 each year from age 67 until her death at age 72 (a total of $900,000). The pension fund still owes her a sizable sum, which will go to her heirs. Under the IRS tables that must be used here, the present value of a $150,000 annuity at age 72 is $858,915.

Blanche's estate owes an excess accumulations tax if Blanche's pension fund is more than $858,915 at her death. Thus, if the fund were $1.3 million, the estate would owe $66,163 of excess accumulations tax (15 percent of $441,085).

This is on top of any regular estate tax. The usual estate tax exemptions (deductions) for bequests to a spouse or to charity aren't available against the tax on excess accumulations.

This is a tax on wealth the plan *owes* the plan participant, not on wealth the participant actually possesses. For example, $441,085 of the $1.3 million in Blanche's fund is subject to the excess tax *because it's in the fund*. If Blanche had collected that $441,085 and held it in a bank account at her death, no excess tax.

So you escape the tax on excess accumulations by withdrawing all or most of your fund before death? Sure. The tax authorities don't mind. The tax shelter ends for funds you withdraw (and maybe the withdrawal suffers the tax on excess distributions).

KEOGHS, INSURANCE, AND YOUR ESTATE

Estate planning advisors for some of the nation's wealthier professionals and business owners sometimes recommend buying life insurance to pay the estate tax on the inherited pension assets. This may be recommended when an individual with large net worth wants to leave more than $600,000 to one or more persons other than his or her spouse or where the estate tax on excess accumulations may apply.

There are ways to reduce estate taxes by giving property away during your lifetime. These techniques don't lend themselves to pension assets. You can't, for example, make annual gifts to your children out of funds in your pension plan. So where large pension assets are concerned, planners suggest buying life insurance to pay the estate tax on the inherited pension. Such a plan makes use of the estate tax relief that life insurance enjoys.

ALL THOSE TAXES

With all his generosity to those who play strictly by his rules, Uncle Sam is something of a disciplinarian to other players. Withdraw from your Keogh *too early* and there's a 10 percent tax (page 131). Withdraw *too late* and there's a 15 percent tax on excess accumulations of large sums (page 142). Withdraw *too much* and there's a 15 percent tax on excess distributions (page 140). Withdraw *too little* and—

We hadn't got to that yet. You may recall your duty to start withdrawing from your plan not later than April 1 following the year you reach age 70½. The tax authorities enforce your duty to withdraw the required amount (see page 122 for details) with a severe penalty if you don't withdraw enough. It's a penalty of 50 percent of the amount you should have withdrawn but didn't.

Example. Say you're 71 and should have withdrawn $18,000. If you withdraw nothing, you owe a penalty tax of $9,000. If you withdraw $10,000, you owe a penalty tax of $4,000 plus a regular tax (say, $2,500) on the $10,000 you withdraw.

All this seems like—and is—a lot of taxes. But they're easier to accept if considered in the right spirit. The regular tax, on an annuity or a lump sum or some other withdrawal, comes only after you have enjoyed many years of tax relief. The taxes on excess distributions and excess accumulations are taxes on great pension wealth. Most of us will find these taxes easy to avoid— unfortunately. And the other taxes, on withdrawals too early or too little, are on abuses of a system designed primarily to provide security for retirement.

KEOGHS AND STATE TAXES

In general, the Keogh tax benefits you get under federal tax law are repeated under state tax law (and under city or county tax laws, where those exist). Any state and local tax benefits you get mean additional tax dollars saved and make Keogh investment worth even more.

Tax rules vary widely among the 50 states, the District of Columbia, and the various cities and counties imposing income taxes. But here's the basic outline of state and local taxation:

1. *Tax deductions when contributions are made*. Many states with income taxes adopt federal Keogh rules exactly. Here, Keogh moves that save federal tax will save additional state tax.

Some states depart from federal Keogh rules to some degree. For example, Massachusetts denies Keogh deduction entirely.

State denials or limitations don't prevent you from contributing the amount you want. They just mean your contribution does not reduce your state tax as much as your federal tax. A few states (e.g., Florida, Nevada, South Dakota, Texas, Washington, Wyoming) impose no personal income tax at all.

2. *Earnings on plan investments*. No state taxes income from plan investments while it remains in the plan. *All* grant the Keogh tax shelter.

3. *Tax when withdrawals are made*. The *federal* tax benefits are forward averaging for lump-sum withdrawals, the credit for the elderly, and the $5,000 of income tax relief for heirs. There is no federal death tax (estate tax) relief.

Many states with income taxes follow the federal rules. Some, such as Pennsylvania, grant special relief to pension or other retirement income.

Some state *death taxes* follow the federal scheme. States with inheritance taxes (rather than estate taxes) indirectly grant relief for pension benefits through the special relief they grant surviving spouses and children.

There's no income tax problem on withdrawals in states with no income tax, and no death tax problem in states with no estate or inheritance tax. A number of states (such as Florida) impose an estate tax but in a way that shifts to that state the tax collections that would otherwise go to the federal government. The effect on the estate is as if there were no state tax, only a federal tax. Thus, these states are often said to have no estate tax.

Summary of Key Tax Rules

Type of Withdrawal	Tax Treatment
Early	Regular tax plus penalty in many cases; lump-sum relief (see below) not available
Annuity	Tax is generally at regular rates, but spread over period annuity is collected
Lump sum	Tax immediately but at reduced rate
Other withdrawals	Tax immediately like other income
"Excess"	If more than $150,000 withdrawn during the year, tax of 15 percent of amount over $150,000 (plus regular tax on amount withdrawn)
After age 70½	If disproportionately small amount withdrawn, tax of 50 percent on amount that should have been withdrawn but wasn't (plus regular tax on amount withdrawn)
Rollover	Not a withdrawal; tax postponed until withdrawal occurs
Withdrawal by spouse or other heirs, after moonlighter's death	Tax treatment generally the same as moonlighter's except: No early withdrawal penalty Modest ($5,000) income tax exemption Possible estate (death) tax
Withdrawals under state tax rules	Like the federal rules above in most states but with many variations

The variations in state tax treatment of Keogh distributions demand close study by persons planning retirement. This
is especially true if you are planning retirement in a state other
than the one you now live in. For example, you could owe
$10,000 of tax on a lump-sum Keogh withdrawal if you're a Maine
resident and no tax if you reside in Florida or Texas. Anything you
get on retirement as an employee in a company plan will raise similar problems and opportunities and will call for equally careful
planning.

HOW IRA TAXES COMPARE

Taxes on IRA withdrawals don't much differ from those on Keogh
withdrawals. Where there's a difference, Keoghs fare better.
Briefly, these are the IRA tax rules:

Early withdrawal. Tax rules are the same as for Keoghs. If a
Keogh withdrawal would trigger a penalty tax, an IRA withdrawal
does likewise.

Withdrawal in annuity form. IRA tax rules are the same as
Keogh rules. If you made *nondeductible* IRA contributions, treat
your IRA annuity as you would a Keogh annuity where nondeductible (employee) Keogh contributions were made. The nondeductible IRA contribution comes back to you tax-free over the IRA
annuity period in the same way nondeductible employee contributions would in a Keogh annuity.[3]

Lump-sum withdrawals. IRAs don't enjoy the forward average
relief granted Keoghs. Otherwise, the tax rules are the same as
for Keoghs. Nondeductible IRA contributions come back tax-free,
as nondeductible employee Keogh contributions do.

Rollovers. Rollovers to or from IRAs aren't taxable because
they are not withdrawals. No rollover is allowed from an IRA to a
Keogh or company plan, though it's OK to park money briefly (up
to 60 days) in an IRA while it's on its way from one Keogh or
company plan to another.

---

[3] With a minor exception if you have more than one IRA.

Other withdrawals. IRA and Keogh rules are the same; again, rules for nondeductible IRA contributions track those for nondeductible employee Keogh contributions.[4]

Tax on your heirs. IRA income taxes on your heirs are the same as for Keoghs, except that IRAs are denied the $5,000 exemption. Rules for nondeductible IRA contributions otherwise follow those for nondeductible employee Keogh contributions.

IRA and Keogh *estate* tax rules are identical.

Tax on millionaires. IRA withdrawals are added to Keogh and company plan withdrawals in figuring the tax on excess *distributions*. IRA *assets* are added to Keogh and company plan assets in figuring the tax on excess *accumulations*.

State tax. As a generalization, state taxes on IRAs will follow the federal rules. But don't trust generalizations; check your own state. A quick way to find your state's income tax rules on IRAs is to glance at the instructions that come with the income tax return form. They may have a brief description of the state's tax rules for IRA contributions and withdrawals. If they are silent about IRAs, the state follows the basic federal rules for taxing IRAs. However, states rarely impose penalty taxes, such as for early withdrawal or excess distribution.

---

[4] With a minor exception if you have more than one IRA.

CHAPTER 15

HOW TO GET STARTED

"I'm sold on Keoghs," Harold says, "I know I need this. So what do I do now? How do I get started?"

Once you know the kind of plan you want, you need something in writing. You need a written Keogh plan, which pension professionals call a *plan document*. And you need a written *trust agreement*.

Both of these are fairly complex legal instruments. In the plan document, you as employer set forth in detail what you will provide. Then you specify the conditions that you *as employee* must meet in order to belong to this plan and benefit from it. You say when and what you will collect. You lay out any options you will have, such as the option to contribute as an employee, the option to take benefits as an annuity or in a lump sum, and so on.

In the trust agreement you as employer set forth what the trustee should do about trust investments and payments to employees (you again). You may of course decide to be trustee. No matter; you still need a written agreement[1] giving yourself directions.

Certain housekeeping details connected with the plan must be handled by the plan administrator—you again. That too calls for something in writing.

Unless you are a lawyer or are well versed in pension matters, you probably won't be able to prepare the various legal documents on your own. Very few moonlighters can do it all themselves. For

---

[1] Trust agreements can be dispensed with in insured plans. See Chapter 9 on such plans.

the great majority of moonlighters, getting started means *adopting a master plan* or having a pension professional draw up a *tailor-made* plan.

WHY YOU MIGHT WANT A MASTER PLAN

A master plan reduces the start-up costs and simplifies your side of the paperwork. With a tailor-made plan, you will have to pay up front for the advice of a pension professional. Besides that, you must pay for having the necessary legal documents drawn up and getting the plan approved by the IRS. With a master plan, no charge is made for advice; you *get* no advice. Nor are you charged for preparing documents; the documents are already prepared. In a master plan, one basic set of plan documents is recycled among all those who adopt that plan.

WHY YOU MIGHT WANT A
TAILOR-MADE PLAN

1. You can directly control all plan investments.
2. You eliminate the middle man. All master plan sponsors (or the financial institutions they use) profit in some way from your investment, by lending out your funds for more than they pay you or by charging you management or transaction fees.
3. You can have a plan that gives you exactly what you want. You have a good chance to find a master money-purchase plan, profit-sharing plan, or both that fit your objectives. But that is less likely with a master defined-benefit plan.

WHO'S WHO IN MASTER PLANS

Master plans are offered by professional associations and trade associations, by law firms and pension firms, and by financial institutions of all types: banks, insurance companies, mutual funds, and securities dealers. In master plan terminology, the firm or institution that offers the plan is the *plan sponsor*. If a moonlighter approves of a master plan's terms and conditions, he or she will adopt the plan *as employer,* and make his or her Keogh contributions to that plan sponsor. An employee covered by the plan is called a *participant*. A moonlighter is a participant in his or her capacity as employee. The *trustee,* the person controlling the investment, will usually be the plan sponsor or someone the sponsor selects.[2]

HOW TO SHOP FOR A MASTER PLAN

Look for these features in *any* kind of plan you consider:

1. *"Employee" contribution.* The plan should allow self-employed persons to make voluntary (nondeductible) contributions as employees. The best plan wording would let you contribute for every year you had the business. This may be expressed as the entire period of your employment. This wording lets you contribute based on the self-employment income you made even before you joined the plan (as well as in later years). A distant second best is wording that lets you contribute with respect to all years you are in the plan. With this wording, your contributions are based only on this year's income and future income.

Either way, you can make catch-up contributions for any year in which you contributed less than you were allowed. The law gives you a splendid catch-up opportunity. Until 1984 a self-employed person with no employees was not allowed to make contributions as employee. From 1984 on, he or she can make such contributions based on *all* prior self-employment earned income, if the *plan* is written to permit this.

Example.   Suppose Elaine has made a total of $50,000 of earned income from her moonlighting activities since she began business. Suppose she made $12,000 of that amount the year she set up her Keogh. If the plan lets her contribute 10 percent of her earnings since she entered the plan, she could contribute $1,200. If it lets her contribute 10 percent of her earnings in the business, she could contribute $5,000.

---

[2] Prototype plans are a kind of master plan in which the employer names the trustee, and so can control the investments.

2. *Withdrawing "employee" contributions.* The plan should let you withdraw your contributions as employee and the earnings thereon, at will.

Some plans say you can withdraw the amounts you contributed as employee or their present value, as increased or decreased by investment earnings or losses, whichever is *less*. That won't do; you can't take out more than you contributed. If your account has suffered investment losses, it's fair that you can't withdraw more than your account has shrunk to. But if you have investment *gains*, you should be free to take those out.

3. *Reliability.* You're investing sums for the long term. You should satisfy yourself that the plan sponsor will be around as long as you are.

4. *IRS approval.* Eventually, your master plan will have to be approved by the IRS. It's better if that approval already has been granted by the IRS. The sponsor will tell you in the fine print whether approval has been granted or not.

But it's not essential to have the approval when you make your contribution. If the sponsor doesn't have approval when you adopt the plan (by December 31), check for the standard clause that your plan contribution will be refunded to you if the plan is not approved. If the plan *is* approved after you've made your contributions, no problem. It's as if it was approved from the start. If it's not approved, you get your money back. But you have no plan and so no deduction for that year.

Sometimes there's a widespread holdup on IRS plan approvals because of some rules changes. So you can sometimes have a hard time finding any worthwhile plan that has been approved at the time you want to contribute. At other times, only new plans are currently unapproved. If a plan you're looking at lacks approval at present, you might be able to find a roughly comparable plan elsewhere that is IRS approved.

How to Shop for a Master Profit-Sharing or Money-Purchase Plan

Look for these features:

1. *Two plans.* Most plan sponsors offer profit-sharing plans; many also offer money-purchase plans. Since a combination of a profit-sharing and a money-purchase plan is a good idea for those who don't want a defined-benefit plan (see Chapter 5), find a sponsor that offers both.

2. *Investment policies.* You may have specific investment goals. No plan sponsor will share those goals exactly, but some will have policies or investment options that come close. For example, some mutual funds sponsors have varied types of portfolios, for income with safety, for long-term growth, and so on (see Chapter 8). Investment policies and the record of investment success may be what counts most in selecting a particular master plan sponsor. The real competition among plan sponsors is in maximizing the return on your investment within the safety/security requirements you have in mind.

3. *Plan sponsor charges* for handling your account are relatively minor nowadays. If the charge is more than nominal (if it's more than, say, $20), make sure the sponsor offers some extra service that you consider worthwhile.

How to Shop for a Master Defined-Benefit Plan

Master defined-benefit plans are offered by insurance companies, some large securities dealers, and some banks and law firms. You'll have to shop carefully. Some plan sponsors may not want your business because your investments (contributions) may seem small in their eyes. Also, most won't offer you all of the options possible, options you would get in a tailor-made plan. As often pointed out in this book, defined-benefit plans offer a great many opportunities to maximize your Keogh wealth. A master plan will limit or foreclose some of those opportunities.

When shopping for a master defined-benefit plan, look for the following key points.

Your flexibility in making contributions. Many moonlighters' incomes fluctuate widely from year to year. A moonlighter in a defined-benefit plan needs some flexibility in how much he or she must contribute each year. Some master defined-benefit plans can be too rigid about this. Be sure the plan you're considering is flexible enough to suit you.

Investment policies. In many cases you will be choosing one sponsor over another based on predictions or projections of investment return on your plan contributions.

Look at the rate of return you get on your investment, not just at the tax deductions. Treat your pension contribution as you would any other investment. The more you pay out, the more you should collect, regardless of the tax deduction for your investment.

Example.   You are looking at two master defined-benefit plans, one from sponsor A, one from sponsor B. In sponsor A's plan, you put in $4,000 a year for 10 years and will get a pension of $8,559 a year at age 65. In sponsor B's plan you put in $5,000 a year over the same period and get a $10,203-a-year pension at 65. The yield on A's plan is better—5 percent better—than on B's. This is so even though the $5,000-a-year investment produces a greater reduction in your tax bill. What counts is what you have left after taxes, not how much your tax bill is reduced. You would need to get a $10,699-a-year pension on a $5,000-a-year investment to match the yield you get on sponsor A's plan.

Plan sponsor charges. These are significantly higher for defined-benefit plans than for other plans. The charges will often be included in (you might say buried within) the investment return. If not, treat them as part of your investment and compute your return on the sum of those amounts. For example, if you invest $3,000 this year and make $300, your return is 10 percent ($300 ÷ $3,000). But if the plan sponsor charges $100 this year, your return is 9.7 percent ($300 ÷ $3,100).

Plan termination, disability, death. With a plan tailor-made for you alone, the amount you would collect on plan termination or disability, or the amount your heir would collect at your death, would be all of your investments plus any uninvested cash contribution. In a master plan a different result could apply. Check.

My own Keogh is tailor-made (by me). Mine is a defined-benefit Keogh. There are no Keogh master plans that offer all of the options I can write for myself or that other pension professionals could write for a person in my situation.

But I have belonged to master plans in the past, before defined-benefit opportunities for moonlighters opened up in 1984.

The master plans I saw, and I saw a good many, were slow to adopt new provisions that could increase plan benefits. A person in a master plan gets only those benefits that *his or her plan* makes possible. It won't help that some new law or IRS ruling increases wealth-building opportunities if the plan does nothing about it. Employer-moonlighters can't *change* a master plan. In most cases, their only option is to leave that master plan for another that has responded better to the new opportunities.

Moving from Plan to Plan

A moonlighter with no employees is free to move from one master plan to another *of the same type* without interference from the government. So you can go from one master profit-sharing to another master profit-sharing plan or from one master money-purchase plan to another master money-purchase plan. That is not terminating or freezing your plan.

The plan you are moving *to* will give you the necessary simple instructions. In essence, you sign the same kinds of papers in the new plan that you signed in the old, and you arrange a transfer of your funds from the old to the new. Some plans may seem to charge a kind of exit fee as you leave them. Actually, that is a feature of the kind of mutual fund in which your money is invested, not part of the plan itself. The charge is some percentage of your investment account, imposed if you withdraw within some prescribed period.

You also can move from a master plan to a tailor-made plan *of the same type*. There's no problem about moving your money there, but you must go through all the formalities connected with starting a new plan.

THE TAILOR-MADE KEOGH

A tailor-made Keogh will give you exactly the kind of plan you want. You have total control over your plan investments. And you can select every favorable option for building up your Keogh fund. Tailor-mades are especially important if you want a defined-benefit plan.

The bad news about tailor-made Keoghs is their upfront costs. You must pay for having a professional design the plan to your specifications (the consultation), draw up the papers (document preparation), and get the IRS to approve it (approval and compliance). An actuary must be brought in at some stage if you have a defined-benefit plan.

There is no standard rate for this kind of work. Most tailor-making is done for companies with employees. Having no employees cuts the consultation time and cost somewhat, especially if you know exactly what you want when consultation begins. But that won't affect costs of document preparation or approval and compliance.

Based on my informal survey, a cost of $1,200 to $1,800 for the complete job would be reasonable, on the low side. The cost of the plan is tax-deductible.

Is a tailor-made Keogh worth it? That depends on the amount of your moonlighting income and the type of plan you want. Though this is a personal opinion, I wouldn't go tailor-made if income in most years is in the $4,000 to $5,000 range or less. Even with larger moonlighting income, some shouldn't go tailor-made in the early years of a money-purchase or profit-sharing plan (or both). The ability to control investments isn't so important while total contributions and earnings thereon are fairly small.

I recommend tailor-made Keoghs especially in two situations: The first is for those who select defined-benefit plans, to get the full range of options for building Keogh wealth. The tax-deductible cost of a tailor-made plan is quickly recovered out of the higher tax-deductible contributions you are allowed and the higher tax-sheltered Keogh earnings.

The second is for start-up operations that may take on employees in the future. A tailor-made plan now can bring future savings in pension costs for employees who are added. See Chapter 18 for Keogh planning for employees.

KEOGH DOCUMENTS

With a tailor-made plan, you need the following documents to get started:

- The Plan
- The Trust Agreement
- IRS Form 5300
- IRS Form 5302 (Employee Census)
- IRS Form 2848 (Power of Attorney, to represent you in discussions with the IRS on plan approval)
- Notice to Employees (that application for approval has been made to the IRS)
- Summary Plan Description, furnished to covered employees and the Department of Labor.

The Plan and Trust Agreement, which are often combined into a single document, are the most important and most complicated. The IRS forms are used to get IRS approval. The other documents communicate certain facts about the plan to the Department of Labor or to yourself in your capacity as employee.

The pension professional you engage is responsible for preparing all of these documents. If you adopt a master plan, the plan sponsor prepares the necessary documents, most of which you never see. You fill in a few blanks on an Adoption Agreement and sign it.

GETTING THE IRS OK

Every master plan will have an IRS OK or will be in the process of getting one. If you have a tailor-made plan, the pension professional you engage to prepare it will advise you to have it approved by the IRS. This is a practical necessity, though not a legal one.

You need IRS approval because you have so much at stake. You will be investing many thousands of dollars because of the many Keogh tax advantages. If you aren't going to get those benefits because of some defect in your plan, you should know that right away.

The IRS has a system designed to let you know in advance whether or not your plan qualifies for all tax benefits. That is, after examining the plan and making sure it meets legal requirements, the IRS will give you a written commitment that its revenue agents will treat the plan as qualified. The commitment usually is called a determination letter, though some call it a ruling. The IRS will do this for existing plans. More important, the IRS will do it for a plan before it goes into effect. The commitment will bind the IRS if you live up to the terms of your plan.

Getting an IRS OK takes time, but it's not a difficult or unfriendly process. It goes like this:

1. Your pension professional submits some IRS forms (see page 156) and a copy of the plan.

2. The IRS sends each of you a notice that the plan is being considered.

3. If the IRS has any problems or questions, an IRS representative gets in touch with your pension professional, and they discuss it, usually over the phone.

4. The IRS representative may require a change. Usually, it's a minor one. Your professional will discuss it with you. If you agree, he or she will amend the plan to reflect the change and send the IRS representative a copy of the change.

5. If the IRS representative accepts the change, the IRS will eventually send you (through your professional) a copy of the determination letter approving the plan. A copy of such a letter begins on page 160. The government charges a fee for reviewing or approving your plan.

The whole process usually takes several months. But don't let it hold up anything you want to do with your Keogh. Make your contributions and investments as if the IRS OK already had been given. The actual OK, when it comes, will treat your plan as approved from the start.

It almost never happens that a self-employed person finds it impossible to accept the IRS conditions. But if that should happen in your case, you will be able to get your money back out of the Keogh plan. Your plan will include wording calling for repayment of all funds if the IRS disapproves the plan. In most cases, your pension professional will include such wording without prompting on your part, but it won't hurt to make sure.

HOW HAROLD GETS STARTED

Harold is 11 years from retirement. He has no time to lose. He wants to build a large Keogh fund in a fairly short time. That means he wants a defined-benefit Keogh plan with all the trimmings. He's looking for a Keogh fund large enough to pay a pension of $10,000 a year. And he wants a plan that offers all of the following opportunities to build a higher Keogh:

- He wants a Keogh fund to buy a *joint-and-full survivor* annuity that will continue the $10,000 a year to his wife after his death. Joint-and-full-survivor costs more than single life paying the same annual amount.
- He wants conservative projections of how fast his Keogh funds grow. Conservative projections will let him put in more.
- He wants to use long joint-and-survivor life expectancies. The longer the expected payout period, the more the projected annuity costs and the more he can put in.
- He wants conservative projections about interest rates at retirement. The lower the projected interest rates at that time, the more the projected annuity cost and the more he can put in.
- He wants the plan to take account of his past service. That will allow him to front-load his contributions if he wishes.
- He wants to make additional Keogh contributions as employee to shelter some investment income from tax.
- He wants to control his investments as plan trustee.

Harold wants a lot. It won't be easy to find everything he wants in a master defined-benefit plan. Harold probably should seek out a pension professional and have a tailor-made plan drawn for him that incorporates all of his requirements.

HOW PETER GETS STARTED

Peter wants to be his own trustee, to control investments that he expects to grow to many hundreds of thousands of dollars. And he wants the opportunity for additional *employee* contributions.

Peter might want his money-purchase plan tailor-made, to be sure he holds investment control. Tailor-made money-purchase plans aren't expensive for self-employed persons with no employees. Or he might find a master plan variant called a prototype plan. This will let him name himself trustee and control his investments directly.

HOW ELAINE GETS STARTED

Elaine expects to put about $3,000 a year into Keoghs. She may not go on moonlighting for long, so she wants no long-term commitments. In her situation maximum Keogh flexibility is obtained by combining a profit-sharing plan and a money-purchase plan. She also would like to make employee contributions to shelter some investment earnings.

A Keogh master plan is just right for Elaine. There are many that offer profit-sharing, money-purchase, and employee contributions. Elaine's primary concern, once these requirements are met, is to find one offering an investment program that fits her own objectives.

Internal Revenue Service   Department of the Treasury
District Director

Date: June 14, 1989

John Jones
112 Fourteenth Avenue
New York, NY 12222

District Office Code and Case Serial Number: 12345432EP
Name of Plan: John Jones
Defined Benefit
Plan & Trust
Application Form: 5300
Date Adopted: October 24 1988
Date Amended:
Employer Identification Number: 13-1234567
Plan Number: 002
File Number: 130000000
Contact Person: W Smith
Contact Phone Number: 718 7801000

Gentlemen:

Based on the information supplied, we have made a favorable determination on your application identifed above. Please keep this letter in your permanent records.

Continued qualification of the plan will depend on its effect in operation under its present form. (See section 1.401-1(b)(3) of the Income Tax Regulations.) The status of the plan in operation will be reviewed periodically.

The enclosed document describes some events that could occur after you receive this letter that would automatically nullify it without specific notice from us. The document also explains how operation of the plan may affect a favorable determination letter, and contains information about filing requirements.

This letter relates only to the status of your plan under the Internal Revenue Code. It is not a determination regarding the effect of other Federal or local statutes.   Letter 835(C)

ATTACHMENT TO 835C LETTER
Plan Name: John Jones   Plan Number: 002

The following items which are checked apply to your plan and are an integral part of our determination.

—   C]   This determination does not indicate that the Internal Revenue Service is in any way passing on the actuarial soundness of the plan or on the reasonableness of the actuarial computations.

x   D]   This determination is subject to your adoption of the proposed amendments submitted in your or your representative's letter dated <u>January 4, 1989.</u> The proposed amendments should be adopted on or before the date prescribed by the regulations under Code section 401(b).

—   E]   This determination does not express an opinion as to whether your plan satisfies the provisions of the Tax Reform Act of 1986.

—   F]   This plan applies only to employees who can retire and obtain benefits during the term of which it is drawn; no other employees are considered covered. Therefore, the provision of Code section 404 will be applied only to covered employees.

—   G]   The trust, not having been created or organized in the United States, is not a qualified trust under Code section 401(a) and is not exempt under section 501(a). Based on the information you submitted, however, we have determined that the trust is part of a plan which meets the requirements of section 401(a) in all other respects and that it would qualify for exemption under section 501(a) except for the fact that it is created or organized outside the United States. Therefore, distributions to beneficiaries will be taxable as though made through an exempt trust, as provided in section 402(c). Deductions for contributions made by the employer, who is a domestic corporation or resident of the United States, are allowable as provided in Code section 404(a)(4).

(over)

—   H]   This determination does not apply beginning with any year in which discrimination prohibited by Code section 401(a)(4) arises because of the years of service weighing factor applied in allocating employer contributions. (See Rev. Rul. 68-653, 1968-2 C.B. 177.)

—   I]   This determination expresses an opinion on whether the amendment(s), in and of itself (themselves), affect(s) the continued qualified status of the plan under Code section 401 and the exempt status of the related trust under section 501(a). This determination should not be construed as an opinion on the qualification of the plan as a whole and the exempt status of the related trust as a whole.

—   J]   Your plan does not consider total compensation for purposes of figuring benefits. The provision may, in operation, discriminate in favor of employees who are stockholders, officers, or highly compensated. If this discrimination occurs, your plan will not remain qualified. (See Rev. Rul. 69-503, 1969-2 C.B. 94.)

—   K]   This determination applies to the plan year(s) beginning after _____.

—   L]   This determination does not express an opinion on any provisions of the Tax Reform Act of 1986.

x   M]   We have sent a copy of this letter to your representative as indicated in the power of attorney.

—   N]

CHAPTER 16

YOUR PLAN IN OPERATION

It's not hard or complicated to operate your plan. You will be able to handle all or most of the duties yourself. Here is what you are in for:

1. You generally must file an annual report with the IRS. If your plan uses the calendar year (which is what most moonlighters choose), the report is due July 31, for the preceding year. A moonlighter with no employees in his plan, files the one-page Form 5500-EZ. A filled-in sample of this form appears on page 169. Even this modest reporting requirement can be excused if you have no more than $100,000 in your Keogh fund (totaling all Keoghs you have).

Many moonlighters with profit-sharing or money-purchase plans will be able to fill out the form without outside help.

If you have two plans, you must report separately for each plan. If professional help is needed, consult a tax accountant or attorney.

If you have a defined-benefit plan, your Form 5500-EZ must be accompanied by the two-page Form 5500 Schedule B (Actuarial Information), together with a statement of actuarial assumptions. Samples of these are on pages 170–172. You can't prepare the Schedule B yourself. It must be prepared and signed by an *enrolled actuary*. For more about this professional, see page 217.

You also must file a brief return from the plan trustee. The easiest way is to file Form 5500 Schedule P. It's a one-page form, filed with 5500-EZ. A sample appears on page 173.

You will need an employer identification number (EIN) for all of your Keogh reports to the IRS. Apply for it on Form SS-4. (See page 174 for a filled-in version of this form.) You can get the form from most IRS and social security offices. Send the application to your local IRS Service Center.

You may already have obtained an EIN if you had an employee in your business. If so, use that number in your Keogh reporting.

2. You handle the fund investments if you are trustee. You as employer (and perhaps as employee) will be making contributions each year, often more than once a year. You as trustee will invest these contributions in some income-producing way. From time to time you will probably sell or redeem some or all of them, and you also will receive payments of interest, dividends, or other investment income, which you will reinvest. Remember that all of your investment actions should be taken as trustee.

You as plan administrator must furnish a summary report of your plan's financial condition to yourself as participant by September 30 of each year. (You got this information from yourself or the trustee.) The report is for the preceding year. A sample appears on pages 177–78.

So much for your annual or recurring duties. You will have further duties in the following special situations.

3. *Withdrawal.* Report withdrawal to social security (and yourself). Withholding is generally required unless waived by the participant (you). Participants usually waive; further reporting requirements apply if they don't.

Up to 90 days before an annuity is to begin, married participants must be notified of their right to waive joint-and-survivor annuity in favor of single life. Notify your spouse that the two of you share this right.

4. *Change.* If you change the terms and conditions of a tailor-made plan, the documents involved when you launched the plan (see page 156) should be amended. If you are just changing the level of plan benefits (in a defined-benefit plan) or the rate of your plan contributions (for other plans), this need not be reported to the IRS. But amendments mandated by new pension laws should be resubmitted to the IRS. You need not submit a revised Summary Plan Description to the Department of Labor, but you should submit one to participants (yourself). This need not be done for somewhat more than five years from the time you make the change.

If the plan changes its name, report that to the IRS.

If the plan administrator changes his or her name (e.g., by marriage) or address, report that to the IRS.

5. *Divorce or separation.* Suppose you are divorced or separated and are served as plan administrator with a "qualified domestic relations order." That can give your spouse a right to certain funds in your plan. Money you pay him or her is a withdrawal, reported as described in (3) above.

6. *After 10 years.* If the plan is not amended, furnish an updated version of the Summary Plan Description to yourself 10 years after the plan begins (technically somewhat more than 10 years) and every 10 years of operation after that.

7. *Adding participants.* If you take on employees who join your plan, you should give each of them a copy of the Summary Plan Description and furnish them with other information if they ask for it.[1] You will have further duties if *they* withdraw funds or become the subject of a qualified domestic relations order.

For the most part, there are no government filing charges or fees connected with your Keogh reporting. However, a penalty is imposed if the annual reporting form (5500-EZ) is filed late.

Certain information about participants (you) should be maintained as part of the basic records of the plan—specifically, your date of birth, sex, employment date (date you started your business), and your net earnings from self-employment for each year. The year you started business will do if you don't remember the exact date. If you don't remember the year and are not covering past service, the date the plan went into effect will do.

The plan also should keep a record of who your beneficiary is. A sample Beneficiary Designation form appears on page 175. Fill out two copies; keep one with your Keogh's documents and one in your file of personal assets or investments.

---

[1] In these pages we have been assuming you are the only participant in your Keogh, so here we'll skip the information you owe other participants. Complete details on this may be found in *The Employee Benefits Compliance Coordinator,* published by The Research Institute of America.

VALUING YOUR INVESTMENTS

If you have a defined-benefit plan, the value of your Keogh determines how much you must contribute this year or in future years. And whatever your plan, you as plan administrator must report the value of Keogh assets each year—to *yourself* as participant.

For most Keogh investments, it's easy to find the value as of a given date. For publicly traded common or preferred stocks, bonds, shares in various types of mutual funds, and so on, the value is what you could get for them on the market on that day. That value fluctuates from day to day.

Cost is even easier to determine and is a constant, but it should not be used unless it represents true worth.

The rule is that your asset valuation method must recognize fair market value. You must use fair market value on the valuation date (see below). Or you must use an "actuarial valuation method" based on a moving average of fair market values computed over several years. The actuarial valuation method is a complex method large plans use to reduce year-to-year fluctuations in values of assets held. Details on acceptable methods are found in U.S. Treasury Regulation Section 1.412(c)(2)-1, reprinted in the *Federal Tax Coordinator 2d*, published by the Research Institute of America. I consider actuarial valuation methods more trouble than they are worth for Keogh plans and use fair market value in all cases.

The valuation date, the date as of which value is determined, is up to you, but you should use the same date each year. Typical dates are the first or last day of the year. It would be appropriate to use the value as of the last day of the preceding year in calculating the current year's contribution. I use the last day.

Here is how I value Keogh assets (valuation as of the last day of the year): For assets traded on exchanges (stocks and bonds) look at the stock or bond quotes for the last trading day in the year. Value is the midpoint between the day's high and low for each item you own. For mutual fund assets, the mutual fund will report the amount in your account as of the last day of the year or the last accounting day. Use that as the value. For bank CDs or other bank deposits, value is the amount in your account including interest credited through year's end.

CHECKLIST OF YOUR DUTIES WHEN YOU HAVE A KEOGH PLAN

Your basic duties
 Investment activities as trustee
 Annual report to IRS
 Annual report to yourself as participant
  Involves annual valuation of plan assets
 Keeping certain basic information in your own files
Your occasional or special duties
 Reporting a withdrawal of funds from the plan
 Reporting a change in the plan
 Reporting and other action when an employee participant is added
 A pro forma report approximately every 10 years

YOUR INCOME TAX RETURN

Your self-employment income and Keogh deductions go on each year's tax returns. Page 176 shows how these items are entered on tax return Form 1040.

Self-employment income is entered on line 12; the Keogh deduction is entered on line 27. The entries are for Peter's moonlighting income and his contribution to his money-purchase plan.

The amount entered on line 12 is arrived at through calculations on Schedule C (see page 107 for a sample involving another taxpayer). There is no form for making or reporting the calculations to arrive at the Keogh *deduction*.

WHEN A KEOGH LOSES QUALIFICATION

A Keogh plan can lose its qualification if it has violated the Keogh rules in some major way. When that happens, "the adverse effect . . . upon both the employer and the participants is immense." So says the IRS guide to IRS agents who examine retirement plans. "Immense" is no exaggeration; disqualification can operate retroactively, back to the time the misbehavior occurred.

Disqualification means the end of deductions for Keogh contributions. And it means that the IRS takes back the tax saved on deductions claimed in past years (seldom more than three years). The moonlighter will therefore owe tax for those past years, with interest.[2] Disqualification also means no averaging for funds withdrawn in a lump sum.

And disqualification retroactively revokes the tax exemption Keogh investment earnings enjoyed in the Keogh trust. Assuming the trust has been filing required returns, the retroactive effect is limited to three years.

While any flagrant violation of the Keogh rules can cause loss of qualification, the two most common offenses are (1) *illegally* favoring the business owner over other employees, and (2) intentionally exceeding the legal limits on plan contributions or benefits, discussed on pages 98 and 102.

PENALTIES

Pension specialists, a group not given to hyperbole, call disqualification "nuking the plan." For lesser breaches of duty, IRS imposes milder punishment in the form of tax penalties on the employer or the trustee. Those in Keogh plans should know about:

- Penalties on those who use plan funds to aid their businesses, or to advance their personal interests, without taking a formal, taxable, employee withdrawal.
- Penalties for making plan contributions as employer that exceed the amount allowed as a deduction.

---

[2] The exact effect of loss of qualification will depend on whether funds vested (see page 105) when they were contributed. But for practical purposes, the effect is a retroactive loss of the Keogh deduction.

Form **5500EZ**	**Annual Return of One-Participant (Owners and Their Spouses) Pension Benefit Plan**	OMB No. 1545-0956
Department of the Treasury Internal Revenue Service	For the calendar year 1990 or fiscal plan year beginning _____, 19 ___, and ending _____, 19 ___.	**19 90**
Please type or machine print		This Form Is Open to Public Inspection

This return is: *(i)* ☐ the first return filed   *(ii)* ☐ an amended return   *(iii)* ☐ the final return

Use IRS label. Otherwise, please type or machine print.

1a Name of employer Susan Turner
Number, street, and room or suite no. (If a P.O. box, see instructions for line 1a.) 6789 Lake Shore Dr.
City or town, state, and ZIP code Chicago, Ill. 60666

1b Employer identification number 139 876543
1c Telephone number of employer (312) 286-4765
1d If plan year has changed since last return, check here ▶ ☐

2a *(i)* Name of plan ▶ Susan Turner defined Benefit Plan and Trust
(ii) ☐ Check if name of plan has changed since last return

2b Date plan first became effective Month 1 Day 1 Year 84
2c Enter three-digit plan number . . ▶ 0 0 1

3a Enter the date the most recent plan amendment was adopted . NA. Month ___ Year ___
b Enter the date of the most recent IRS determination letter . . . . Month 3 Year 85
c Is a determination letter request pending with IRS? [Yes/No] X

4a Enter the number of other qualified pension benefit plans maintained by the employer . . . ▶ ____
b If you have more than one pension plan and the total assets of all plans are more than $100,000, check this box . ▶ ☐
5 Type of plan: **a** ☐ Defined benefit pension plan (attach Schedule B (Form 5500)) **b** ☐ Money purchase plan
c ☐ Profit-sharing plan **d** ☐ Stock bonus plan **e** ☐ ESOP plan (attach Schedule E (Form 5500))
6 Were there any noncash contributions made to the plan during the plan year? X

7 Enter the number of participants in each category listed below: | Number
a Under age 59½ at the end of the plan year | **7a** 1
b Age 59½ or older at the end of the plan year, but under age 70½ at the beginning of the plan year . . . | **7b** 0
c Age 70½ or older at the beginning of the plan year | **7c** 0

8a A fully insured plan with no trust and which is funded entirely by allocated insurance contracts that fully guarantee the amount of benefit payments should check the box at the right and not complete 8b through 10d . . . . ▶ ☐
b Contributions received for this plan year . . . . . | **8b** 7,500
c Net plan income other than from contributions . . . . | **8c** 3,000
d Plan distributions . . . . | **8d** 0
e Plan expenses other than distributions . . . . | **8e** 10
9a Total plan assets at the end of the year . . . | **9a**
b Total plan liabilities at the end of the year . . . | **9b**

10 During the plan year, if any of the following transactions took place between the plan and a party-in-interest (see instructions), check "Yes" and enter amount. Otherwise, check "No." | Yes | Amount | No
a Sale, exchange, or lease of property | 10a |
b Loan or extension of credit | 10b |
c Acquisition or holding of employer securities | 10c |
d Payment by the plan for services | 10d |

| | Yes | No |

11a Does your business have any employees other than you and your spouse (and your partners and their spouses)? . . . .
If "No," do NOT complete the rest of this question; go to question 12.
b Total number of employees (including you and your spouse and your partners and their spouses) ▶ _____
c Does this plan meet the coverage test of Code section 410(b)? . . . .
See the specific instructions for line 11c.

12 Answer these questions only if there was a benefit payment, loan, or distribution of an annuity contract made during the plan year and the plan is subject to the spousal consent requirements (see instructions).
a Was there consent of the participant's spouse to any benefit payment or loan within the 90-day period prior to such payment or loan?
b If "No," check the reason for no consent: *(i)* ☐ the participant was not married
(ii) ☐ the benefit payment made was part of a qualified joint and survivor annuity *(iii)* ☐ other
c Were any annuity contracts purchased by the plan and distributed to the participants? . . . .

Under penalties of perjury and other penalties set forth in the instructions, I declare that I have examined this return, including accompanying schedules and statements, and to the best of my knowledge and belief, it is true, correct, and complete

Signature of employer/plan sponsor ▶ Susan Turner   Date ▶ 7/29/91

For Paperwork Reduction Act Notice, see page 1 of the instructions.   Form **5500EZ** (1990)
1/2/91 page 748,195

SCHEDULE B (Form 5500) Department of the Treasury Internal Revenue Service Department of Labor Pension and Welfare Benefits Administration Pension Benefit Guaranty Corporation	**Actuarial Information** This schedule is required to be filed under section 104 of the Employee Retirement Income Security Act of 1974, referred to as ERISA, and section 6059(a) of the Internal Revenue Code, referred to as the Code. ▶ **Attach to Form 5500, 5500-C/R, or 5500EZ if applicable.** ▶ **See separate instructions.**	OMB No. 1210-0016 19**90** This Form Is Open to Public Inspection

For calendar plan year 1990 or fiscal plan year beginning _____, 1990, and ending _____, 19 ____

▶ **Read the specific Instructions** before attempting to complete this form.
▶ **Please complete every Item on this form. If an item does not apply, enter "N/A."** ▶ **Round off amounts to nearest dollar.**
▶ **Caution: A penalty of $1,000 will be assessed for late filing of this report unless reasonable cause is established.**

Name of plan sponsor as shown on line 1a of Form 5500, 5500-C/R, or 5500EZ
JOHN JONES

Employer identification number
13 : 1234567

Name of plan
JOHN JONES DEFINED BENEFIT PLAN

Enter three-digit plan number ▶ **00:2**

		Yes	No
1	Has a waiver of a funding deficiency for this plan year been approved by the IRS? . . . . If "Yes," attach a copy of the IRS approval letter.		✓
2	Is a waived funding deficiency of a prior plan year being amortized in this plan year?		✓
3	Have any of the periods of amortization for charges described in Code section 412(b)(2)(B) been extended by IRS? . . . If "Yes," attach a copy of the IRS approval letter.		✓
4a	Was the shortfall funding method the basis for this plan year's funding standard account computations?		✓
b	Is this plan a multiemployer plan which is, for this plan year, in reorganization as described in Code section 418 or ERISA section 4241? . . . If "Yes," you are required to attach the information described in the instructions.		✓
5	Has a change been made in funding method for this plan year? . . . . If "Yes," attach either a copy of the letter showing IRS approval or state the applicable Revenue Procedure authorizing approval if used.		✓

6 Operational information:
a Enter the most recent actuarial valuation date ▶ _____
b Enter date(s) and amount of contributions received this plan year for prior plan years and not previously reported:
  Date(s) ▶ _____ Amount ▶
c Current value of the assets accumulated in the plan as of the beginning of this plan year . . . . .

d Current liability as of beginning of plan year:	(1) No. of Persons	(2) Vested Benefits	(3) Total Benefits
(i) For retired participants and beneficiaries receiving payments			
(ii) For terminated vested participants			
(iii) For active participants			
(iv) Total			

e Expected current liability increase as of mo. __**1**__ day __**1**__ yr. __**90**__ attributable to benefits accruing during the plan year . . . .
f Expected benefit payments . . . .

7 Contributions made to the plan for the plan year by employer(s) and employees:

(a) Month Day Year	(b) Amount paid by employer	(c) Amount paid by employees	(a) Month Day Year	(b) Amount paid by employer	(c) Amount paid by employees
			Total . . .		

Statement by Enrolled Actuary (see instructions before signing):
To the best of my knowledge, the information supplied in this schedule and on the accompanying statements, if any, is complete and accurate, and in my opinion each assumption used in combination, represents my best estimate of anticipated experience under the plan. Furthermore, in the case of a plan other than a multiemployer plan, each assumption used (a) is reasonable (taking into account the experience of the plan and reasonable expectations) or (b) would, in the aggregate, result in a total contribution equivalent to that which would be determined if each such assumption were reasonable. In the case of a multiemployer plan, the assumptions used, in the aggregate, are reasonable (taking into account the experience of the plan and reasonable expectations).

Arthur E. Lewis .... Date **5/24/91**
Signature of actuary

Arthur E. Lewis .... Enrollment number **1147**
Print or type name of actuary

4545 DUKE ST. Bronx, N.Y. 10499 (**212**) **123-4567**
Firm name and address .... Telephone number (including area code)

For Paperwork Reduction Act Notice, see the instructions for Form 5500 ____ Schedule B (Form 5500) 1990

Schedule B (Form 5500) 1990   Page **2**

8 Funding standard account and other information:

a Accrued liability as determined for funding standard account as of (enter date) ▶ ....   N/A

b Value of assets as determined for funding standard account as of (enter date) ▶ .... \1/1/90   25,531

c Unfunded liability for spread-gain methods with bases as of (enter date) ▶ 1/1/90   28,907

d (i) Actuarial gains or (losses) for period ending ▶ ....   N/A

J (ii) Shortfall gains or (losses) for period ending ▶ ....

e Amount of contribution certified by the actuary as necessary to reduce the funding deficiency to zero, from
     9o or 10h (or the attachment for 4b if required)   0

9 Funding standard account statement for this plan year ending ▶ .... 12/31/90 ....

Charges to funding standard account:

a Prior year funding deficiency, if any . . . .

b Employer's normal cost for plan year as of mo. ..... 1 day ..1.. yr. ..90   1,417

c Amortization charges: Balance

       (i) Funding waivers (outstanding balance as of mo. .... day .... yr. ......▶$ ....)

       (ii) Other than waivers (outstanding balance as of mo. ...1... day ..1.. yr. ..90.▶$ .28,795...)   2,056

d Interest as applicable on a, b, and c   208

e Additional funding charge, if applicable (see line 13, page 3) . . . .

f Additional interest charge due to late quarterly contributions   3,681

g Total charges (add a through f)   4,888

Credits to funding standard account:

h Prior year credit balance, if any   5,516

I Employer contributions (total from column (b) of item 7) . . . .

J Amortization credits (outstanding balance as of mo. .... day .... yr. ......▶$ ....)

k Interest as applicable to end of plan year on h, I, and J   293

l Miscellaneous credits:

       (i) FFL credit before reflecting 150% of current liability component . . . . . _____

       (ii) Additional credit due to 150% of current liability component . . . . _____

       (iii) Waived funding deficiency . . . . _____

       (iv) Total . . . . _____

m Total credits (add h through l)   10,697

Balance:

n Credit balance: if m is greater than g, enter the difference   7,016

o Funding deficiency: if g is greater than m, enter the difference.   0

Reconciliation:

p Current year's accumulated reconciliation account:

       (i) Due to additional funding charge as of the beginning of the plan year . . . . _____

       (ii) Due to additional interest charges as of the beginning of the plan year . . . . _____

       (iii) Due to waived funding deficiency:

            (a) Reconciliation outstanding balance as of mo. .... day .... yr. ...... _____

            (b) Reconciliation amount (9c(I) balance minus 9p(III)(a)) . . . . . _____

       (iv) Total as of mo. ...... day ...... yr. ......

10 Alternative minimum funding standard account (omit if not used):

a Was the entry age normal cost method used to determine entries in line 9, above . . . .   ☐ Yes   ☒ No
     If "No," do not complete b through h.

b Prior year alternate funding deficiency, if any . . . . _____

c Normal cost . . . . _____

d Excess, if any, of value of accrued benefits over market value of assets . . . . _____   N/A

e Interest on b, c, and d . . . . _____

f Employer contributions (total from columns (b) of item 7) . . . . _____

g Interest on f . . . . _____

h Funding deficiency: if the sum of b through e is greater than the sum of f and g, enter difference . . . .

John Jones Defined Benefit Plan
002
13-1234567
Schedule B, Form 5500
Statement of Actuarial Assumptions and Methods
Year ending 12/31/90

I. ACTUARIAL ASSUMPTIONS

   A. Mortality
      UP 1984 Table
   B. Interest
      6% compounded annually
   C. Turnover
      0
   D. Assets
      Market Value

II. METHOD OF FUNDING

   Frozen Initial Liability Method

Eligibility—6 months service and 21st birthday

Retirement Date—Age 65

Annual Retirement Benefit—3.4% of compensation for each year of service

Ordinary Form of Retirement Benefits—Life

Disability Benefit—100% of present value of accrued benefit

Termination Benefit—100% vesting after 3 years of service

Death Benefit—Value of total prior contribution

SCHEDULE P (Form 5500)	Annual Return of Fiduciary of Employee Benefit Trust	OMB No. 1210-0016
Department of the Treasury Internal Revenue Service	▶ File as an attachment to Form 5500, 5500-C/R, or 5500EZ. ▶ For the Paperwork Reduction Notice, see page 1 of the Form 5500 instructions.	19**90**

For trust calendar year 1990 or fiscal year beginning _____ , 1990, and ending _____ , 19 _____

Please type or print

1a Name of trustee or custodian

John Jones

b Number, street, and room or suite no. (If a P.O. box, see the instructions for Form 5500, 5500-C/R, or 5500EZ.)

112 Fourteenth Avenue

c City or town, state, and ZIP code

New York, New York 10999

2 Name of trust

John Jones Defined Benefit Plan and Trust

3 Name of plan if different from name of trust

4 Have you furnished the participating employee benefit plan(s) with the trust financial information required to be reported by the plan(s)? . . . . ☒ Yes ☐ No

5 Enter the plan sponsor's employer identification number as shown on Form 5500, 5500-C/R, or 5500EZ . . . . ▶ 13 1234567

Under penalties of perjury, I declare that I have examined this schedule, and to the best of my knowledge and belief it is true, correct, and complete.

Signature of fiduciary ▶ 5/24/91   Date ▶ John Jones

Instructions

(Section references are to the Internal Revenue Code.)

A. Purpose of Form

You may use this schedule to satisfy the requirements under section 6033(a) for an annual information return from every section 401(a) organization exempt from tax under section 501(a).

Filing this form will start the running of the statute of limitations under section 6501(a) for any trust described in section 401(a), which is exempt from tax under section 501(a).

B. Who May File

(1) Every trustee of a trust created as part of an employee benefit plan as described in section 401(a).

(2) Every custodian of a custodial account described in section 401(f).

C. How To File

File Schedule P (Form 5500) for the trust year ending with or within any participating plan's plan year. Attach it to the Form 5500, 5500-C/R, or 5500EZ filed by the plan for that plan year.

Schedule P (Form 5500) must be filed only as an attachment to a Form 5500, 5500-C/R, or 5500EZ. A separately filed Schedule P (Form 5500) will not be accepted.

If the trust or custodial account is used by more than one plan, file one Schedule P (Form 5500). File it as an attachment to one of the participating plan's returns/reports. If a plan uses more than one trust or custodial account for its funds, file one Schedule P (Form 5500) for each trust or custodial account.

D. Signature

The fiduciary (trustee or custodian) must sign this schedule. If there is more than one fiduciary, one of them, authorized by the others, may sign.

E. Other Returns and Forms That May Be Required

(1) Form 990-T.—For trusts described in section 401(a), a tax is imposed on income derived from business that is unrelated to the purpose for which the trust received a tax exemption. Report such income and tax on **Form 990-T,** Exempt Organization Business Income Tax Return. (See sections 511 through 514 and the related regulations.)

(2) Forms W-2P and 1099-R.—If you made payments or distributions to individual beneficiaries of a plan, report these payments on Forms W-2P or 1099-R. (See sections 6041 and 6047 and the related regulations.)

(3) Forms 941 or 941E.—If you made payments or distributions to individual beneficiaries of a plan, you are required to withhold income tax from those payments unless the payee elects not to have the tax withheld. Report any withholding tax on Form 941 or 941E. (See Form 941 or 941E, and Circular E, Pub. 15.)

Schedule P (Form 5500) 1990

Form **SS-4** — Application for Employer Identification Number

(Rev. April 1991)
Department of the Treasury
Internal Revenue Service

(For use by employers and others. Please read the attached instructions before completing this form.)

EIN

OMB No. 1545-0003
Expires 4-30-94

1 Name of applicant (True legal name) (See instructions.) — *John Jones*

2 Trade name of business, if different from name in line 1

3 Executor, trustee, "care of" name

4a Mailing address (street address) (room, apt., or suite no.) — *112 Fourteenth Ave*

5a Address of business (See instructions.)

4b City, state, and ZIP code — *New York, N.Y. 10999*

5b City, state, and ZIP code

6 County and state where principal business is located — *New York, N.Y.*

7 Name of principal officer, grantor, or general partner (See instructions.) ▶ *JOHN JONES*

8a Type of entity (Check only one box.) (See instructions.)
☒ Individual SSN *123 45 6789*

9 Reason for applying (Check only one box.)
☒ Created a pension plan (specify type) ▶ *Defined Benefit*

10 Date business started or acquired (Mo., day, year) (See instructions.) — *6/3/85*

11 Enter closing month of accounting year. (See instructions.) — *DEC*

12 First date wages or annuities were paid or will be paid — *N/A*

13 Enter highest number of employees expected in the next 12 months. — Nonagricultural *0* Agricultural *0* Household *0*

14 Principal activity (See instructions.) ▶ *CONSULTING*

15 Is the principal business activity manufacturing? ☒ No

16 To whom are most of the products or services sold? ☐ Public (retail)

17a Has the applicant ever applied for an identification number for this or any other business? ☒ No

Name and title (Please type or print clearly.) ▶ *John Jones*

Telephone number (include area code) — *212-765-4321*

Signature ▶ *John Jones*   Date ▶ *4/4/91*

JOHN JONES
DEFINED BENEFIT PLAN AND TRUST
DESIGNATION OF BENEFICIARY FORM

I hereby designate as the beneficiary of any amount payable under the plan by reason of my death (hereby revoking and rescinding any designation heretofore made by me):

1. (   ) My spouse _____

2. (√) My spouse <u>Janet Jones</u>   , if living at the time of my death and if my spouse is not then living, then to my issue, as provided in paragraph 3 below.

3. (   ) My surviving issue, to be divided into as many shares as there are children of mine who survive me, plus children of mine who are deceased at the time of my death but who have issue who survive me; and one of these shares shall be paid to each of my children who survive me and one of such shares shall be paid to the surviving issue of each then deceased child of mine, per stirpes.

4. (   ) Other: (Name) _____ ,
whose address is _____ ,
if living at the time of my death, or if not, then _____
whose address is _____ .

EXECUTED this _____16_____ day of __November__ ,
19 _90_ .

WITNESS: _____ EMPLOYEE _John. Jones_

_____ S.S. No. _898-44-4321_
Birth date ___7/6/40_____

Form **1040**	Department of the Treasury - Internal Revenue Service **U.S. Individual Income Tax Return** 19**90**	(0)		

For the year Jan.–Dec. 31, 1990, or other tax year beginning _____ , 1990, ending _____ , 19 ____ OMB No. 1545-0074

Label (See Instructions on page 8) Use IRS label. Otherwise, please print or type.	Your first name and initial Last name *Peter Thorn*	Your social security number
	If a joint return, spouse's first name and initial Last name	Spouse's social security number
	Home address (number and street) (If you have a P.O. box, see page 9) Apt. no	**For Privacy Act and Paperwork Reduction Act Notice, see Instructions.**
	City, town or post office, state, and ZIP code (If you have a foreign address, see page 9)	

Presidential Election Campaign (See page 9.) ▶ Do you want $1 to go to this fund? . . . . . | Yes | No
If joint return, does your spouse want $1 to go to this fund? . . | Yes | No

Note: Checking "Yes" will not change your tax or reduce your refund.

Filing Status

Check only one box

1 ☐ Single (See page 10 to find out if you can file as head of household.)
2 ☐ Married filing joint return (even if only one had income)
3 ☐ Married filing separate return. Enter spouse's social security no. above and full name here. ▶ ____
4 ☐ Head of household (with qualifying person). (See page 10.) If the qualifying person is your child but not your dependent, enter this child's name here. ▶ ____
5 ☐ Qualifying widow(er) with dependent child (year spouse died ▶ 19 ____). (See page 10.)

Exemptions

(See Instructions on page 10)

If more than 6 dependents, see Instructions on page 11

6a ☐ **Yourself** If your parent (or someone else) can claim you as a dependent on his or her tax return, do not check box 6a. But be sure to check the box on line 33b on page 2 .
b ☐ **Spouse** . . . .
c **Dependents:**

(1) Name (first, initial, and last name)	(2) Check if under age 2	(3) If age 2 or older, dependent's social security number	(4) Dependent's relationship to you	(5) No. of months lived in your home in 1990

No. of boxes checked on 6a and 6b ____
No. of your children on 6c who:
• lived with you
• didn't live with you due to divorce or separation (see page 11)
No. of other dependents on 6c ____
Add numbers entered on lines above ▶

d If your child didn't live with you but is claimed as your dependent under a pre-1985 agreement, check here ▶ ☐
e Total number of exemptions claimed . . . .

Income

Attach Copy B of your Forms W-2, W-2G, and W-2P here.

If you do not have a W-2, see page 8.

Attach check or money order on top of any Forms W-2, W-2G, or W-2P.

7	Wages, salaries, tips, etc. (attach Form(s) W-2)	7	
8a	**Taxable** interest income (also attach Schedule B if over $400) .	8a	
b	Tax-exempt interest income (see page 13) DON'T include on line 8a	8b	
9	Dividend income (also attach Schedule B if over $400)	9	
10	Taxable refunds of state and local income taxes, if any, from worksheet on page 14	10	
11	Alimony received	11	
12	Business income or (loss) (attach Schedule C)	12	*30,000*
13	Capital gain or (loss) (attach Schedule D)	13	
14	Capital gain distributions not reported on line 13 (see page 14).	14	
15	Other gains or (losses) (attach Form 4797)	15	
16a	Total IRA distributions . 16a ____ 16b Taxable amount (see page 14)	16b	
17a	Total pensions and annuities 17a ____ 17b Taxable amount (see page 14)	17b	
18	Rents, royalties, partnerships, estates, trusts, etc. (attach Schedule E) . .	18	
19	Farm income or (loss) (attach Schedule F)	19	
20	Unemployment compensation (insurance) (see page 16) . . .	20	
21a	Social security benefits . 21a ____ 21b Taxable amount (see page 16)	21b	
22	Other income (list type and amount—see page 16)	22	
23	Add the amounts shown in the far right column for lines 7 through 22. This is your **total income ▶**	23	

Adjustments to Income

(See Instructions on page 17.)

24a	Your IRA deduction, from applicable worksheet on page 17 or 18	24a		
b	Spouse's IRA deduction, from applicable worksheet on page 17 or 18	24b		
25	One-half of self-employment tax (see page 18)	25		
26	Self-employed health insurance deduction, from worksheet on page 18	26		
27	Keogh retirement plan and self-employed SEP deduction .	27	*6,000*	
28	Penalty on early withdrawal of savings	28		
29	Alimony paid. Recipient's SSN ▶	29		
30	Add lines 24a through 29. These are your **total adjustments** . . . . . . ▶	30	

Adjusted Gross Income

31 Subtract line 30 from line 23. This is your **adjusted gross income.** If this amount is less than $20,264 and a child lived with you, see page 23 to find out if you can claim the "Earned Income Credit" on line 57 . . . . ▶ | 31 |

12/18/90 page 728,111

SUMMARY ANNUAL REPORT FOR THE JOHN JONES DEFINED-BENEFIT PLAN

This is a summary of the annual report for the John Jones Defined Benefit Plan for 1990. The annual report has been filed with the Internal Revenue Service, as required under the Employee Retirement Income Security Act of 1974 (ERISA).

Basic Financial Statement

Benefits under the plan are provided by a trust. Plan expenses were $0. These expenses included $0 in benefits paid to participants and beneficiaries and $0 in other expenses. A total of 1 persons were participants in or beneficiaries of the plan at the end of the plan year, although not all of these persons had yet earned the right to receive benefits.

The value of plan assets, after subtracting liabilities of the plan, was $32,318 as of December 31, 1990, compared to $25,531 as of January 1, 1990. During the plan year the plan experienced an increase in its net assets of $6,787. This increase includes unrealized appreciation or depreciation in the value of plan assets; that is, the difference between the value of the plan's assets at the end of the year and the value of the assets at the beginning of the year or the cost of assets acquired during the year. The plan had total income of $6,787, including employer contributions of $5,000, employee contributions of $0, gains of $0 from the sale of assets, and earnings from investments of $1,787.

Minimum Funding Standards

An actuary's statement shows that enough money was contributed to the plan to keep it funded in accordance with the minimum funding standards of ERISA.

Your Rights to Additional Information

You have the right to receive a copy of the full annual report or any part thereof on request. The item listed below is included in that report:

Actuarial information regarding the funding of the plan.

To obtain a copy of the full annual report or any part thereof, write or call the office of John Jones, who is the plan administrator, 112 Fourteenth Avenue, New York, NY 12222, (212) 765-4321. The charge to cover copying costs will be $0 for the full annual report, or $0 per page for any part thereof.

You also have the right to receive from the plan administrator, on request and at no charge, a statement of the assets and liabilities of the plan and accompanying notes, a statement of income and expenses of the plan and accompanying notes, or both. If you request a copy of the full annual report from the plan administrator, these two statements and accompanying notes will be included as part of that report.

You also have the legally protected right to examine the annual report at the main office of the plan, 112 Fourteenth Avenue, New York, NY, and at the U.S. Department of Labor in Washington, D.C., or to obtain a copy from the U.S. Department of Labor upon payment of copying costs.

Requests to the Department should be addressed to: Public Disclosure Room, N4677, Pension and Welfare Benefit Programs, Department of Labor, 200 Constitution Avenue, NW, Washington, D.C. 20216.

CHAPTER 17

COMPUTING YOUR KEOGH WEALTH: HOW TO DO YOUR OWN CALCULATIONS

I'm no mathematician, no statistician, no accountant, no actuary. I have no special skill with numbers. If I dare to explain how you can do your own computations for your own Keogh planning, it's because it's something anyone can learn.

The tools you will need, apart from pencil and paper, are a pocket calculator and a book of compound interest and annuity tables. Such books are available in general libraries as well as in hard cover and paperback in most bookstores. I have used *Comprehensive Compound Interest Tables,* Sherman (Contemporary Books, Inc.). Tables taken from that book, with permission of the publisher, appear beginning on page 191.

Pensions or annuities are usually figured and paid on a monthly basis—for example, as $800 per month rather than $9,600 per year. On the other hand, Keogh owners rarely pay into their plans on a monthly basis. More often the payments are made two or three times during the year, sometimes corresponding to when funds are received from self-employment work.

Rates of return on investment are sometimes calculated or paid on a daily or monthly basis (such as certificates of deposit), sometimes quarterly (as with dividends on stocks), and sometimes semiannually (such as bond interest).

For convenience—mine and, I hope, yours—all payments, annuities, and rates of return in these pages are on an annual basis, with annual compounding, except as otherwise noted.

Books of compound interest and annuity tables will show annual compounding and compounding for shorter periods, usually monthly, quarterly, and semiannually. Be sure you are using a table reflecting the proper compounding period.

FIGURING WHAT YOUR KEOGH WEALTH WILL BE AT ANY DATE

For this computation, you first must answer three questions:

a. How much will I put in each year?
b. What rate of return (interest rate) will I receive on my money?
c. For how many years?

Up to now my calculations have assumed the moonlighter puts in the same amount each year and gets the same rate of return throughout the period. I'll show how to figure this way first and then how to figure assuming changes in contributions or interest rates.

Exercise 1:

a. Amount put in each year: $4,000.
b. Interest rate: 10 percent.
c. Number of years: 20.

To solve, use the "Future Value Per Period" table,[1] (Your compound interest book might call this "Amount of 1 per Annum at Compound Interest.") Find the column in that table for the interest rate involved (here, 10 percent). Look down the row for the number of years involved (here, 20).

The figure where the years row intersects with the interest column—here, 57.2749—is what $1 per annum grows to at 10 percent in 20 years. Since you are investing $4,000 a year, multiply this number by $4,000. The result, $229,099, is your answer.

---

[1] Table 1 at the end of this chapter.

Exercise 2: To vary the assumptions, you will put in $4,000 a year for eight years. That will earn at the rate of 10 percent for that period. Then from the 9th through the 20th year you will put in $5,000 a year. That money, plus all previous investments, will earn at the rate of 8 percent a year from the ninth year.

First step:

a. Amount put in each year: $4,000.
b. Interest rate: 10 percent.
c. Number of years [at rate in (b)]: 8.

To solve, use the "Future Value Per Period" table. Intersection of (b) and (c) yields 11.4358. 11.4358 × $4,000 equals $45,743, the Keogh fund after eight years at 10 percent.

Second step:

a. Amount put in each year in years 9 to 20: $5,000.
b. Interest rate: 8 percent.
c. Number of years [at rate in (b)]: 12.

To solve, use the "Future Value Per Period" table.[2] Intersection of (b) and (c) yields 18.9771. 18.9771 × $5,000 = $94,886.

Third step: Find what the amount in the first step has grown to, invested at 8 percent for 12 years.

To solve, use the "Future Value" table[3] (sometimes called "Compound Amount of 1.") Find the column for 8 percent and the row for 12 years. The number where these intersect is 2.5181. This is what *1* becomes at 8 percent in 12 years. Multiply this by the $45,753 from the first step. The result is $115,185.

The answer to exercise 2 is $210,071, that is, $94,886 from the second step plus $115,185 from the third step.

You use those computations to figure what your Keogh wealth will be with a money-purchase pension plan, a profit-sharing plan, or both. Peter and Elaine use the computation in exercise 1.

---

[2] Table 2 at the end of this chapter.
[3] Table 11 at the end of this chapter.

FIGURING WHAT A GIVEN ANNUITY WILL COST FOR YOUR LIFE EXPECTANCY

Figuring this requires answers to these questions:

a. How much do I want each year?
b. At what age will the annuity start?
c. What is my life expectancy at that time?
d. What interest rate does the annuity pay?

In these pages I have assumed you are buying your annuity when you retire. If that's what you mean to do, you must, one way or another, come up with an answer to all of these questions. On the other hand, you could start buying your annuity now if you go into an insured plan. If you know how much you want and when you want to start collecting it, insurance companies can quote you a price today. You can pay for it each year in installments over whatever period you choose, up to the time the annuity is to start.

But let's say that you don't want an insured plan. You might still want to know what insurance companies are currently charging. This would give you *an idea* of what your annuity would cost when you retire *if* interest rates and life expectancies are at that time about what they are now. Examples from several companies appear on page 193.

Exercise 1: Find the amount the X Insurance Company charges for a single life annuity of $12,000 starting at age 62.

a. Amount each year: $12,000.
b. Age when payment starts: 62.
c. Life expectancy: Built into insurance company table.
d. Interest rate: Built into insurance company table.

To solve, use the "Single Premium Immediate Annuities" table.[4] Find the age column and the row for the insurance company of your choice. Assume that's Washington National. Tables are by sex; assume the moonlighter is male. As noted in Chapter 9, insur-

---

[4] Table 3 at the end of this chapter. Company sales charges and related expenses are ignored in this calculation.

ance companies sell annuities in multiples of $10 a month. Convert the annual pension to monthly ($1,000 a month) and divide by 10, which equals $100. Multiply this by annuity cost per $10 monthly (here, $1,024). The result, $102,400, is your answer for $12,000 a year paid monthly.

But you may want to run your own computation. You may believe that interest rates will be higher or lower when you retire than they are today.

Or you may believe that life expectancies when you come to retire will be longer than now. So you might choose to run your computation using one of the tables showing somewhat longer life expectancies than those currently in standard use. So now for how to figure the cost of an annuity using *your own* interest assumptions and *your own* choice of life expectancy.

Exercise 2: Find the amount you will need to buy an annuity of $12,000 for your life expectancy, starting at age 62 and assuming a 7 percent interest rate.

    a. Amount each year: $12,000.
    b. Age when payment starts: 62.
    c. Life expectancy: 17.

You may select life expectancy from a variety of mortality tables. Tables can be by sex, or they can be unisex. The figure 17 is from a unisex table.

    d. Interest rate: 7 percent.

To solve, use the "Present Value Per Period" table.[5] Find the column in the table for the interest rate (here, 7 percent). Look down the row for the number of years (here, 17).

The figure where the years row intersects with the interest column (here, 9.7632) is what you would pay for an annuity of $1 a year for 17 years. Since you want an annuity of $12,000, multiply 9.7632 by $12,000. The result, $117,158, is your answer.

You can find tables that combine items (c) and (d). For example, unisex pension (UP) 1984 tables combine interest rate with life

---

[5] Table 4 at the end of this chapter.

expectancy, merging figures for both sexes. That table[6] yields $112,729 as the cost of a $12,000 annuity, paid $1,000 a month, regardless of sex, for a person age 62 using a 7 percent interest rate. Of course, if you decide to use UP 1984, it means you are selecting the life expectancies contemplated in those tables.

You would use one of those computations to figure what your defined-benefit pension would cost you at retirement. Putting this thought another way, you use the computation to figure how high you can build your defined-benefit Keogh.

Exercise 3: Find the amount you will need to buy an annuity of $10,000 for your life and then for the life of your spouse if he or she survives you. The annuity assumes a 7 percent interest rate and will start when you are age 65 and your spouse is age 63.

  a. Amount each year: $10,000.
  b. Age when payment starts: 65 and 63.
  c. Life expectancy: 26.
  d. Interest rate: 7 percent.

Figuring the cost of a joint-and-survivor annuity is the same as for a single life annuity except for using a joint-and-survivor life expectancy. Joint-and-survivor life expectancy is taken from the table "Ordinary Joint and Last Survivor Annuities; Two Lives— Expected Return Multiples,"[7] a unisex table. ("Expected return multiples" is another way of saying life expectancies.)

The figure where the column for age 65 intersects with the row for age 63 (here, 26) is their joint-and-survivor life expectancy.

To solve, use the "Present Value Per Period" table.[8] The figure where the column for the interest rate (7 percent) intersects with the years row (26) (here, 11.8257) is what you would pay for an annuity of $1 a year for 26 years. Since you want an annuity of $10,000, multiply 11.8257 by $10,000. The result, $118,257, is your answer.

This computation is used in defined-benefit plans to figure the cost of a joint-and-full survivor annuity. Harold would make such a

---

[6] Table 5 at the end of this chapter.
[7] Table 6 at the end of this chapter.
[8] Table 4 at the end of this chapter.

computation; the ages used in the life expectancy calculation are his and Judy's ages when Harold retires.

FIGURING ANNUAL CONTRIBUTIONS NEEDED TO REACH A GIVEN SUM

You intend to invest an amount at interest each year to build toward a given sum (your goal).

    a. Your goal.
    b. Your interest rate.
    c. Number of years.

Exercise: Find the amount needed each year for 15 years at 9 percent to reach $120,000.

    a. Goal: $120,000.
    b. Interest rate: 9 percent.
    c. Number of years: 15.

To solve, use the "Sinking Fund" table[9] (sometimes called "Annuity Whose Accumulation at Compound Interest Is 1.") Find the column for the interest rate involved (here, 9 percent). Look down the row for the number of years involved (here, 15). The figure where the years row intersects with the interest column (here, .0340) is what you would need to put in each year to reach $1. Since your goal is $120,000, multiply this number by $120,000. The result, $4,080, is your answer.

This calculation is used in defined-benefit plans. The moonlighter will first have computed the amount needed to buy a particular annuity (page 182). He or she then makes *this* computation to figure how much must be put in each year, on a level basis, to reach that sum. Harold makes this computation.

More complex computations are required if you want the smallest contribution possible or if you would rather front-load your contributions. These are illustrated on pages 54–57.

---

[9] Table 7 at the end of this chapter.

FIGURING THE PENSION A GIVEN SUM WILL BUY

Figuring the pension you would get, starting immediately, with a given investment, requires this information:

    a. Amount to be invested.
    b. Interest rate.
    c. Life expectancy (period over which pension will be paid).

Exercise:

    a. Amount to be invested: $100,000.
    b. Interest rate: 7.5 percent.
    c. Life expectancy: 15 years (taken from Table 8 at the end of this chapter and rounded to the nearest full year)

To solve, use the "Partial Payment to Amortize" table[10] (sometimes called "Annuity Whose Present Value at Compound Interest Is 1.") The figure where the interest column for 7.5 percent intersects the years row for 15 (here, the figure is .1132) is the pension that $1 would buy at 7.5 percent. Multiply this by $100,000. The result, $11,320, is your answer.

This calculation could be used, for example, to find the pension that a money-purchase or profit-sharing Keogh fund could buy at retirement and so might be used by Peter or Elaine.

FIGURING WHAT A GIVEN INVESTMENT WILL GROW TO OVER A PERIOD

To figure this, you need to provide:

    a. The amount invested.
    b. The rate of interest.
    c. Number of years invested.

Exercise:
You have an investment fund of $150,000 that you will invest for five years at 10 percent.

---

[10] Table 9 at the end of this chapter.

a. Amount invested: $150,000.

b. Rate: 10 percent.

c. Number of years invested: five.

To solve this exercise, use the "Future Value" table.[11] Find the column in the table for the interest rate involved (here, 10 percent). Look down the row for the number of years involved (here, five). The figure where the years row intersects with the interest column (here, 1.6105) is what $1 would grow to at 10 percent for five years. Since you have $150,000, you multiply 1.6105 by $150,000. The result, $241,575 is your answer.

You make this computation when no further contributions will be made to the Keogh and no withdrawals will be made for some years. Such computations are made when a Keogh plan is frozen, to compute what the frozen funds will grow to at retirement. Peter would make such a computation. He froze his profit-sharing plan when he set up his money-purchase plan. Such computations also are made when the moonlighter ceases moonlighting at a younger age but postpones withdrawal until age 70½, to maximize the Keogh tax shelter (page 121). And they are made when defined-benefit plans are fully funded before the moonlighter retires (page 28).

FIGURING THE AMOUNT NEEDED TO PAY OFF (AMORTIZE) A GIVEN SUM

You make this calculation if you will give credit for past service in a defined-benefit pension plan (see Chapter 6). To figure this, you need:

a. The amount your fund would have today if you had contributed level amounts from the start.

b. The number of years you intend to pay off this amount.

c. The rate of interest.

Exercise: You will start your defined-benefit plan this year. It will run for 11 years, and you mean to give yourself credit for 9 years of past service in your business.

---

[11] Table 12 at the end of this chapter.

You have determined your "normal cost," the level amount to put in each year over 20 years. (This is done under "Figuring Annual Contributions Needed to Reach a Given Sum.") Using this normal cost, you have determined what that sum each year would grow to in nine years (under "Figuring What Your Keogh Wealth Will Be at Any Date"). That amount is $40,000. You will pay off $40,000 over 10 years at 6.5 percent.

   a. Amount your fund should have: $40,000.
   b. Number of years to pay off: 10.
   c. Interest rate: 6.5 percent.

To solve, use the "Partial Payment to Amortize" table.[12]

Find the column for the interest rate (here, 6.5 percent). Look down the row for the number of years involved (here, 10). The figure where the years row intersects with the interest column (here, .1391) is what you would have to pay each year at 6.5 percent interest to pay off a debt of $1 in 10 years. Since your "debt" is $40,000, you multiply .1391 by $40,000. The result, $5,564 is your answer.

This amount, your annual past service cost, is added to the normal cost you determined to arrive at your annual contribution (for 10 years) where you give credit for past service.

FIGURING THE AFTER-TAX RETURN ON A GIVEN INVESTMENT

In these pages I have often compared what your investment reaches tax-free in a Keogh with what you would have in a taxable investment. To compute after-tax return on a taxable investment, you need to know.

   a. Amount invested.
   b. Period invested.
   c. The investor's tax bracket[13] over that period.
   d. The pre-tax percentage rate of investment return.

---

[12] Table 12 at the end of this chapter.
[13] The tax bracket is rarely constant throughout the period. Treat this as an average.

Exercise 1:

a. Amount invested: $10,000.

b. Period invested: 10 years.

c. Tax bracket: 35 percent. (See Chapter 19 for more information on tax brackets.)

d. Pre-tax rate of investment return: 10 percent.

For all three of these exercises, you must find the *after-tax* rate of investment return. That is the percentage left after taxes—here, 65 percent (100 percent minus 35 percent)—times the pre-tax investment return—here, 10 percent. So the after-tax rate is 6.5 percent (65 percent times 10 percent).

Now, to solve, use the "Future Value" table.[14] Look down to where the interest rate column for 6.5 percent intersects with the years row for 10 years. The result (here, 1.8771) shows what 1 grows to at 6.5 percent for 10 years. Since you have $10,000, multiply by $10,000. The result, $18,771, is your answer.

Exercise 2: Find what a given amount invested *each year* earns after tax.

a. Amount invested each year: $1,500.

b. Number of years invested: 10.

c. Tax bracket: 35 percent.

d. Pre-tax rate of investment return: 10 percent.

The after-tax rate is found the same way as in Exercise 1. Exercise 2 is solved the same way as on page 180 (with the "Future Value Per Period" table) but using 6.5 percent instead of 10 percent and 10 years instead of 20. The result using 6.5 percent for 10 years is $20,242.

Exercise 3: These pages also have pointed out that moonlighters have more to invest with a Keogh than without one. They pay no tax on the money put into the Keogh (until they collect, years later). Their non-Keogh investments are made with funds from which tax has been taken.

---

[14] Table 10 at the end of this chapter.

Thus, $4,000 earned by a person in the 35 percent bracket becomes $2,600 available for investment after tax.

a. Amount invested each year: $2,600.
b. Number of years invested: 15.
c. Tax bracket: 35 percent.
d. Pre-tax rate of investment return: 10 percent.

After-tax rate is 6.5 percent. Solve the same way as in exercise 2 but using 15 years and $2,600. Result is $62,873.

Compare investing $4,000 in a Keogh:

a. Amount invested each year: $4,000.
b. Number of years invested: 15.
c. Tax bracket: 0.
d. Pre-tax rate of investment return: 10 percent.

After-tax rate is also 10 percent. Solve the same way as in exercise 3 except for using 10 percent instead of 6.5 percent and $4,000 instead of $2,600. The result is $127,089. Tax must be paid on this when it is withdrawn. For tax on withdrawals, see Chapter 14.

TABLE 1

	FUTURE VALUE PER PERIOD					ANNUAL
SECTION 2						COMPOUNDING

YRS	9.75% ANNUAL RATE	10.00% ANNUAL RATE	10.25% ANNUAL RATE	10.50% ANNUAL RATE	10.75% ANNUAL RATE	11.00% ANNUAL RATE	YRS
1	1.000 000	1.000 000	1.000 000	1.000 000	1.000 000	1.000 000	1
2	2.097 500	2.100 000	2.102 500	2.105 000	2.107 500	2.110 000	2
3	3.302 006	3.310 000	3.318 006	3.326 025	3.334 056	3.342 100	3
4	4.623 952	4.641 000	4.658 102	4.675 258	4.692 467	4.709 731	4
5	6.074 787	6.105 100	6.135 557	6.166 160	6.196 908	6.227 801	5
6	7.667 079	7.715 610	7.764 452	7.813 606	7.863 075	7.912 860	6
7	9.414 619	9.487 171	9.560 308	9.634 035	9.708 356	9.783 274	7
8	11.332 544	11.435 888	11.540 240	11.645 609	11.752 004	11.859 434	8
9	13.437 468	13.579 477	13.723 114	13.868 398	14.015 344	14.163 972	9
10	15.747 621	15.937 425	16.129 734	16.324 579	16.521 994	16.722 009	10
11	18.283 014	18.531 167	18.783 031	19.038 660	19.298 108	19.561 430	11
12	21.065 607	21.384 284	21.708 292	22.037 720	22.372 655	22.713 187	12
13	24.119 504	24.522 712	24.933 392	25.351 680	25.777 715	26.211 638	13
14	27.471 156	27.974 983	28.489 065	29.013 607	29.548 820	30.094 918	14
15	31.149 594	31.772 482	32.409 194	33.060 035	33.725 318	34.405 359	15
16	35.186 679	35.949 730	36.731 136	37.531 339	38.350 789	39.189 948	16
17	39.617 380	40.544 703	41.496 078	42.472 130	43.473 499	44.500 843	17
18	44.480 075	45.599 173	46.749 426	47.931 703	49.146 900	50.395 936	18
19	49.816 882	51.159 090	52.541 242	53.964 532	55.430 192	56.939 488	19
20	55.674 028	57.274 999	58.926 719	60.630 808	62.388 938	64.202 832	20
21	62.102 246	64.002 499	65.966 708	67.997 043	70.095 749	72.265 144	21
22	69.157 215	71.402 749	73.728 295	76.136 732	78.631 042	81.214 309	22
23	76.900 043	79.543 024	82.285 446	85.131 089	88.083 879	91.147 884	23
24	85.397 797	88.497 327	91.719 704	95.069 854	98.552 895	102.174 151	24
25	94.724 083	98.347 059	102.120 974	106.052 188	110.147 332	114.413 307	25
26	104.959 681	109.181 765	113.588 373	118.187 668	122.988 170	127.998 771	26
27	116.193 249	121.099 942	126.231 182	131.597 373	137.209 398	143.078 636	27
28	128.522 091	134.209 936	140.169 878	146.415 097	152.959 408	159.817 286	28
29	142.052 995	148.630 930	155.537 290	162.788 683	170.402 545	178.397 187	29
30	156.903 162	164.494 023	172.479 862	180.881 494	189.720 818	199.020 878	30
31	173.201 221	181.943 425	191.159 048	200.874 051	211.115 806	221.913 174	31
32	191.088 340	201.137 767	211.752 851	222.965 827	234.810 756	247.323 624	32
33	210.719 453	222.251 544	234.457 518	247.377 238	261.052 912	275.529 222	33
34	232.264 599	245.476 699	259.489 414	274.351 848	290.116 100	306.837 437	34
35	255.910 398	271.024 368	287.087 078	304.158 792	322.303 581	341.589 555	35
36	281.861 661	299.126 805	317.513 504	337.095 466	357.951 215	380.164 406	36
37	310.343 173	330.039 486	351.058 638	373.490 489	397.430 971	422.982 490	37
38	341.601 633	364.043 434	388.042 148	413.706 991	441.154 801	470.510 564	38
39	375.907 792	401.447 778	428.816 469	458.146 225	489.578 942	523.266 726	39
40	413.558 802	442.592 556	473.770 157	507.251 579	543.208 678	581.826 066	40
41	454.880 785	487.851 811	523.331 598	561.512 994	602.603 611	646.826 934	41
42	500.231 662	537.636 992	577.973 087	621.471 859	668.383 499	718.977 896	42
43	550.004 249	592.400 692	638.215 328	687.726 404	741.234 725	799.065 465	43
44	604.629 663	652.640 761	704.632 399	760.937 676	821.917 458	887.962 666	44
45	664.581 055	718.904 837	777.857 220	841.836 132	911.273 585	986.638 559	45
46	730.377 708	791.795 321	858.587 585	931.228 926	1010.235 495	1096.168 801	46
47	802.589 534	871.974 853	947.592 813	1030.007 963	1119.835 811	1217.747 369	47
48	881.842 014	960.172 338	1045.721 076	1139.158 800	1241.218 160	1352.699 580	48
49	968.821 610	1057.189 572	1153.907 486	1259.770 473	1375.649 113	1502.496 533	49
50	1064.281 717	1163.908 529	1273.183 003	1393.046 373	1524.531 392	1668.771 152	50

Source: Michael Sherman, *Comprehensive Compound Interest Tables* (Chicago: Contemporary Books, 1986), p. 87.

TABLE 2

	FUTURE VALUE PER PERIOD				ANNUAL COMPOUNDING	
SECTION 2						

YRS	6.75% ANNUAL RATE	7.00% ANNUAL RATE	7.25% ANNUAL RATE	7.50% ANNUAL RATE	7.75% ANNUAL RATE	8.00% ANNUAL RATE	YRS
1	1.000 000	1.000 000	1.000 000	1.000 000	1.000 000	1.000 000	1
2	2.067 500	2.070 000	2.072 500	2.075 000	2.077 500	2.080 000	2
3	3.207 056	3.214 900	3.222 756	3.230 625	3.238 506	3.246 400	3
4	4.423 533	4.439 943	4.456 406	4.472 922	4.489 490	4.506 112	4
5	5.722 121	5.750 739	5.779 496	5.808 391	5.837 426	5.866 601	5
6	7.108 364	7.153 291	7.198 509	7.244 020	7.289 827	7.335 929	6
7	8.588 179	8.654 021	8.720 401	8.787 322	8.854 788	8.922 803	7
8	10.167 881	10.259 803	10.352 630	10.446 371	10.541 034	10.636 628	8
9	11.854 213	11.977 989	12.103 196	12.229 849	12.357 964	12.487 558	9
10	13.654 372	13.816 448	13.980 677	14.147 087	14.315 707	14.486 562	10
11	15.576 042	15.783 599	15.994 276	16.208 119	16.425 174	16.645 487	11
12	17.627 425	17.888 451	18.153 861	18.423 728	18.698 125	18.977 126	12
13	19.817 276	20.140 643	20.470 016	20.805 508	21.147 229	21.495 297	13
14	22.154 942	22.550 488	22.954 093	23.365 921	23.786 140	24.214 920	14
15	24.650 401	25.129 022	25.618 264	26.118 365	26.629 566	27.152 114	15
16	27.314 303	27.888 054	28.475 588	29.077 242	29.693 357	30.324 283	16
17	30.158 019	30.840 217	31.540 069	32.258 035	32.994 592	33.750 226	17
18	33.193 685	33.999 033	34.826 724	35.677 388	36.551 673	37.450 244	18
19	36.434 259	37.378 965	38.351 661	39.353 192	40.384 428	41.446 263	19
20	39.893 571	40.995 492	42.132 156	43.304 681	44.514 221	45.761 964	20
21	43.586 387	44.865 177	46.186 738	47.552 532	48.964 073	50.422 921	21
22	47.528 468	49.005 739	50.535 276	52.118 972	53.758 788	55.456 755	22
23	51.736 640	53.436 141	55.199 084	57.027 895	58.925 035	60.893 296	23
24	56.228 863	58.176 671	60.201 017	62.304 987	64.491 789	66.764 759	24
25	61.024 311	63.249 038	65.565 591	67.977 862	70.489 903	73.105 940	25
26	66.143 452	68.676 470	71.319 096	74.076 201	76.952 870	79.954 415	26
27	71.608 135	74.483 823	77.489 731	80.631 916	83.916 718	87.350 768	27
28	77.441 684	80.697 691	84.107 736	87.679 310	91.420 264	95.338 830	28
29	83.668 998	87.346 529	91.205 547	95.255 258	99.505 334	103.965 936	29
30	90.316 655	94.460 786	98.817 949	103.399 403	108.216 997	113.283 211	30
31	97.413 030	102.073 041	106.982 251	112.154 358	117.603 815	123.345 868	31
32	104.988 409	110.218 154	115.738 464	121.565 935	127.718 110	134.213 537	32
33	113.075 127	118.933 425	125.129 503	131.683 380	138.616 264	145.950 620	33
34	121.707 698	128.258 765	135.201 392	142.559 633	150.359 024	158.626 670	34
35	130.922 967	138.236 878	146.003 492	154.251 606	163.011 849	172.316 804	35
36	140.760 268	148.913 460	157.588 746	166.820 476	176.645 267	187.102 148	36
37	151.261 586	160.337 402	170.013 930	180.332 012	191.335 275	203.070 320	37
38	162.471 743	172.561 020	183.339 940	194.856 913	207.163 759	220.315 945	38
39	174.438 566	185.640 292	197.632 085	210.471 181	224.218 950	238.941 221	39
40	187.213 190	199.635 112	212.960 411	227.256 520	242.595 919	259.056 519	40
41	200.850 080	214.609 570	229.400 041	245.300 759	262.397 103	280.781 040	41
42	215.407 461	230.632 240	247.031 544	264.698 315	283.732 878	304.243 523	42
43	230.947 464	247.776 496	265.941 331	285.550 689	306.722 176	329.583 005	43
44	247.536 418	266.120 851	286.222 078	307.966 991	331.493 145	356.949 646	44
45	265.245 127	285.749 311	307.973 178	332.064 515	358.183 864	386.505 617	45
46	284.149 173	306.751 763	331.301 234	357.969 354	386.943 113	418.426 067	46
47	304.329 242	329.224 386	356.320 573	385.817 055	417.931 204	452.900 152	47
48	325.871 466	353.270 093	383.153 815	415.753 334	451.320 873	490.132 164	48
49	348.867 789	378.999 000	411.932 466	447.934 835	487.298 240	530.342 737	49
50	373.416 365	406.528 929	442.797 570	482.529 947	526.063 854	573.770 156	50

Source: Michael Sherman, *Comprehensive Compound Interest Tables* (Chicago: Contemporary Books, 1986), p. 85.

TABLE 3

SINGLE PREMIUM IMMEDIATE ANNUITIES (Cont.)
$10 MONTHLY

Annuity Age		40	50	55	60	62	65	68	70	75	80
United Farm Bur Family, Gtd Cost; $100 pol fee											
LIFE	M	1389	1279	1209	1129	1093	1033	967	919	790	653
	F	1439	1355	1295	1221	1189	1133	1066	1016	873	714
IR	M	1401	1307	1248	1179	1148	1098	1042	1001	892	774
	F	1443	1368	1316	1252	1222	1172	1114	1071	951	820
United Founders, Ok, Gtd Cost; $75 pol fee*											
LIFE	M	1908	1704	1572	1420	1351	1239	1117	1033	820	621
	F	1984	1815	1704	1572	1515	1420	1316	1239	1033	820
IR	M	1931	1748	1634	1497	1437	1340	1239	1168	991	823
	F	2000	1848	1748	1634	1582	1497	1406	1340	1168	991
United of Omaha, Gtd Cost; $100*											
LIFE	M	1684	1525	1429	1304	1250	1165	1075	1013	857	711
	F	1743	1619	1534	1427	1376	1292	1201	1137	973	816
IR	M	1701	1558	1473	1357	1306	1226	1147	1096	973	863
	F	1758	1640	1565	1452	1401	1320	1240	1185	1051	934
USAA Life, Gtd Cost											
LIFE	M	1359	1255	1192	1117	1082	1027	965	923	809	691
	F	1404	1318	1261	1193	1163	1114	1057	1016	902	772
IR	M	1434	1335	1255	1167	1136	1086	1033	996	898	796
	F	1479	1393	1337	1252	1209	1160	1109	1072	971	859
Washington National Ins, Gtd Cost; $80 pol fee*											
LIFE		1254	1174	1121	1055	1024	974	918	879	771	655
IR		1258	1185	1136	1076	1049	1004	956	922	831	735
West Coast Life, Gtd Cost; $100 pol fee*											
LIFE	M	1757	1571	1459	1330	1272	1181	1085	1020	858	700
	F	1843	1685	1583	1462	1408	1322	1229	1164	987	804
Western Farm Bureau, Gtd Cost; $75 pol fee											
LIFE	M	1325	1233	1174	1103	1071	1016	955	910	789	657
	F	1362	1299	1248	1186	1157	1107	1048	1001	868	717
IR	M	1333	1258	1209	1149	1121	1075	1025	987	887	776
	F	1366	1311	1267	1214	1189	1144	1092	1053	942	818
Western Life, Mn, Gtd Cost*											
LIFE	M	1115	1064	1027	978	954	912	863	828	730	622
	F	1138	1104	1075	1036	1017	982	942	910	815	699
IR	M	1122	1078	1046	1004	983	949	909	881	803	717
	F	1141	1110	1086	1052	1035	1005	970	944	865	772
Western National, Gtd Cost; No policy fee*											
LIFE	M			1231	1151	1115	1055	989	941	812	674
	F	...		1315	1242	1209	1154	1088	1038	896	736
IR	M			1271	1203	1171	1121	1066	1026	919	802
	F			1337	1274	1244	1195	1137	1095	977	847
Western-Southern Companies, Gtd Cost *; $100 pol fee											
LIFE	M	1505	1428	1372	1304	1271	1221	1167	1132	1046	974
	F	1538	1480	1436	1378	1350	1303	1249	1210	1110	1014
Western States, Gtd Cost; $100 pol fee*											
LIFE	M	1623	1450	1346	1245	1197	1115	1031	975	830	680
	F	1692	1544	1449	1354	1312	1238	1151	1087	925	751
IR	M	1635	1489	1396	1299	1256	1188	1125	1083	966	843
	F	1698	1565	1478	1393	1354	1289	1217	1167	1038	901
William Penn Life, Gtd Cost; No pol fee											
LIFE	M	1372	1292	1238	1166	1132	1073	1009	963	839	708
	F	1399	1337	1292	1224	1197	1150	1093	1053	939	787

*ADD PREMIUM TAX WHERE APPLICABLE

Taken from *1988 Life Rates & Data,* published by the National Underwirter Co., Cincinnati, Ohio. Reproduced with permission of the publisher.

TABLE 4

	PRESENT VALUE PER PERIOD	ANNUAL

SECTION 5 — ANNUAL COMPOUNDING

YRS	6.75% ANNUAL RATE	7.00% ANNUAL RATE	7.25% ANNUAL RATE	7.50% ANNUAL RATE	7.75% ANNUAL RATE	8.00% ANNUAL RATE	YRS
1	0.936 768	0.934 579	0.932 401	0.930 233	0.928 074	0.925 926	1
2	1.814 303	1.808 018	1.801 772	1.795 565	1.789 396	1.783 265	2
3	2.636 349	2.624 316	2.612 375	2.600 526	2.588 767	2.577 097	3
4	3.406 416	3.387 211	3.368 182	3.349 326	3.330 642	3.312 127	4
5	4.127 790	4.100 197	4.072 897	4.045 885	4.019 157	3.992 710	5
6	4.803 551	4.766 540	4.729 974	4.693 846	4.658 151	4.622 880	6
7	5.436 581	5.389 289	5.342 633	5.296 601	5.251 184	5.206 370	7
8	6.029 584	5.971 299	5.913 877	5.857 304	5.801 563	5.746 639	8
9	6.585 091	6.515 232	6.446 505	6.378 887	6.312 355	6.246 888	9
10	7.105 471	7.023 582	6.943 128	6.864 081	6.786 409	6.710 081	10
11	7.592 947	7.498 674	7.406 180	7.315 424	7.226 365	7.138 964	11
12	8.049 600	7.942 686	7.837 930	7.735 278	7.634 678	7.536 078	12
13	8.477 377	8.357 651	8.240 495	8.125 840	8.013 622	7.903 776	13
14	8.878 105	8.745 468	8.615 846	8.489 154	8.365 310	8.244 237	14
15	9.253 494	9.107 914	8.965 824	8.827 120	8.691 703	8.559 479	15
16	9.605 146	9.446 649	9.292 143	9.141 507	8.994 620	8.851 369	16
17	9.934 563	9.763 223	9.596 404	9.433 960	9.275 750	9.121 638	17
18	10.243 151	10.059 087	9.880 097	9.706 009	9.536 659	9.371 887	18
19	10.532 225	10.335 595	10.144 612	9.959 078	9.778 802	9.603 599	19
20	10.803 021	10.594 014	10.391 247	10.194 491	10.003 528	9.818 147	20
21	11.056 695	10.835 527	10.621 209	10.413 480	10.212 091	10.016 803	21
22	11.294 327	11.061 240	10.835 626	10.617 191	10.405 653	10.200 744	22
23	11.516 934	11.272 187	11.035 549	10.806 689	10.585 293	10.371 059	23
24	11.725 465	11.469 334	11.221 957	10.982 967	10.752 012	10.528 758	24
25	11.920 811	11.653 583	11.395 764	11.146 946	10.906 740	10.674 776	25
26	12.103 804	11.825 779	11.557 822	11.299 485	11.050 338	10.809 978	26
27	12.275 226	11.986 709	11.708 925	11.441 381	11.183 609	10.935 165	27
28	12.435 809	12.137 111	11.849 814	11.573 378	11.307 293	11.051 078	28
29	12.586 238	12.277 674	11.981 178	11.696 165	11.422 082	11.158 406	29
30	12.727 155	12.409 041	12.103 663	11.810 386	11.528 614	11.257 783	30
31	12.859 162	12.531 814	12.217 867	11.916 638	11.627 484	11.349 799	31
32	12.982 821	12.646 555	12.324 352	12.015 478	11.719 243	11.434 999	32
33	13.098 662	12.753 790	12.423 638	12.107 421	11.804 402	11.513 888	33
34	13.207 177	12.854 009	12.516 213	12.192 950	11.883 436	11.586 934	34
35	13.308 831	12.947 672	12.602 529	12.272 511	11.956 785	11.654 568	35
36	13.404 057	13.035 208	12.683 011	12.346 522	12.024 858	11.717 193	36
37	13.493 262	13.117 017	12.758 052	12.415 370	12.088 036	11.775 179	37
38	13.576 826	13.193 473	12.828 021	12.479 414	12.146 669	11.828 869	38
39	13.655 107	13.264 928	12.893 259	12.538 989	12.201 085	11.878 582	39
40	13.728 437	13.331 709	12.954 088	12.594 409	12.251 587	11.924 613	40
41	13.797 131	13.394 120	13.010 805	12.645 962	12.298 456	11.967 235	41
42	13.861 481	13.452 449	13.063 687	12.693 918	12.341 955	12.006 699	42
43	13.921 762	13.506 962	13.112 995	12.738 528	12.382 325	12.043 240	43
44	13.978 231	13.557 908	13.158 970	12.780 026	12.419 791	12.077 074	44
45	14.031 130	13.605 522	13.201 837	12.818 629	12.454 562	12.108 402	45
46	14.080 684	13.650 020	13.241 806	12.854 539	12.486 833	12.137 409	46
47	14.127 104	13.691 608	13.279 073	12.887 943	12.516 782	12.164 267	47
48	14.170 589	13.730 474	13.313 821	12.919 017	12.544 577	12.189 136	48
49	14.211 325	13.766 799	13.346 220	12.947 922	12.570 373	12.212 163	49
50	14.249 485	13.800 746	13.376 429	12.974 812	12.594 314	12.233 485	50

Source: Michael Sherman, *Comprehensive Compared Interest Tables* (Chicago: Contemporary Books, 1986), p. 223.

TABLE 5

**ANNUITY PURCHASE RATES—
MALES AND FEMALES BASED UPON
THE 1984 UNISEX PENSION MORTALITY
TABLE WITH 7% INTEREST**

Cost of $1.00 Monthly Annuity			Cost of $1.00 Monthly Annuity		
Age	No Refund	10 C&C	Age	No Refund	10 C&C
55	129.392	133.707	70	91.227	106.147
56	127.193	131.905	71	88.421	104.486
57	124.930	130.076	72	85.586	102.880
58	122.605	128.226	73	82.728	101.338
59	120.224	126.361	74	79.863	99.869
60	117.781	124.481	75	77.000	98.478
61	115.281	122.593	76	74.149	97.169
62	112.729	120.700	77	71.323	95.945
63	110.132	118.809	78	69.535	94.811
64	107.497	116.927	79	65.768	93.764
65	104.831	115.058	80	63.033	92.808
66	102.142	113.210	81	60.340	91.942
67	99.445	111.391	82	57.703	91.168
68	96.735	109.606	83	55.120	90.483
69	94.000	107.857	84	52.581	89.884
			85 +	50.077	89.367

TABLE 6

ORDINARY JOINT LIFE AND LAST SURVIVOR ANNUITIES; TWO LIVES—EXPECTED RETURN MULTIPLES—Continued

Ages	45	46	47	48	49	50	51	52	53	54
51	41.6	41.0	40.4	39.8	39.3	38.7	38.2	37.8	37.3	36.9
52	41.3	40.6	40.0	39.4	38.8	38.3	37.8	37.3	36.8	36.4
53	41.0	40.3	39.7	39.0	38.4	37.9	37.3	36.9	36.3	35.8
54	40.7	40.0	39.3	38.7	38.1	37.5	36.9	36.4	35.8	35.3
55	40.4	39.7	39.0	38.4	37.7	37.1	36.5	35.9	35.4	34.9
56	40.2	39.5	38.7	38.1	37.4	36.8	36.1	35.6	35.0	34.4
57	40.0	39.2	38.5	37.8	37.1	36.4	35.8	35.2	34.6	34.0
58	39.7	39.0	38.2	37.5	36.8	36.1	35.5	34.8	34.2	33.6
59	39.6	38.8	38.0	37.3	36.6	35.9	35.2	34.5	33.9	33.3
60	39.4	38.6	37.8	37.1	36.3	35.6	34.9	34.2	33.6	32.9
61	39.2	38.4	37.6	36.9	36.1	35.4	34.6	33.9	33.3	32.6
62	39.1	38.3	37.5	36.7	35.9	35.1	34.4	33.7	33.0	32.3
63	38.9	38.1	37.3	36.5	35.7	34.9	34.2	33.5	32.7	32.0
64	38.8	38.0	37.2	36.3	35.5	34.8	34.0	33.2	32.5	31.8
65	38.7	37.9	37.0	36.2	35.4	34.6	33.8	33.0	32.3	31.6
66	38.6	37.8	36.9	36.1	35.2	34.4	33.6	32.9	32.1	31.4
67	38.5	37.7	36.8	36.0	35.1	34.3	33.5	32.7	31.9	31.2
68	38.4	37.6	36.7	35.8	35.0	34.2	33.4	32.5	31.8	31.0
69	38.4	37.5	36.6	35.7	34.9	34.1	33.2	32.4	31.6	30.8
70	38.3	37.4	36.5	35.7	34.8	34.0	33.1	32.3	31.5	30.7
71	38.2	37.3	36.5	35.6	34.7	33.9	33.0	32.2	31.4	30.5
72	38.2	37.3	36.4	35.5	34.6	33.8	32.9	32.1	31.2	30.4
73	38.1	37.2	36.3	35.4	34.6	33.7	32.8	32.0	31.1	30.3
74	38.1	37.2	36.3	35.4	34.5	33.6	32.8	31.9	31.1	30.2
75	38.1	37.1	36.2	35.3	34.5	33.6	32.7	31.8	31.0	30.1
76	38.0	37.1	36.2	35.3	34.4	33.5	32.6	31.8	30.9	30.1
77	38.0	37.1	36.2	35.3	34.4	33.5	32.6	31.7	30.8	30.0
78	38.0	37.0	36.1	35.2	34.3	33.4	32.5	31.6	30.8	29.9
79	37.9	37.0	36.1	35.2	34.3	33.4	32.5	31.6	30.7	29.9
80	37.9	37.0	36.1	35.2	34.2	33.4	32.5	31.6	30.7	29.8
81	37.9	37.0	36.0	35.1	34.2	33.3	32.4	31.5	30.7	29.8
82	37.9	36.9	36.0	35.1	34.2	33.3	32.4	31.5	30.6	29.7
83	37.9	36.9	36.0	35.1	34.2	33.3	32.4	31.5	30.6	29.7
84	37.8	36.9	36.0	35.0	34.2	33.2	32.3	31.4	30.6	29.7
85	37.8	36.9	36.0	35.1	34.1	33.2	32.3	31.4	30.5	29.6
86	37.8	36.9	36.0	35.0	34.1	33.2	32.3	31.4	30.5	29.6
87	37.8	36.9	35.9	35.0	34.1	33.2	32.3	31.4	30.5	29.6
88	37.8	36.9	35.9	35.0	34.1	33.2	32.3	31.4	30.5	29.6
89	37.8	36.9	35.9	35.0	34.1	33.2	32.3	31.4	30.5	29.6
90	37.8	36.9	35.9	35.0	34.1	33.2	32.3	31.3	30.5	29.6
91	37.8	36.8	35.9	35.0	34.1	33.2	32.2	31.3	30.4	29.5
92	37.8	36.8	35.9	35.0	34.1	33.2	32.2	31.3	30.4	29.5
93	37.8	36.8	35.9	35.0	34.1	33.1	32.2	31.3	30.4	29.5
94	37.8	36.8	35.9	35.0	34.1	33.1	32.2	31.3	30.4	29.5
95	37.8	36.8	35.9	35.0	34.0	33.1	32.2	31.3	30.4	29.5
96	37.8	36.8	35.9	35.0	34.0	33.1	32.2	31.3	30.4	29.5
97	37.8	36.8	35.9	35.0	34.0	33.1	32.2	31.3	30.4	29.5
98	37.8	36.8	35.9	35.0	34.0	33.1	32.2	31.3	30.4	29.5
99	37.8	36.8	35.9	35.0	34.0	33.1	32.2	31.3	30.4	29.5
101	37.8	36.8	35.9	35.0	34.0	33.1	32.2	31.3	30.4	29.5
102	37.8	36.8	35.9	35.0	34.0	33.1	32.2	31.3	30.4	29.5
103	37.7	36.8	35.9	34.9	34.0	33.1	32.2	31.3	30.4	29.5
104	37.7	36.8	35.9	34.9	34.0	33.1	32.2	31.3	30.4	29.5
105	37.7	36.8	35.9	34.9	34.0	33.1	32.2	31.3	30.4	29.5
106	37.7	36.8	35.9	34.9	34.0	33.1	32.2	31.3	30.4	29.5
107	37.7	36.8	35.9	34.9	34.0	33.1	32.2	31.3	30.4	29.5
108	37.7	36.8	35.9	34.9	34.0	33.1	32.2	31.3	30.4	29.5
109	37.7	36.8	35.9	34.9	34.0	33.1	32.2	31.3	30.4	29.5
110	37.7	36.8	35.9	34.9	34.0	33.1	32.2	31.3	30.4	29.5
111	37.7	36.8	35.9	34.9	34.0	33.1	32.2	31.3	30.4	29.5
112	37.7	36.8	35.9	34.9	34.0	33.1	32.2	31.3	30.4	29.5
113	37.7	36.8	35.9	34.9	34.0	33.1	32.2	31.3	30.4	29.5
114	37.7	36.8	35.9	34.9	34.0	33.1	32.2	31.3	30.4	29.5
115	37.7	36.8	35.9	34.9	34.0	33.1	32.2	31.3	30.4	29.5

ORDINARY JOINT LIFE AND LAST SURVIVOR ANNUITIES; TWO LIVES—EXPECTED RETURN MULTIPLES

Ages	55	56	57	58	59	60	61	62	63	64
55	34.4	33.9	33.5	33.1	32.7	32.3	32.0	31.7	31.4	31.1
56	33.9	33.4	33.0	32.5	32.1	31.7	31.4	31.0	30.7	30.4
57	33.5	33.0	32.5	32.0	31.6	31.2	30.8	30.4	30.1	29.8
58	33.1	32.5	32.0	31.5	31.1	30.6	30.2	29.9	29.5	29.2
59	32.7	32.1	31.6	31.1	30.6	30.1	29.7	29.3	28.9	28.6
60	32.3	31.7	31.2	30.6	30.1	29.7	29.2	28.8	28.4	28.0
61	32.0	31.4	30.8	30.2	29.7	29.2	28.7	28.3	27.8	27.4
62	31.7	31.0	30.4	29.9	29.3	28.8	28.3	27.8	27.3	26.9
63	31.4	30.7	30.1	29.5	28.9	28.4	27.8	27.3	26.9	26.4
64	31.1	30.4	29.8	29.2	28.6	28.0	27.4	26.9	26.4	25.9
65	30.9	30.2	29.5	28.9	28.2	27.6	27.1	26.5	26.0	25.5
66	30.6	29.9	29.2	28.6	27.9	27.3	26.7	26.1	25.6	25.1
67	30.4	29.7	29.0	28.3	27.6	27.0	26.4	25.8	25.2	24.7
68	30.2	29.5	28.8	28.1	27.4	26.7	26.1	25.5	24.9	24.3
69	30.1	29.3	28.6	27.8	27.1	26.5	25.8	25.2	24.6	24.0
70	29.9	29.1	28.4	27.6	26.9	26.2	25.6	24.9	24.3	23.7
71	29.7	29.0	28.2	27.5	26.7	26.0	25.3	24.7	24.0	23.4
72	29.6	28.8	28.1	27.3	26.5	25.8	25.1	24.4	23.8	23.1
73	29.5	28.7	27.9	27.1	26.4	25.6	24.9	24.2	23.5	22.9
74	29.4	28.6	27.8	27.0	26.2	25.5	24.7	24.0	23.3	22.7
75	29.3	28.5	27.7	26.9	26.1	25.3	24.6	23.8	23.1	22.4

TABLE 7

		SINKING FUND			ANNUAL COMPOUNDING

SECTION 3

YRS	8.25% ANNUAL RATE	8.50% ANNUAL RATE	8.75% ANNUAL RATE	9.00% ANNUAL RATE	9.25% ANNUAL RATE	9.50% ANNUAL RATE	YRS
1	1.000 000	1.000 000	1.000 000	1.000 000	1.000 000	1.000 000	1
2	0.480 192	0.479 616	0.479 042	0.478 469	0.477 897	0.477 327	2
3	0.307 285	0.306 539	0.305 796	0.305 055	0.304 316	0.303 580	3
4	0.221 103	0.220 288	0.219 477	0.218 669	0.217 864	0.217 063	4
5	0.169 609	0.168 766	0.167 927	0.167 092	0.166 262	0.165 436	5
6	0.135 459	0.134 607	0.133 761	0.132 920	0.132 084	0.131 253	6
7	0.111 218	0.110 369	0.109 527	0.108 691	0.107 860	0.107 036	7
8	0.093 169	0.092 331	0.091 499	0.090 674	0.089 857	0.089 046	8
9	0.079 248	0.078 424	0.077 607	0.076 799	0.075 998	0.075 205	9
10	0.068 214	0.067 408	0.066 610	0.065 820	0.065 039	0.064 266	10
11	0.059 280	0.058 493	0.057 715	0.056 947	0.056 187	0.055 437	11
12	0.051 919	0.051 153	0.050 397	0.049 651	0.048 914	0.048 188	12
13	0.045 767	0.045 023	0.044 289	0.043 567	0.042 854	0.042 152	13
14	0.040 564	0.039 842	0.039 132	0.038 433	0.037 745	0.037 068	14
15	0.036 119	0.035 420	0.034 734	0.034 059	0.033 396	0.032 744	15
16	0.032 289	0.031 614	0.030 951	0.030 300	0.029 661	0.029 035	16
17	0.028 964	0.028 312	0.027 673	0.027 046	0.026 432	0.025 831	17
18	0.026 059	0.025 430	0.024 815	0.024 212	0.023 623	0.023 046	18
19	0.023 507	0.022 901	0.022 309	0.021 730	0.021 165	0.020 613	19
20	0.021 254	0.020 671	0.020 102	0.019 546	0.019 005	0.018 477	20
21	0.019 256	0.018 695	0.018 149	0.017 617	0.017 098	0.016 594	21
22	0.017 478	0.016 939	0.016 415	0.015 905	0.015 409	0.014 928	22
23	0.015 889	0.015 372	0.014 870	0.014 382	0.013 909	0.013 449	23
24	0.014 466	0.013 970	0.013 489	0.013 023	0.012 571	0.012 134	24
25	0.013 187	0.012 712	0.012 251	0.011 806	0.011 376	0.010 959	25
26	0.012 036	0.011 580	0.011 140	0.010 715	0.010 305	0.009 909	26
27	0.010 996	0.010 560	0.010 140	0.009 735	0.009 345	0.008 969	27
28	0.010 056	0.009 639	0.009 238	0.008 852	0.008 481	0.008 124	28
29	0.009 204	0.008 806	0.008 423	0.008 056	0.007 703	0.007 364	29
30	0.008 431	0.008 051	0.007 686	0.007 336	0.007 001	0.006 681	30
31	0.007 728	0.007 365	0.007 018	0.006 686	0.006 368	0.006 064	31
32	0.007 089	0.006 742	0.006 412	0.006 096	0.005 795	0.005 507	32
33	0.006 506	0.006 176	0.005 861	0.005 562	0.005 276	0.005 004	33
34	0.005 974	0.005 660	0.005 361	0.005 077	0.004 806	0.004 549	34
35	0.005 488	0.005 189	0.004 905	0.004 636	0.004 380	0.004 138	35
36	0.005 045	0.004 760	0.004 490	0.004 235	0.003 993	0.003 764	36
37	0.004 639	0.004 368	0.004 112	0.003 870	0.003 642	0.003 426	37
38	0.004 267	0.004 010	0.003 767	0.003 538	0.003 322	0.003 119	38
39	0.003 926	0.003 682	0.003 452	0.003 236	0.003 032	0.002 840	39
40	0.003 614	0.003 382	0.003 164	0.002 960	0.002 767	0.002 587	40
41	0.003 327	0.003 107	0.002 901	0.002 708	0.002 527	0.002 357	41
42	0.003 064	0.002 856	0.002 661	0.002 478	0.002 308	0.002 148	42
43	0.002 823	0.002 625	0.002 441	0.002 268	0.002 108	0.001 958	43
44	0.002 601	0.002 414	0.002 239	0.002 077	0.001 926	0.001 785	44
45	0.002 397	0.002 220	0.002 055	0.001 902	0.001 759	0.001 627	45
46	0.002 209	0.002 042	0.001 886	0.001 742	0.001 608	0.001 484	46
47	0.002 037	0.001 878	0.001 731	0.001 595	0.001 470	0.001 353	47
48	0.001 878	0.001 728	0.001 589	0.001 461	0.001 343	0.001 234	48
49	0.001 732	0.001 590	0.001 459	0.001 339	0.001 228	0.001 126	49
50	0.001 597	0.001 463	0.001 340	0.001 227	0.001 123	0.001 027	50

Source: Michael Sherman, *Comprehensive Compound Interest Tables* (Chicago: Contemporary Books, 1986), p. 132.

TABLE 8

ORDINARY LIFE ANNUITIES ONE LIFE—EXPECTED RETURN MULTIPLES—Continued		ORDINARY LIFE ANNUITIES ONE LIFE—EXPECTED RETURN MULTIPLES—Continued		ORDINARY LIFE ANNUITIES ONE LIFE—EXPECTED RETURN MULTIPLES—Continued	
Age	Multiple	Age	Multiple	Age	Multiple
27	55.1	57	26.8	87	6.1
28	54.1	58	25.9	88	5.7
29	53.1	59	25.0	89	5.3
30	52.2	60	24.2	90	5.0
31	51.2	61	23.3	91	4.7
32	50.2	62	22.5	92	4.4
33	49.3	63	21.6	93	4.1
34	48.3	64	20.8	94	3.9
35	47.3	65	20.0	95	3.7
36	46.4	66	19.2	96	3.4
37	45.4	67	18.4	97	3.2
38	44.4	68	17.6	98	3.0
39	43.5	69	16.8	99	2.8
40	42.5	70	16.0	100	2.7
41	41.5	71	15.3	101	2.5
42	40.6	72	14.6	102	2.3
43	39.6	73	13.9	103	2.1
44	38.7	74	13.2	104	1.9
45	37.7	75	12.5	105	1.8
46	36.8	76	11.9	106	1.6
47	35.9	77	11.2	107	1.4
48	34.9	78	10.6	108	1.3
49	34.0	79	10.0	109	1.1
50	33.1	80	9.5	110	1.0
51	32.2	81	8.9	111	.9
52	31.3	82	8.4	112	.8
53	30.4	83	7.9	113	.7
54	29.5	84	7.4	114	.6
55	28.6	85	6.9	115	.5
56	27.7	86	6.5		

TABLE 9

	PARTIAL PAYMENT TO AMORTIZE				ANNUAL
SECTION 6					COMPOUNDING

YRS	6.75% ANNUAL RATE	7.00% ANNUAL RATE	7.25% ANNUAL RATE	7.50% ANNUAL RATE	7.75% ANNUAL RATE	8.00% ANNUAL RATE	YRS
1	1.067 500	1.070 000	1.072 500	1.075 000	1.077 500	1.080 000	1
2	0.551 176	0.553 092	0.555 009	0.556 928	0.558 848	0.560 769	2
3	0.379 312	0.381 052	0.382 793	0.384 538	0.386 284	0.388 034	3
4	0.293 564	0.295 228	0.296 896	0.298 568	0.300 242	0.301 921	4
5	0.242 260	0.243 891	0.245 525	0.247 165	0.248 808	0.250 456	5
6	0.208 179	0.209 796	0.211 418	0.213 045	0.214 677	0.216 315	6
7	0.183 939	0.185 553	0.187 174	0.188 800	0.190 433	0.192 072	7
8	0.165 849	0.167 468	0.169 094	0.170 727	0.172 367	0.174 015	8
9	0.151 858	0.153 486	0.155 123	0.156 767	0.158 419	0.160 080	9
10	0.140 737	0.142 378	0.144 027	0.145 686	0.147 353	0.149 029	10
11	0.131 701	0.133 357	0.135 022	0.136 697	0.138 382	0.140 076	11
12	0.124 230	0.125 902	0.127 585	0.129 278	0.130 981	0.132 695	12
13	0.117 961	0.119 651	0.121 352	0.123 064	0.124 788	0.126 522	13
14	0.112 637	0.114 345	0.116 065	0.117 797	0.119 541	0.121 297	14
15	0.108 067	0.109 795	0.111 535	0.113 287	0.115 052	0.116 830	15
16	0.104 111	0.105 858	0.107 618	0.109 391	0.111 178	0.112 977	16
17	0.100 659	0.102 425	0.104 206	0.106 000	0.107 808	0.109 629	17
18	0.097 626	0.099 413	0.101 214	0.103 029	0.104 859	0.106 702	18
19	0.094 947	0.096 753	0.098 574	0.100 411	0.102 262	0.104 128	19
20	0.092 567	0.094 393	0.096 235	0.098 092	0.099 965	0.101 852	20
21	0.090 443	0.092 289	0.094 151	0.096 029	0.097 923	0.099 832	21
22	0.088 540	0.090 408	0.092 288	0.094 187	0.096 102	0.098 032	22
23	0.086 829	0.088 714	0.090 616	0.092 535	0.094 471	0.096 422	23
24	0.085 284	0.087 189	0.089 111	0.091 050	0.093 006	0.094 978	24
25	0.083 887	0.085 811	0.087 752	0.089 711	0.091 686	0.093 679	25
26	0.082 619	0.084 561	0.086 521	0.088 500	0.090 495	0.092 507	26
27	0.081 465	0.083 426	0.085 405	0.087 402	0.089 417	0.091 448	27
28	0.080 413	0.082 392	0.084 390	0.086 405	0.088 438	0.090 489	28
29	0.079 452	0.081 449	0.083 464	0.085 498	0.087 550	0.089 619	29
30	0.078 572	0.080 586	0.082 620	0 084 671	0.086 741	0.088 827	30
31	0.077 766	0.079 797	0.081 847	0.083 916	0.086 003	0.088 107	31
32	0.077 025	0.079 073	0.081 140	0.083 226	0.085 330	0.087 451	32
33	0.076 344	0.078 408	0.080 492	0.082 594	0.084 714	0.086 852	33
34	0.075 716	0.077 797	0.079 896	0.082 015	0.084 151	0.086 304	34
35	0.075 138	0.077 234	0.079 349	0.081 483	0.083 635	0.085 803	35
36	0.074 604	0.076 715	0.078 846	0.080 994	0.083 161	0.085 345	36
37	0.074 111	0.076 237	0.078 382	0.080 545	0.082 726	0.084 924	37
38	0.073 655	0.075 795	0.077 954	0.080 132	0.082 327	0.084 539	38
39	0.073 233	0.075 387	0.077 560	0.079 751	0.081 960	0.084 185	39
40	0.072 842	0.075 009	0.077 196	0.079 400	0.081 622	0.083 860	40
41	0.072 479	0.074 660	0.076 859	0.079 077	0.081 311	0 083 561	41
42	0.072 142	0.074 336	0.076 548	0.078 778	0.081 024	0 083 287	42
43	0.071 830	0.074 036	0.076 260	0.078 502	0.080 760	0 083 034	43
44	0.071 540	0.073 758	0.075 994	0.078 247	0.080 517	0.082 802	44
45	0.071 270	0.073 500	0.075 747	0.078 011	0.080 292	0.082 587	45
46	0.071 019	0.073 260	0.075 518	0.077 794	0.080 084	0.082 390	46
47	0.070 786	0.073 037	0.075 306	0.077 592	0.079 893	0.082 208	47
48	0.070 569	0.072 831	0.075 110	0.077 405	0.079 716	0.082 040	48
49	0.070 366	0.072 639	0.074 928	0.077 232	0.079 552	0.081 886	49
50	0.070 178	0.072 460	0.074 758	0.077 072	0.079 401	0.081 743	50

Source: Michael Sherman, *Comprehensive Compound Interest Tables* (Chicago: Contemporary Books, 1986), p. 269.

TABLE 10

	FUTURE VALUE				ANNUAL COMPOUNDING	

SECTION 1

YRS	5.25% ANNUAL RATE	5.50% ANNUAL RATE	5.75% ANNUAL RATE	6.00% ANNUAL RATE	6.25% ANNUAL RATE	6.50% ANNUAL RATE	YRS
1	1.052 500	1.055 000	1.057 500	1.060 000	1.062 500	1.065 000	1
2	1.107 756	1.113 025	1.118 306	1.123 600	1.128 906	1.134 225	2
3	1.165 913	1.174 241	1.182 609	1.191 016	1.199 463	1.207 950	3
4	1.227 124	1.238 825	1.250 609	1.262 477	1.274 429	1.286 466	4
5	1.291 548	1.306 960	1.322 519	1.338 226	1.354 081	1.370 087	5
6	1.359 354	1.378 843	1.398 564	1.418 519	1.438 711	1.459 142	6
7	1.430 720	1.454 679	1.478 981	1.503 630	1.528 631	1.553 987	7
8	1.505 833	1.534 687	1.564 023	1.593 848	1.624 170	1.654 996	8
9	1.584 889	1.619 094	1.653 954	1.689 479	1.725 681	1.762 570	9
10	1.668 096	1.708 144	1.749 056	1.790 848	1.833 536	1.877 137	10
11	1.755 671	1.802 092	1.849 627	1.898 299	1.948 132	1.999 151	11
12	1.847 844	1.901 207	1.955 980	2.012 196	2.069 890	2.129 096	12
13	1.944 856	2.005 774	2.068 449	2.132 928	2.199 258	2.267 487	13
14	2.046 961	2.116 091	2.187 385	2.260 904	2.336 712	2.414 874	14
15	2.154 426	2.232 476	2.313 160	2.396 558	2.482 756	2.571 841	15
16	2.267 533	2.355 263	2.446 167	2.540 352	2.637 928	2.739 011	16
17	2.386 579	2.484 802	2.586 821	2.692 773	2.802 799	2.917 046	17
18	2.511 874	2.621 466	2.735 563	2.854 339	2.977 974	3.106 654	18
19	2.643 748	2.765 647	2.892 858	3.025 600	3.164 097	3.308 587	19
20	2.782 544	2.917 757	3.059 198	3.207 135	3.361 853	3.523 645	20
21	2.928 628	3.078 234	3.235 101	3.399 564	3.571 969	3.752 682	21
22	3.082 381	3.247 537	3.421 120	3.603 537	3.795 217	3.996 606	22
23	3.244 206	3.426 152	3.617 834	3.819 750	4.032 418	4.256 386	23
24	3.414 527	3.614 590	3.825 860	4.048 935	4.284 445	4.533 051	24
25	3.593 789	3.813 392	4.045 846	4.291 871	4.552 222	4.827 699	25
26	3.782 463	4.023 129	4.278 483	4.549 383	4.836 736	5.141 500	26
27	3.981 043	4.244 401	4.524 495	4.822 346	5.139 032	5.475 697	27
28	4.190 047	4.477 843	4.784 654	5.111 687	5.460 222	5.831 617	28
29	4.410 025	4.724 124	5.059 772	5.418 388	5.801 486	6.210 672	29
30	4.641 551	4.983 951	5.350 708	5.743 491	6.164 079	6.614 366	30
31	4.885 233	5.258 069	5.658 374	6.088 101	6.549 333	7.044 300	31
32	5.141 707	5.547 262	5.983 731	6.453 387	6.958 667	7.502 179	32
33	5.411 647	5.852 362	6.327 795	6.840 590	7.393 583	7.989 821	33
34	5.695 758	6.174 242	6.691 643	7.251 025	7.855 682	8.509 159	34
35	5.994 786	6.513 825	7.076 413	7.686 087	8.346 663	9.062 255	35
36	6.309 512	6.872 085	7.483 307	8.147 252	8.868 329	9.651 301	36
37	6.640 761	7.250 050	7.913 597	8.636 087	9.422 600	10.278 636	37
38	6.989 401	7.648 803	8.368 629	9.154 252	10.011 512	10.946 747	38
39	7.356 345	8.069 487	8.849 825	9.703 507	10.637 231	11.658 286	39
40	7.742 553	8.513 309	9.358 690	10.285 718	11.302 058	12.416 075	40
41	8.149 037	8.981 541	9.896 814	10.902 861	12.008 437	13.223 119	41
42	8.576 861	9.475 525	10.465 881	11.557 033	12.758 964	14.082 622	42
43	9.027 147	9.996 679	11.067 669	12.250 455	13.556 400	14.997 993	43
44	9.501 072	10.546 497	11.704 060	12.985 482	14.403 675	15.972 862	44
45	9.999 078	11.126 554	12.377 044	13.764 611	15.303 904	17.011 098	45
46	10.524 872	11.738 515	13.088 724	14.590 487	16.260 398	18.116 820	46
47	11.077 427	12.384 133	13.841 325	15.465 917	17.276 673	19.294 413	47
48	11.658 992	13.065 260	14.637 201	16.393 872	18.356 465	20.548 550	48
49	12.271 089	13.783 849	15.478 841	17.377 504	19.503 744	21.884 205	49
50	12.915 322	14.541 961	16.368 874	18.420 154	20.722 728	23.306 679	50

Source: Michael Sherman, *Comprehensive Compound Interest Tables* (Chicago: Contemporary Books, 1986), p. 38.

TABLE 11

| | | FUTURE VALUE | | | ANNUAL |
| | SECTION 1 | | | | COMPOUNDING |

YRS	6.75% ANNUAL RATE	7.00% ANNUAL RATE	7.25% ANNUAL RATE	7.50% ANNUAL RATE	7.75% ANNUAL RATE	8.00% ANNUAL RATE	YRS
1	1.067 500	1.070 000	1.072 500	1.075 000	1.077 500	1.080 000	1
2	1.139 556	1.144 900	1.150 256	1.155 625	1.161 006	1.166 400	2
3	1.216 476	1.225 043	1.233 650	1.242 297	1.250 984	1.259 712	3
4	1.298 588	1.310 796	1.323 089	1.335 469	1.347 936	1.360 489	4
5	1.386 243	1.402 552	1.419 013	1.435 629	1.452 401	1.469 328	5
6	1.479 815	1.500 730	1.521 892	1.543 302	1.564 962	1.586 874	6
7	1.579 702	1.605 781	1.632 229	1.659 049	1.686 246	1.713 824	7
8	1.686 332	1.718 186	1.750 566	1.783 478	1.816 930	1.850 930	8
9	1.800 159	1.838 459	1.877 482	1.917 239	1.957 742	1.999 005	9
10	1.921 670	1.967 151	2.013 599	2.061 032	2.109 467	2.158 925	10
11	2.051 383	2.104 852	2.159 585	2.215 609	2.272 951	2.331 639	11
12	2.189 851	2.252 192	2.316 155	2.381 780	2.449 105	2.518 170	12
13	2.337 666	2.409 845	2.484 076	2.560 413	2.638 910	2.719 624	13
14	2.495 459	2.578 534	2.664 172	2.752 444	2.843 426	2.937 194	14
15	2.663 902	2.759 032	2.857 324	2.958 877	3.063 791	3.172 169	15
16	2.843 715	2.952 164	3.064 480	3.180 793	3.301 235	3.425 943	16
17	3.035 666	3.158 815	3.286 655	3.419 353	3.557 081	3.700 018	17
18	3.240 574	3.379 932	3.524 937	3.675 804	3.832 755	3.996 019	18
19	3.459 312	3.616 628	3.780 495	3.951 489	4.129 793	4.315 701	19
20	3.692 816	3.869 684	4.054 581	4.247 851	4.449 852	4.660 957	20
21	3.942 081	4.140 562	4.348 538	4.566 440	4.794 716	5.033 834	21
22	4.208 172	4.430 402	4.663 808	4.908 923	5.166 306	5.436 540	22
23	4.492 223	4.740 530	5.001 934	5.277 092	5.566 695	5.871 464	23
24	4.795 448	5.072 367	5.364 574	5.672 874	5.998 114	6.341 181	24
25	5.119 141	5.427 433	5.753 505	6.098 340	6.462 967	6.848 475	25
26	5.464 683	5.807 553	6.170 634	6.555 715	6.963 847	7.396 353	26
27	5.833 549	6.213 868	6.618 005	7.047 394	7.503 546	7.988 061	27
28	6.227 314	6.648 838	7.097 811	7.575 948	8.085 070	8.627 106	28
29	6.647 657	7.114 257	7.612 402	8.144 144	8.711 663	9.317 275	29
30	7.096 374	7.612 255	8.164 301	8.754 955	9.386 817	10.062 657	30
31	7.575 380	8.145 113	8.756 213	9.411 577	10.114 296	10.867 669	31
32	8.086 718	8.715 271	9.391 039	10.117 445	10.898 154	11.737 083	32
33	8.632 571	9.325 340	10.071 889	10.876 253	11.742 760	12.676 050	33
34	9.215 270	9.978 114	10.802 101	11.691 972	12.652 824	13.690 134	34
35	9.837 300	10.676 581	11.585 253	12.568 870	13.633 418	14.785 344	35
36	10.501 318	11.423 942	12.425 184	13.511 536	14.690 008	15.968 172	36
37	11.210 157	12.223 618	13.326 010	14.524 901	15.828 484	17.245 626	37
38	11.966 843	13.079 271	14.292 146	15.614 268	17.055 191	18.625 276	38
39	12.774 605	13.994 820	15.328 326	16.785 339	18.376 969	20.115 298	39
40	13.636 890	14.974 458	16.439 630	18.044 239	19.801 184	21.724 521	40
41	14.557 380	16.022 670	17.631 503	19.397 557	21.335 775	23.462 483	41
42	15.540 004	17.144 257	18.909 787	20.852 374	22.989 298	25.339 482	42
43	16.588 954	18.344 355	20.280 747	22.416 302	24.770 969	27.366 640	43
44	17.708 708	19.628 460	21.751 101	24.097 524	26.690 719	29.555 972	44
45	18.904 046	21.002 452	23.328 055	25.904 839	28.759 249	31.920 449	45
46	20.180 069	22.472 623	25.019 339	27.847 702	30.988 091	34.474 085	46
47	21.542 224	24.045 707	26.833 242	29.936 279	33.389 668	37.232 012	47
48	22.996 324	25.728 907	28.778 652	32.181 500	35.977 368	40.210 573	48
49	24.548 576	27.529 930	30.865 104	34.595 113	38.765 614	43.427 419	49
50	26.205 605	29.457 025	33.102 824	37.189 746	41.769 949	46.901 613	50

TABLE 11 (concluded)

	FUTURE VALUE				ANNUAL COMPOUNDING	
	9.75% ANNUAL RATE	**10.00%** ANNUAL RATE	**10.25%** ANNUAL RATE	**10.50%** ANNUAL RATE	**10.75%** ANNUAL RATE	**11.00%** ANNUAL RATE
YRS						YRS
1	1.097 500	1.100 000	1.102 500	1.105 000	1.107 500	1.110 000	1
2	1.204 506	1.210 000	1.215 506	1.221 025	1.226 556	1.232 100	2
3	1.321 946	1.331 000	1.340 096	1.349 233	1.358 411	1.367 631	3
4	1.450 835	1.464 100	1.477 455	1.490 902	1.504 440	1.518 070	4
5	1.592 292	1.610 510	1.628 895	1.647 447	1.666 168	1.685 058	5
6	1.747 540	1.771 561	1.795 856	1.820 429	1.845 281	1.870 415	6
7	1.917 925	1.948 717	1.979 932	2.011 574	2.043 648	2.076 160	7
8	2.104 923	2.143 589	2.182 875	2.222 789	2.263 340	2.304 538	8
9	2.310 153	2.357 948	2.406 619	2.456 182	2.506 650	2.558 037	9
10	2.535 393	2.593 742	2.653 298	2.714 081	2.776 114	2.839 421	10
11	2.782 594	2.853 117	2.925 261	2.999 059	3.074 547	3.151 757	11
12	3.053 897	3.138 428	3.225 100	3.313 961	3.405 060	3.498 451	12
13	3.351 652	3.452 271	3.555 673	3.661 926	3.771 104	3.883 280	13
14	3.678 438	3.797 498	3.920 129	4.046 429	4.176 498	4.310 441	14
15	4.037 085	4.177 248	4.321 942	4.471 304	4.625 472	4.784 589	15
16	4.430 701	4.594 973	4.764 941	4.940 791	5.122 710	5.310 894	16
17	4.862 695	5.054 470	5.253 348	5.459 574	5.673 401	5.895 093	17
18	5.336 807	5.559 917	5.791 816	6.032 829	6.283 292	6.543 553	18
19	5.857 146	6.115 909	6.385 477	6.666 276	6.958 746	7.263 344	19
20	6.428 218	6.727 500	7.039 989	7.366 235	7.706 811	8.062 312	20
21	7.054 969	7.400 250	7.761 588	8.139 690	8.535 293	8.949 166	21
22	7.742 828	8.140 275	8.557 150	8.994 357	9.452 837	9.933 574	22
23	8.497 754	8.954 302	9.434 258	9.938 764	10.469 017	11.026 267	23
24	9.326 285	9.849 733	10.401 270	10.982 335	11.594 436	12.239 157	24
25	10.235 598	10.834 706	11.467 400	12.135 480	12.840 838	13.585 464	25
26	11.233 569	11.918 177	12.642 808	13.409 705	14.221 228	15.079 865	26
27	12.328 842	13.109 994	13.938 696	14.817 724	15.750 010	16.738 650	27
28	13.530 904	14.420 994	15.367 412	16.373 585	17.443 136	18.579 901	28
29	14.850 167	15.863 093	16.942 572	18.092 812	19.318 274	20.623 691	29
30	16.298 058	17.449 402	18.679 186	19.992 557	21.394 988	22.892 297	30
31	17.887 119	19.194 342	20.593 802	22.091 775	23.694 949	25.410 449	31
32	19.631 113	21.113 777	22.704 667	24.411 412	26.242 156	28.205 599	32
33	21.545 147	23.225 154	25.031 896	26.974 610	29.063 188	31.308 214	33
34	23.645 798	25.547 670	27.597 665	29.806 944	32.187 481	34.752 118	34
35	25.951 264	28.102 437	30.426 426	32.936 673	35.647 635	38.574 851	35
36	28.481 512	30.912 681	33.545 134	36.395 024	39.479 756	42.818 085	36
37	31.258 459	34.003 949	36.983 510	40.216 501	43.723 829	47.528 074	37
38	34.306 159	37.404 343	40.774 320	44.439 234	48.424 141	52.756 162	38
39	37.651 010	41.144 778	44.953 688	49.105 354	53.629 736	58.559 340	39
40	41.321 983	45.259 256	49.561 441	54.261 416	59.394 933	65.000 867	40
41	45.350 877	49.785 181	54.641 489	59.958 864	65.779 888	72.150 963	41
42	49.772 587	54.763 699	60.242 241	66.254 545	72.851 226	80.087 569	42
43	54.625 414	60.240 069	66.417 071	73.211 272	80.682 733	88.897 201	43
44	59.951 392	66.264 076	73.224 821	80.898 456	89.356 127	98.675 893	44
45	65.796 653	72.890 484	80.730 365	89.392 794	98.961 910	109.530 242	45
46	72.211 827	80.179 532	89.005 227	98.779 037	109.600 316	121.578 568	46
47	79.252 480	88.197 485	98.128 263	109.150 836	121.382 350	134.952 211	47
48	86.979 596	97.017 234	108.186 410	120.611 674	134.430 952	149.796 954	48
49	95.460 107	106.718 957	119.275 517	133.275 900	148.882 280	166.274 619	49
50	104.767 467	117.390 853	131.501 258	147.269 969	164.887 125	184.564 827	50

Source: Michael Sherman, *Comprehensive Compound Interest Tables* (Chicago: Contemporary Books, 1986), pp. 39, 41.

TABLE 12

| | PARTIAL PAYMENT TO AMORTIZE | | | | | ANNUAL | |
| SECTION 6 | | | | | | COMPOUNDING | |

YRS	5.25% ANNUAL RATE	5.50% ANNUAL RATE	5.75% ANNUAL RATE	6.00% ANNUAL RATE	6.25% ANNUAL RATE	6.50% ANNUAL RATE	YRS
1	1.052 500	1.055 000	1.057 500	1.060 000	1.062 500	1.065 000	1
2	0.539 711	0.541 618	0.543 527	0.545 437	0.547 348	0.549 262	2
3	0.368 930	0.370 654	0.372 381	0.374 110	0.375 841	0.377 576	3
4	0.283 651	0.285 794	0.286 941	0.288 591	0.290 245	0.291 903	4
5	0.232 573	0.234 176	0.235 784	0.237 396	0.239 013	0.240 635	5
6	0.198 595	0.200 179	0.201 768	0.203 363	0.204 963	0.206 568	6
7	0.174 389	0.175 964	0.177 546	0.179 135	0.180 730	0.182 331	7
8	0.156 289	0.157 864	0.159 446	0.161 036	0.162 633	0.164 237	8
9	0.142 261	0.143 839	0.145 427	0.147 022	0.148 626	0.150 238	9
10	0.131 082	0.132 668	0.134 263	0.135 868	0.137 482	0.139 105	10
11	0.121 975	0.123 571	0.125 177	0.126 793	0.128 419	0.130 055	11
12	0.114 422	0.116 029	0.117 648	0.119 277	0.120 917	0.122 568	12
13	0.108 064	0.109 684	0.111 316	0.112 960	0.114 616	0.116 283	13
14	0.102 645	0.104 279	0.105 926	0.107 585	0.109 257	0.110 940	14
15	0.097 977	0.099 626	0.101 288	0.102 963	0.104 651	0.106 353	15
16	0.093 919	0.095 583	0.097 260	0.098 952	0.100 658	0.102 378	16
17	0.090 363	0.092 042	0.093 736	0.095 445	0.097 168	0.098 906	17
18	0.087 225	0.088 920	0.090 630	0.092 357	0.094 098	0.095 855	18
19	0.084 439	0.086 150	0.087 877	0.089 621	0.091 380	0.093 156	19
20	0.081 952	0.083 679	0.085 423	0.087 185	0.088 962	0.090 756	20
21	0.079 721	0.081 465	0.083 226	0.085 005	0.086 800	0.088 613	21
22	0.077 712	0.079 471	0.081 249	0.083 046	0.084 860	0.086 691	22
23	0.075 894	0.077 670	0.079 465	0.081 278	0.083 111	0.084 961	23
24	0.074 243	0.076 036	0.077 848	0.079 679	0.081 529	0.083 398	24
25	0.072 741	0.074 549	0.076 378	0.078 227	0.080 095	0.081 981	25
26	0.071 368	0.073 193	0.075 039	0.076 904	0.078 790	0.080 695	26
27	0.070 111	0.071 952	0.073 814	0.075 697	0.077 600	0.079 523	27
28	0.068 957	0.070 814	0.072 693	0.074 593	0.076 513	0.078 453	28
29	0.067 896	0.069 769	0.071 663	0.073 580	0.075 517	0.077 474	29
30	0.066 917	0.068 805	0.070 716	0.072 649	0.074 603	0.076 577	30
31	0.066 013	0.067 917	0.069 843	0.071 792	0.073 763	0.075 754	31
32	0.065 176	0.067 095	0.069 038	0.071 002	0.072 989	0.074 997	32
33	0.064 400	0.066 335	0.068 292	0.070 273	0.072 275	0.074 299	33
34	0.063 680	0.065 630	0.067 603	0.069 598	0.071 617	0.073 656	34
35	0.063 011	0.064 975	0.066 963	0.068 974	0.071 007	0.073 062	35
36	0.062 388	0.064 366	0.066 369	0.068 395	0.070 443	0.072 513	36
37	0.061 807	0.063 800	0.065 817	0.067 857	0.069 921	0.072 005	37
38	0.061 265	0.063 272	0.065 303	0.067 358	0.069 436	0.071 535	38
39	0.060 759	0.062 780	0.064 825	0.066 894	0.068 985	0.071 099	39
40	0.060 286	0.062 320	0.064 379	0.066 462	0.068 567	0.070 694	40
41	0.059 844	0.061 891	0.063 963	0.066 059	0.068 177	0.070 318	41
42	0.059 429	0.061 489	0.063 574	0.065 683	0.067 815	0.069 968	42
43	0.059 040	0.061 113	0.063 211	0.065 333	0.067 478	0.069 644	43
44	0.058 676	0.060 761	0.062 872	0.065 006	0.067 163	0.069 341	44
45	0.058 333	0.060 431	0.062 554	0.064 700	0.066 869	0.069 060	45
46	0.058 012	0.060 122	0.062 256	0.064 415	0.066 596	0.068 797	46
47	0.057 710	0.059 831	0.061 978	0.064 148	0.066 340	0.068 553	47
48	0.057 425	0.059 559	0.061 716	0.063 898	0.066 101	0.068 325	48
49	0.057 158	0.059 302	0.061 471	0.063 664	0.065 878	0.068 112	49
50	0.056 906	0.059 061	0.061 241	0.063 444	0.065 669	0.067 914	50

Source: Michael Sherman, *Comprehensive Compound Interest Tables* (Chicago: Contemporary Books, 1986), p. 268.

CHAPTER 18

KEOGH PLANNING WHEN YOU HAVE EMPLOYEES

What's good for you about Keoghs will be good for your employees as well, if they are in your Keogh plan. But your employee gets into your Keogh only because you pay his or her way, out of your business income. *You* provide the money used for your employee's Keogh benefits. This increases the costs of running your self-employment business.

And you may not have the choice of including employees or leaving them out. In many cases, you can't have a Keogh for yourself unless your employees are part of it.

Keogh planning where there are employees is a large and complex subject. *Complete* coverage of so weighty a topic is more than a book this size can handle. But we can examine the basic issues and rough out a plan of action for you to pursue with a pension professional.

The law says that if you have a Keogh for yourself, you generally must include your employees in your Keogh. And it says you can't favor yourself in your plan at the expense of your employees. In the technical phrase, your plan can't "discriminate" in your favor and against others in the plan.

It may seem that any money you put in for your employees is money taken from yourself, from your own share of the Keogh or from your business profits. This is, in fact, the way I see it.

Of course, it's not an *extra* cost to you if your employees count what you put in for them as part of their pay and therefore expect less in the way of current wages. But that's not the way the world that most of us know works. Employees—you yourself if you are an employee—want at least a standard level of cash pay *in addition* to retirement benefits.

So Keogh for your employees represents an additional cost of doing business. And if you are like most business owners, you will want to keep this cost as low as possible. Keogh planning when you have employees means finding ways to build your own Keogh as high as possible while saving as much as possible on Keogh costs for employees.

This may seem like a tall order when your plan, by law, can't "discriminate" in your favor. However, there are a number of things your plan can legally do for you that might seem like discrimination to persons unfamiliar with the rules. This chapter will point out the opportunities that matter most to small businesses.

In this chapter you will see two familiar words, *discrimination* and *integration,* in unfamiliar contexts. In pension parlance, discrimination and integration have nothing to do with racial matters or with discrimination based on sex, age, religion, or handicap. Discrimination for any of these reasons may be punishable under a variety of federal or state laws, but not under the Keogh law. In Keogh plans discrimination means *illegally* favoring the business owner over his employees. Integration, explained at greater length below, means working the effect of social security into a Keogh contribution or Keogh pension.

EMPLOYEES YOU LEAVE OUT SAVE KEOGH EXPENSES

You are allowed to leave some of your employees out of your Keogh. Naturally, you have no Keogh costs for employees you don't cover. You can always exclude the following:

1. Employees younger than 21.

2. Employees who work for you part-time. Plans normally define full-time as 1,000 hours a year or more, so part-time is less than 1,000. If your business is a sideline for you, you would define full-time to include yourself—say, 500 hours or more a year—and part-time as less than that.

3. Employees who have worked for you less than one year. *Or* employees who have worked for you less than *two* years if they are fully vested (see page 104 on vesting) in all you contribute for them upon two years' service.

There are other more complex situations in which you may exclude employees. Two opportunities that small businesses can use are discussed later in this chapter. They are plans where you have to contribute for an employee only if the employee contributes for himself or herself (see page 211) and 401(k) plans (see page 207).

There are additional opportunities typically available only to larger businesses. They arise where the employer has union employees or employees working in different lines of business. These options are best discussed with a pension professional.

WHICH TYPE OF PLAN WHEN YOU HAVE EMPLOYEES?

As a moonlighter, alone in your business, your choice of plan may turn on how close you are to retirement age. Close to retirement, you would choose a defined-benefit plan, which lets you make large tax-deductible contributions over a short period. Farther from retirement, you would choose a money-purchase plan, alone or combined with a profit-sharing plan, which gives you many years of contributions and investment earnings.

These considerations still matter when you have employees, but now you must also consider *their* ages (or closeness to retirement age). If you select a defined-benefit plan because you're close to retirement age, and your employees are close to retirement age too, you may be stuck with heavy contributions on their behalf as well.

If you and your employees are relatively young, in a money-purchase plan you will have many years ahead of you, contributing for them as well as yourself.

So it's best if you can pick a plan that fits you better than it does your employees. In borderline cases, where defined-benefit and money-purchase might seem equally good, you would take money-purchase if your employees are older than you and defined-benefit if they are younger.

Not that you should pick a plan that's unsuitable for *you* simply to cut down what you must put in for your employees. There are several ways to keep costs down even where your employees are about as close to retirement as you are. These ways—integration, target benefit, and delayed vesting—are considered later in this chapter.

Profit-Sharing with Employees

Business owners can use profit-sharing as a reward and incentive for employees. For example, you might promise to put 10 percent of salary into a plan for your employees if your profit exceeded $200,000 but nothing if it was less than that.

Would this get them to work harder and smarter? You're the best judge of that with your own employees. No outsider's guess is worth much. *If* it produces that result, the Keogh cost may be well worth it.

This course of action is designed to enrich your business, not your Keogh. A richer business may be what really matters, but it also helps your Keogh indirectly. The larger your business earnings—after any contributions for employees, of course—the more you can contribute for yourself.

One way to combine business and Keogh goals is by adopting both a profit-sharing plan and a money-purchase pension plan. You make a modest commitment to the money-purchase plan segment: You will put, say, 6 percent of what an employee earns into a Keogh for his or her benefit. The amount could be less than 6 percent for some but still 6 percent (of earned income) for yourself, under a target-benefit plan (see page 212). Add a profit-sharing plan, and you can contribute up to an additional 15 percent of pay or earned income out of profits. You would make this contribution if you think your employees' efforts produced something extra. Of course, you could contribute for yourself only if you also contributed for employees in the plan.

Cut Keogh Costs with a 401(k)

I discussed 401(k) plans for self-employed persons without employees in Chapter 5. We return to them here because of their cost-cutting uses when you have employees.

Except in rare cases, 401(k)s are profit-sharing plans. One type of 401(k) is called a salary-reduction plan. When one of these is installed, employees get to choose between continuing to take all of their salary in cash or diverting some of it into the 401(k) profit-sharing plan.

The owner is the real winner with a *pure* 401(k) plan. He or she gets a profit-sharing plan without any additional cost for employees. He or she is offering employees the same amount as before. If the employee takes it all in cash, the owner is *exactly* where he or she was before. If the employee defers collecting some by diverting it to the 401(k) profit-sharing plan, he or she pays less tax now, and has less money now.

But there aren't many *pure* 401(k)s around. Owners aren't allowed to keep their 401(k)s unless *some* employees defer. To encourage employees to defer, owners typically offer a modest matching contribution. For every, say, $3 or $5 an employee diverts into the 401(k), the owner will add $1 more. Any matching contribution the owner makes adds to his or her business cost.

So in reality 401(k)s are a *low-cost* way to provide profit-sharing benefits for owner and employees—low cost, not free.

HOW KEOGHS CAN FAVOR THE BUSINESS OWNER

Business owners usually make more than those who work for them. And they are usually in their businesses longer than anyone who works for them. Use these facts of business life as key elements of your Keogh planning in the following ways.

Using How Much You Make

1. Contributions to a money-purchase Keogh or a profit-sharing Keogh are a percentage of your earnings or compensation. So if you make more than your employee, you put in more for yourself than for your employee. You don't violate the law prohibiting discrimination in your favor when you make Keogh contributions proportionate to earnings or compensation, even though you get much more than your employees do that way.

2. A defined-benefit Keogh pension can be a percentage (up to 100 percent) of certain earned income or compensation. Here, too, you aren't discriminating illegally if you make your pension 100 percent of your earned income and an employee's pension 100 percent of his or hers. That is true even if it means your pension is $90,000 and an employee's is $8,000.

Using How Long You Work

1. In a money-purchase or profit-sharing plan you put in money each year based on that year's compensation. Employees who join you after your Keogh has begun get nothing for past years, years contributions were made for *you*.

2. A defined-benefit plan can base the retirement pension on length of service (as well as pay). For example, it can give a pension equal to 4 percent of earned income or compensation for each year of service. Using this method, the owner who works 25 years before retirement gets a pension equal to 100 percent of his or her earnings; an employee who works 12 years gets 48 percent of his or her earnings. And you can work this technique to recognize service before the plan was set up. For example, the owner just mentioned might set up the plan 11 years before retirement. The plan would provide a pension for the owner's *14* years of past service and the employee's 1 year of past service, assuming they retire at the same time.

LATE VESTING CUTS KEOGH COSTS

Your Keogh plan can require participants to be in the plan for some specified minimum period before they become absolutely entitled to its benefits; that is, before the benefits become vested. If employment ends before that period is up, the participant forfeits all rights. This period for vesting is in addition to any waiting period before the employee is included in the plan (becomes a participant). Benefits can be made to vest a certain percentage each year.

Vested amounts are amounts participants can take with them when they leave or collect when they reach retirement age whether or not they work for you at that time. Amounts that are forfeited stay in the plan when the participant leaves.

For economic reasons, owners want to postpone the time when employees' shares vest. That increases the possibility that they will forfeit all or part of their shares. You can apply what they forfeit against your future plan contributions, thereby decreasing your future pension costs. (In money-purchase and profit-sharing plans, you could instead share out what departing employees forfeit among those who remain, including yourself, thereby increasing your share of the total fund.)

Employers tend to believe that their most valued employees are those who stay with them the longest. This also encourages employers to postpone vesting.

Your vesting and forfeiture expectations get figured into your calculations of how much pension or profit-sharing you can afford. With delayed vesting and high turnover, a plan that includes employees may not cost much more than a plan for yourself alone.

Not that you necessarily want a high turnover. An employee's departure may hurt your business more than it helps your Keogh. You're the best judge of that. But if you want to keep an employee, it helps to have him or her in a plan, one with delayed vesting.

Your vesting options. Except in rare cases, you have only two options in a Keogh plan:

(*a*). Everything must vest by the end of the participant's third year of service. That means that if you wish you can postpone any vesting to the end of that third year.

(*b*). Vest 20 percent after two years of service and 20 percent at the end of each succeeding year's service, so that it's all fully vested at the end of six year's service.

Sometimes (a) postpones the greater dollar amount; sometimes (b) does. It depends on your employee mix.

You are free to adopt any faster vesting method. For example, you could have 100 percent vesting after two years or 25 percent the first year and 25 percent in each succeeding year.

Exactly what and how much vests depends on the type of plan you have. In money-purchase and profit-sharing plans, what vests is the amount in the employee's account at that time, that is, the contributions and earnings up to that point. For example, if you put in $6,000, which has earned $2,000, and 60 percent vests, the employee is vested in $4,800 (60 percent of $8,000).

With a defined-benefit plan, what vests is the pension earned to date. For example, if participants earn a pension of 3 percent of compensation each year, one whose pay averaged $30,000 a year over three years would, under option (a), have a vested right to receive a pension of $2,700 a year (9 percent of $30,000) on reaching the retirement age specified in the plan.

Delayed vesting doesn't apply with amounts employees put in out of their own pocket or deferred amounts in 401(k) plans. Such amounts vest immediately.

CUT KEOGH COSTS THROUGH MANDATORY CONTRIBUTIONS

Chapter 7 covered Keogh plans to which moonlighters contributed in their capacity as employees. Employee contributions may be either mandatory (the employee must contribute if he wants to participate in the plan) or voluntary. A mandatory plan is a cost-cutting device for owners with employees. You contribute only for employees who contribute for themselves. For example, if you have six employees but only four of them contribute on their own behalf, you don't have to contribute for the others. You may put in one employer dollar per employee dollar, or two for one, or one for two, and so on.

Making an employee contribute a lot in order to be included is a way to keep down the number of employees you must make contributions for. But there are limits on your power to keep employees out of your plan through this device. The limits are complex, and should be discussed with a pension professional.

You can couple this plan with one permitting a further *voluntary* contribution. For example, you could have this mandatory plan: Anyone who put up 5 percent of salary or earned income gets another 10 percent ($2 for $1) from you as employer. Then you could add a voluntary feature, which you match on a $1-for-$1 basis. Such a plan would let you put in a tax-deductible 15 percent of your earned income for yourself, plus the nondeductible 10 percent you contribute in your capacity as employee. You would have to put in a further tax-deductible 15 percent of salary for any employee who paid in a *non*deductible 10 percent of salary out of his or her own pocket.

For flexibility and employee incentive, the mandatory part could be a money-purchase plan and the voluntary part a profit-sharing plan. You as employer would match the voluntary 5 percent only where employee efforts produced extra profits for your business. Here, too, there are limits to be discussed with a pension professional.

TARGET-BENEFIT PLANS REDUCE COSTS

A target-benefit plan is a special type of money-purchase plan. It's another way to keep down contributions for employees, and it works even in cases where the owner and the employee earn the same income.

The owner determines the retirement benefit: for example, 25 percent of the average of the participant's final five years' earnings. The benefit will be paid for through the owner's contributions and the investment earnings on those contributions. The owner (or the actuary he or she hires) will compute what the contributions and rate of return on investment must be to pay for the targeted pension. Though this is much like a defined-benefit plan, no annual recalculations are made to reflect differences between assumed and actual investment returns. Contribution and deduction ceilings are those for a money-purchase plan.

A business owner might use a target-benefit plan if the persons to be benefited earn about the same amount but are of widely differing ages: an owner aged 57 and an employee aged 31, for example. A target-benefit plan to fund a particular benefit level at age 65 might cost a tax deductible 20 percent of earnings for the owner (with only 8 years remaining before retirement) but 1.34 percent of salary (with 34 years to go) for the employee, even if their salaries are the same.

Of course, if the employee earned less than the owner, the contribution on the employee's behalf would be that much less.

With "age-weighting," profit-sharing plans can do something similar. Age-weighted profit-sharing is a new concept, not yet fully developed, that IRS approved in principle in 1990.

INTEGRATION WITH SOCIAL SECURITY
CUTS COSTS

In Keogh lingo, "integration," like "discrimination," has no racial overtones. Integration with social security is a complex device used to keep down Keogh contributions for lower-paid employees. The concept, much oversimplified, is this:

Social security is our basic retirement system. That system contemplates paying you something like $1 a year of pension for every $3 of wages that you and your employer paid social security tax on in an average year. If you (and your employer) paid a social security tax on wages averaging $30,000, you would get a $10,000 Social Security pension.

If wages were more than $30,000 you (and your employer) paid no social security tax on the excess, and you get no social security benefits for that excess. (Income subject to social security tax has been rising annually by law so that wages above $30,000 have been taxed since 1982. But social security is based on wages over a working life. The $30,000 figure is a rough approximation of what average taxable wages would be for many people now working.)

It's here that the integration concept comes in. A business owner (Dentist Walker) decides he will give himself and his employees a pension of 30 percent of pay, but he will count what social security provides as part of the pension. He feels entitled to count the social security portion since he paid toward that portion when he paid the employer's share of social security taxes. He will make up through his Keogh contributions whatever is necessary to provide a retirement benefit of 30 percent of pay, counting social security as part of that benefit.

Consider how this might work for Dentist Walker and his two aides, Janet and Regina. Walker makes $120,000, Janet makes $27,000, and Regina makes $21,000. Social security will pay Janet $9,000 a year, Regina $7,000 a year, and Walker $10,000 a year (one-third of the $30,000 he paid tax on). But Walker's plan gives him a pension of $36,000—that is, 30 percent of $120,000, but including the $10,000 of social security. So he can put enough into his Keogh to buy an additional $26,000 of pension a year. What about Janet and Regina? Walker need not put *anything* in for them.

He owes them a 30 percent pension *counting social security*. They've got that without his Keogh help, through social security alone.

Integration is a key concept in pension planning when you have employees. It is widely used in company and other private pension plans, as well as in self-employed plans: It's used in Harold's company plan.

My explanation greatly oversimplifies the concept. In fact, Walker would have to put in *something* for Janet and Regina, though not much; and Walker's pension might be a percentage of some amount less than (or greater than) $120,000. There are many possible refinements. You could have a pension that is, say, 60 percent of pay, so you contribute something for all employees but proportionately more for yourself. In this scenario Walker buys himself a pension of $62,000 ($72,000 minus $10,000), Janet one of $7,200, and Regina one of $5,600.[1]

"LEASING" YOUR EMPLOYEES

The employee-leasing concept has been around for years and is an approved technique for minimizing pension costs. The concept is much like going to an agency for temporary help but winding up with a long-term staff of persons on *your* premises doing *your* work who are employed by someone else. An early use of employee leasing (and the way I learned about it) was in the offices of incorporated medical practices. The corporation leased staff instead of employing them directly, so they wouldn't be employees to be included in the rich pension plans designed for the doctors.

Employee leasing is perfectly legal. Within limits, leased employees need not be included in your plan *if* they are included in a plan of the leasing agency. The agency must provide them with a certain level of pension benefit.

Leasing does not have to mean just leasing *new* staff. Some business owners have worked out arrangements to terminate their

---

[1] These contributions reduce Walker's business profits or earned income, of course, and so may reduce the size of the pension he can have.

employees, who are then immediately hired by the leasing agency to continue the same work in the same place.

Although employee leasing saves you pension or profit-sharing costs, the leasing approach *can* cost your business more than if you had employees and included them in your plan. The leasing agency does certain things for you: it relieves you of payroll duties and some personnel administration. You pay for these services in a charge that will also indirectly include the cost of pension benefits the agency provides.

You may or may not be better off using the leasing approach. Costs, business efficiency, and staff relationships are all factors that must figure in your decision.

USE SELF-EMPLOYED HELP INSTEAD OF EMPLOYEES?

You don't have to provide Keogh benefits for persons who work for you if they aren't your employees. Whether to hire your own staff or use outside help will depend on many business-related factors, including payroll taxes and workers' compensation duties. Possible Keogh cost savings is only one element, and a small one, in the decision-making process.

OTHER KEOGH CONCERNS

You face more than just extra Keogh costs when you have employees. Keoghs that include employees are also more trouble than Keoghs for owners only.

If you are plan *trustee,* you must be extra careful about the investments you make. You now owe others solid performance.

As plan *administrator,* your reporting duties to the IRS, the Department of Labor, and the employees themselves become more onerous. Also, you may need grievance and review procedures in your plan so employees will feel they are being fairly treated.

If you have a defined-benefit plan, you may need plan termination insurance to protect employees against loss of their vested benefits because of something you do. Insurance is provided by a government agency, the Pension Benefit Guarantee Corporation. The premiums are paid by you.

Your decision to withdraw your own funds from a pension plan could hurt its financial position because you're taking out most of the assets. If you withdraw your entire account within 10 years after the plan was set up, you may have to provide a kind of guarantee that remaining participants will get their due, perhaps by posting a bond covering what's needed for them.

HOW TO GET STARTED WHEN YOU HAVE EMPLOYEES

So Keoghs when you have employees may mean extra costs and trouble. Don't let that discourage you. There are many tens of thousands of Keoghs for owners with employees—many more such Keoghs than those for moonlighters only. Keogh benefits usually are too good to pass up, despite the added burdens.

You may already have the Keogh and now have added, or are thinking of adding, an employee. Or you may already have one or more employees and are thinking of adopting a Keogh. In either case, the way to start Keogh planning with employees is to consult a pension professional after you have read what this book has to say about Keoghs. The Keogh consultation will be time and money well spent. You and your business have a lot at stake.

CHAPTER 19

SPEAKING KEOGH

No one has ever asked me to "say something in Keogh," but Keogh lingo can sound exotic at times. Here are definitions of terms you may hear from pension professionals and Keogh investors who know the ropes.

actuary A mathematician or statistician in insurance. As applied to pensions, the work involves calculations of actual and projected rates of investment return, mortality, and employee turnover. An *enrolled actuary* is a person enrolled with the federal Joint Board for the Enrollment of Actuaries. An enrolled actuary is needed to complete IRS Form 5500, Schedule B, which must be filed by defined-benefit plans. Actuaries are listed in the telephone Yellow Pages.

beneficiary In pension industry usage, this is a person, *other than the Keogh plan participant,* who may become entitled to benefits under the plan. A beneficiary may be made a co-annuitant with the participant under a joint-and-survivor annuity or may receive benefits on the participant's death. In most cases, the Keogh participant selects the person who is to be the beneficiary. In legal usage, the term also includes the plan participant, who is a beneficiary of the Keogh trust.

compensation Payment for services. Usually used for payment to employees, but in Keogh plans the term also means earned income of self-employed persons. Pension and profit-sharing plan benefits and contributions are based on compensation.

contributions Amounts paid into the plan, from which plan investments are made.

deferred compensation Compensation earned in one year and received in one or more later years. Pension and profit-sharing plans are *tax-favored* deferred-compensation plans.

defined-benefit plan   A pension plan that states (defines) the participant's pension benefit at retirement, or the method of determining that benefit. The typical corporate pension plan is a defined-benefit plan.

defined-contribution plan   A plan that states (defines) the contribution to be made for participants. Usually the contributions are a percentage of the participant's compensation. Money-purchase plans and profit-sharing plans are defined-contribution plans. A defined-contribution plan provides a separate account for each participant. The participant's benefit is the sum of the following amounts: contributions to the account; investment profits less losses and expenses; and in certain cases, forfeitures from other accounts (of other participants who leave) allocated to the account. No forteitures arise if the moonlighter has no employees.

fiduciary   A person with trustee-type responsibilities to look out for the interests of certain designated persons called beneficiaries. Keogh plan trustees and plan administrators are fiduciaries.

fund   As a noun ("a Keogh fund"), the sum of investments and uninvested contributions; as a verb ("to fund a pension"), the act of paying in (contributing for investment) amounts needed to provide future benefits.

interest   As applied to Keogh plans, often used for the rate of return on investments, whether from interest, dividends, rents, or gains (less losses) on sales of investments.

Keogh investor   As used in this book, the self-employed owner of a business, who makes tax-deductible contributions to (investments in) a Keogh plan on his or her own behalf and on behalf of covered employees if any. Technically, Keogh investors also include partners who contribute to partnership Keoghs. Partnership Keoghs are not discussed in this book.

Keogh plan   A pension or profit-sharing plan covering self-employed persons. It was named for the late Representative Eugene Keogh, Democrat of New York. Until 1962, pension and profit-sharing tax benefits were available only for employees. Legislation sponsored by Rep. Keogh extended these benefits to self-employed persons by treating them as both employees and employers. Keogh plans also are called Self-Employed Retirement Plans and HR 10 plans (after the number of Rep. Keogh's House of Representatives proposal).

Some use the term *Keogh plan* to mean only self-employed *profit-sharing* plans, which was the standard form of self-employed plan for many years. As used in this book, "Keogh" and "self-employed" are interchangeable, and "Keogh plans" include defined-benefit and money-purchase pension plans as well as profit-sharing plans.

life expectancy Length of time a person of a given age is expected to live. The period is a statistical average, based on mortality tables showing rate of death at each age. It does not seek to predict the life span of any particular individual.

master plan A model Keogh plan (or company plan) that specifies the trust to be used. A prototype plan is a model plan under which the employer selects the trust. A pattern plan is a model plan designed by a law firm, to be used by several different clients. The most common model plans are master plans.

participant An employee (including for this purpose, a self-employed person) entitled to benefits under the plan.

past service Employment or self-employment in a business before a plan went into effect.

pattern plan See master plan.

plan administrator The person who operates or administers the plan; in a Keogh plan often the self-employed person himself or herself.

plan sponsor The employer (self-employed person) who established a tailor-made plan or the institution that establishes a master plan.

prototype plan See master plan.

rollover Funds withdrawn from one Keogh plan and invested in another Keogh plan, in an IRA, or (less often) in a company plan. The term also is used for (*a*) funds withdrawn from a company plan and invested in any of the above and (*b*) funds withdrawn from one IRA and invested in another.

tax bracket With our progressive tax system, tax rates rise as taxable income rises. When a person speaks of his tax bracket, he means the highest rate of tax he pays, that is, the rate on his last dollar of taxable income.

In many cases—and generally in this book—the term is used to mean the highest rate of tax that person pays when federal and state taxes are combined. Tax calculations in these pages generally assume a combined federal-state tax bracket of 35 percent.

tax deduction An amount by which you reduce your income subject to tax. The dollar value of a tax deduction is the dollar amount of tax you save. For example, in the 35 percent tax bracket, a $4,000 tax deduction saves $1,400 of tax. If the $4,000 tax deduction involves a $4,000 out-of-pocket cash outlay, as it usually does, the true cost of the item being deducted is $2,600, or 65 percent of $4,000.

Tax deductions reduce costs; they don't eliminate costs. Tax deductibility is desirable if the outlay is for something the taxpayer would want in any case; the deduction makes it cheaper.

tax shelter   Any type of investment offering tax benefits. As applied to Keogh plans, it refers to the fact that Keogh investment earnings are exempt from tax until they are withdrawn.

vested benefits   Benefits are vested if they must be paid, now or in the future, regardless of the participant's future service. Benefits that do not vest are forfeited, which means they are shared among other participants or used to reduce future employer contributions.

Some entries in this chapter are derived from the glossary in the "Pension Costs" section of Accounting Principles Board Opinion 8, Appendix B, of the American Institute of Certified Public Accountants.